About the authors

Paul Higate is a senior lecturer in the Department of Politics, University of Bristol. He spent eight years in the Royal Air Force before becoming involved in critical military sociology. Since then, his academic research has focused on the gendered culture of the military.

Marsha Henry is a lecturer in the Department of Politics, University of Bristol. Her research has looked at various aspects of gender in South Asia, focusing on connections between the 'developed' and 'developing' worlds. Her recent research examines gender relations and perceptions of security in peacekeeping missions.

insecure SPACES

Peacekeeping, power and performance in Haiti, Kosovo and Liberia

PAUL HIGATE & MARSHA HENRY

Zed Books

LONDON | NEW YORK

Insecure Spaces: Peacekeeping, Power and Performance in Haiti, Kosovo and Liberia was first published in 2009 by Zed Books Ltd, 7 Cynthia Street, London NI 9JF, UK and Room 400, 175 Fifth Avenue, New York, NY 10010, USA

www.zedbooks.co.uk

Designed and typeset in Monotype Ehrhardt
by illuminati, Grosmont, www.illuminatibooks.co.uk
Index by John Barker
Cover designed by Andrew Corbett
Printed and bound in the UK by the MPG Books Group

Distributed in the USA exclusively by Palgrave Macmillan, at division of St Martin's Press, LLC, 175 Fifth Avenue, New York, NY 10010, USA

A catalogue record for this book is available from the British Library
Library of Congress Cataloging in Publication Data available

ISBN 978 1 84277 886 9 Hb
ISBN 978 1 84277 887 6 Pb

Contents

Acknowledgements

This book owes its existence to the kindness, generosity and encouragement of many people, including those who were frank in revealing their feelings towards peacekeepers and the peacekeeping project. That they did so with humility, patience and dignity to complete strangers is in itself a testament to the human spirit of those living in the challenging conditions of post-conflict societies.

It is impossible to name all of those who helped both directly and indirectly with the fieldwork. In Haiti they include: Nadine, Natalie and all of the UN civilian and military staff who provided transportation, guidance, advice and who often participated as respondents. Numerous women's and gender organizations, most of which wish to remain anonymous, and staff members from international organizations, including Oxfam, MSF and ICRC, gave generously of their time. Many Haitians bravely shared their thoughts, feelings and perceptions on the topic of security, despite their sense of pessimism about the possibility of change in the country. In Kosovo, we thank Habit and family, Michael, Tony, Digi, Tilly, Tamara and all of the UN, OSCE, ICTY and KFOR personnel who gave up much of their time assisting us in our research. Women's organizations in Kosovo also spared time to meet and discuss the much neglected gendered side of post-conflict Kosovo. In Liberia, we thank all of the staff at the Royal Hotel in Monrovia, Sam 'The Organizer', Jordan, Aine, Sandra, Evariste, Josephine, John and our courageous driver Paul, who shared with us his experiences of living through the many years of civil war in the country. In addition, organizations such as MSF, Norwegian Refugee Council, Oxfam, Save the Children and groups affiliated with a number of churches enabled us to conduct fieldwork in hard-to-access or neglected spaces and communities.

Excellent research assistance over and above the call of (fieldwork) duty was provided by Gurchathen Sanghera, to whom we also owe a debt for his accomplished input into the critical peacekeeping literature sketched in the Introduction. Others who helped facilitate fieldwork include Jamie Munn, James Korovilas, Mimi Sheller and Jean Pretlove. More broadly, our ongoing support from and conversations with Cynthia Enloe, Cynthia Cockburn, Ruth Jacobson, Carol Cohn, Deborah Heifetz-Yahar, Nada Ghandour-Demiri, Christina Rowley, Laura Shepherd, Suruchi Thapar-Bjorkert, Stuart Croft, Anthony Forster, Neil Cooper, Paul Williams, Mark Duffield, Tim Edmunds, Michael Pugh, Martin Gainsborough, Elke Krahmann, Richard Little, Eric Herring, Jutta Weldes, Tony King, Victoria Basham, Rachel Woodward, Tom Slater and Nadine Puechguirbal have shaped our thinking in the pages that follow, though of course we take full responsibility for what has ended up on the page.

The project on which this book is based was made possible with the support of the Economic and Social Research Council. Their award provided for the numerous field visits as well as participation in conferences and workshops throughout many locations around the world. The ideas in this book evolved through academic engagement at many of these events. Administrative support was generously provided by the School for Policy Studies and the Department of Politics, University of Bristol. Colleagues from PRIO, Utrecht University, the Netherlands Defence Academy, and the University of West of England commented on earlier ideas and concepts that shaped the book. To all, a big 'thank you'.

Finally, this book would not have been possible without the support of family, friends and colleagues. Many worried for our safety and sent supportive emails and 'debriefed' with us on our arrival home. In particular, we acknowledge Katinka, Mo, Anya and Frankie, alongside Jonathan, Theo and Audrey. We dedicate the book to you, who, more than likely, know the contents better than we.

Acronyms and abbreviations

ANT	Actor network theory
AU	African Union
ASBO	Anti-Social Behaviour Order
BBC	British Broadcasting Corporation
CIMIC	Civil–Military Cooperation
DDRR	Disarmament, Demobilization, Reintegration and Rehabilitation
DPKO	Department of Peacekeeping Operations
DRC	Democratic Republic of Congo
ECOMIL	ECOWAS Military Mission to Liberia
ECOMOG	ECOWAS Monitoring Group
ECOWAS	Economic Community of West African States
EU	European Union
FRY	Federal Republic of Yugoslavia
HCS	Humanitarian Common Service
ICRC	International Committee of the Red Cross
IDP	Internally displaced person
IMF	International Monetary Fund
INPFL	Independent National Patriotic Front of Liberia
KFOR	Kosovo Force
KLA	Kosovo Liberation Army
KPS	Kosovo Police Service
LPC	Liberia Peace Council

LURD	Liberians United for Reconciliation and Democracy
MINUSTAH	United Nations Stabilization Mission in Haiti
MNF	Multinational force
MODEL	Movement for Democracy in Liberia
NATO	North Atlantic Treaty Organization
NGO	Non-governmental organization
NPFL	National Patriotic Front of Liberia
OAS	Organization of American States
OCHA	Office for the Coordination of Humanitarian Affairs
OSCE	Organization for Security and Co-operation in Europe
PNH	Police Nationale d'Haiti
PRC	People's Redemption Council
PSO	Peace Support Operations
QRF	Quick Reaction Force
SALW	Small arms and light weapons
SCFUK	Save the Children Fund United Kingdom
SEA	Sexual exploitation and abuse
SRSG	Special Representative to the Secretary-General (UN)
ULIMO–J	United Liberation Movement of Liberia for Democracy – Johnson
ULIMO–K	United Liberation Movement of Liberia for Democracy – Kromah
UN	United Nations
UNDP	United Nations Development Programme
UNFICYP	United Nations Peacekeeping Force in Cyprus
UNICEF	United Nations Children's Fund
UNMIH	United Nations Mission in Haiti
UNMIK	United Nations Mission in Kosovo
UNMIL	United Nations Mission in Liberia
UNOMIL	United Nations Observer Administration in Liberia
UNPOL	United Nations Police
UNTAET	United Nations Transitional Administration in East Timor
USAID	United States Agency for International Development

Maps

SIERRA
LEONE

GUINEA

Voinjama

ZONE 2

Sanniquelle

HQ

Tubmanburg

Gbarnga

HQ ZONE 3

CÔTE
D'IVOIRE

Monrovia HQ ZONE 1

Buchanan

ZONE 4 HQ
Tchien

River Cess

LIBERIA

ATLANTIC OCEAN

Greenville

Barclayville

LIBERIA

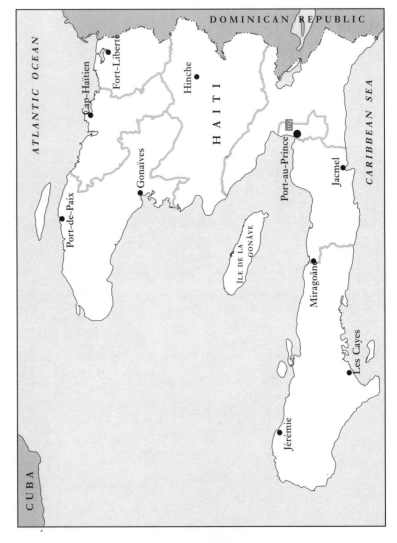

HAITI

KOSOVO

Introduction

For many, the military peacekeeper sporting an iconic blue helmet or beret is a potent image. There is something strangely compelling about the warrior-humanitarian that evokes deep-seated and contradictory feelings of fear and risk, safety and security. Peacekeepers can be seen as something of a quixotic presence – their deployment in relatively small numbers to vast territories such as the Democratic Republic of Congo may appear at first glance to make little sense. Yet the extent to which they are instantly recognized as peace soldiers speaks to the powerful symbolism they carry with them onto the world stage. Wherever they go, audiences – whether in the flesh or via the media – will have some sense that their arrival is in response to matters of life and death. In the UN/AU mission in the Darfur region of Sudan, there are lives to be saved, rape and looting to be prevented and a general sense of violent anarchy to be quelled. The only people who seem able to tackle these profound insecurities are peacekeepers, and it is to them that the international community turns when all else has failed. Yet, despite the centrality of peacekeepers to the day-to-day security activities of those post-conflict sites selected for UN or NATO missions, their interest to researchers has been somewhat marginal. More specifically, the everyday security work they do and the responses it evokes in their audiences (whether they be international staff working in the mission site or members of the host population), tend not to have captured the analytical interest of scholars interested in the ethnographic or social aspects of peacekeeper practice. There are exceptions to this, however, demonstrated most recently in the 'feel good' survey conducted by Professor Krasno and her team in Liberia (2006) for the Department of Peacekeeping Operations (DPKO).[1] Here, it was found that:

> Ninety-four percent of the [Liberian] respondents said the security situation has improved under UNMIL, [and] a further 91 percent said UNMIL had done a good or very good job at making them feel safe ... 91 percent said that the professional conduct of UNMIL had been good or very good.

Whilst these figures are undoubtedly impressive, we need to ask what lies beyond them. What is a 'good job'? How might the nature of the power interaction between 'honoured researcher' and 'the local' shape this 'hard' data? Somewhat disappointingly, a close examination of Krasno's survey reveals that at least half of the questions addressed to Liberians about their feelings towards UNMIL were heavily loaded in favour of a positive response. More than that, its support by DPKO throws into question the extent to which the work can be described as independent and therefore reliable. Further evidence for social researchers' relative neglect of peacekeeping can be traced to a number of spheres, including more broadly the under-utilization of sociological and human-geographical ways of seeing and thinking about peacekeeping. Given that peacekeepers can be framed as somewhat enigmatic individuals deployed to spaces of exception, which – fortunately – many of us will never experience in our lifetimes, it is even more striking that the Blue Helmets and the work they do have failed to stimulate innovative social scientific perspectives. In this book, we seek to address the lack of engagement between peacekeeping and particular strands of contemporary social theory that pay close attention to the routine, mundane and taken-for-granted aspects of daily life in three Peace Support Operations (PSOs). This we do comparatively across the mission sites of Haiti, Kosovo and Liberia.

What approach do we use to bring everyday perceptions of security into view? If nothing else, peacekeeping is about space, how it is seen, the ways it is reconfigured by peacekeepers going about their security work, and, crucially, the impact these spatial-security practices have on those living and working in missions. The first part of the book considers peacekeeping through the spatial lens, engaging concerns of organizational ideology as well as the substantive spatial practices of peacekeepers on the ground. Peacekeeping is also about the performance, symbolism and ritual that reside in the ways these generally military-trained individuals choose to present themselves to their audiences. Seeing peacekeepers as performers of embodied security dramas perceived through their national identity, together with their impact on gender relations, represent the concerns of the second part of the book. Ultimately, then, peacekeeping practice has both spatial and performative dimensions, a consideration of which has the potential to illuminate perceptions of security in new and interesting ways. In sum, this book aims to add depth and sociological weight to critical understandings of peacekeeping, to build bridges between disparate theoretical frameworks and to engender news ways of thinking about peacekeeping.

Background

The fieldwork on which this book is based was derived from a series of one- to two-month visits to the post-conflict sites of Haiti, Kosovo and Liberia between 2004 and 2007. Here, the three-person research team carried out a total of 268 interviews with female and male members of the host population, as well as internationals[2] deployed to these sites as part of the wider 'peace presence'. We also facilitated eighteen focus groups together with slightly more than a hundred informal interviews. We were rarely, if ever, out of the field, and would take every opportunity to ask people how they felt about security – whether it be the driver during the short duration of a taxi ride, or locals and internationals in numerous hotel bars, or indeed in the local people's homes in which we were accommodated.

Interviews conducted in Haiti and Kosovo made use of local translators, while in Liberia we were able to work in English. Extensive use was made of gatekeepers to facilitate contact with the sample; these included UN military and civilian staff, local and international

NGO employees, and local residents through whom we recruited further interviewees. Whilst we were fortunate to access a diverse range of respondents, readers will note that at certain points in the text accounts from international staff employed by the OSCE, NGOs and other international organizations dominate. There are numerous reasons for this, not least of which were the difficulty in moving about insecure sites to talk to local people, and taking advantage of those situations in which others were able to make themselves available at short notice. It should also be noted that many NGO staff could be described as both 'locals' and employees; they may or may not have been educated in the West and they invariably discussed a mix of personal and organizational views in interview. Given that a significant proportion of the local population had endured physical and mental trauma as a result of conflict, it was not always possible to arrange a formal interview with recording equipment as this tended to create a sense of unease as intimate and sensitive concerns came to the fore. Similar difficulties emerged when recording UN and NATO staff, who frequently expressed a desire to talk 'off the record'. Meticulous notes were taken in all cases, often by more than one researcher. In the face of relatively high degrees of illiteracy in some situations, it was often difficult, if not impossible, to obtain written consent for interviews, and in these cases we went about securing verbal agreement. At this point we explained that we were hoping to make their concerns regarding security and peacekeepers known to DPKO, with the longer-term aim of ensuring that the voice of these less powerful individuals could play a part in improving operations.

Conducting fieldwork in peacekeeping missions is a notoriously difficult business. First, relatively little sociologically or anthropologically informed qualitative fieldwork has been conducted in mission sites, and as such there is little in the literature to help researchers navigate the challenges of these unique contexts, though there are exceptions (including Ghosh 1994; Rubinstein 1998; Ben-Ari and Elron 2001; Sion 2008). Second, while there is a literature dealing with the process of conducting fieldwork in conflict zones (Robben and Nordstrom 1996; Hoffman 2003), there is no comparable contribution to assist researchers in their negotiation of the difficulties of insecure post-conflict sites, where civil unrest may rumble on and infrastructural damage frequently curtails freedom of movement.

Haiti was the most insecure post-conflict site in relation to our own freedom of movement as well as to the safety of any informants that we might arrange to meet. The threat of kidnap or being caught in inter-gang crossfire often framed the ways in which both we and our interviewees experienced security. Moving through the field site and talking to people in public or private places was severely limited by informal curfews intended to restrict movement after dark. Without the protection of a UN vehicle, for example, we were frequently left with little option but to venture into leisure sites – for example, bars and clubs – as independent researchers largely devoid of protection or, indeed, any form of security.

The fieldwork experiences of Haiti differed from those of Liberia, where in this sub-Saharan context the dangers posed to us and our informants was altogether less dramatic; here public health concerns tended to be prioritized in regard to the possible contracting of malaria. Respondents in Liberia tended not to stress current threats to their physical well-being, as noted in Haiti, but rather touched on the emotional trauma of the brutal fourteen-year civil war. Numerous of these interviews were psychologically exhausting for all concerned since they invoked memories of the conflict as one way in which security was framed in the present. The ethnically divided province of Kosovo generated a different set of difficulties linked to the recruitment of translators, who could not be deemed 'neutral' in their intermediary role between informants and members of the fieldwork team. In these circumstances, we had necessarily to rely on a greater proportion of those among the international presence, alongside those Kosovar Albanians, ethnic Serbs, Ashkalis and Roma able to speak English.

At least one significant 'security' event took place during each fieldwork visit. In turn, these incidents shaped accounts underscoring the situated nature of our findings. Charles Taylor, the former president of Liberia exiled to Nigeria after he reluctantly resigned, unexpectedly left his accommodation in 2006 during one of our fieldwork trips to UNMIL. He was subsequently transported by the UN to The Hague to stand trial for alleged war crimes perpetrated in Sierra Leone. His temporary disappearance – or, more accurately, escape – resulted in a clampdown on security in both Monrovia and outlying areas of the country for a short period. Prior to news being received that he had been captured at a border crossing point, reports of Taylor being 'on the loose' exacted a profound, albeit short-lived, influence on the ways that members of the host population and the international community thought and felt about security. Similarly, a few hours before a visit to interview members of the Serbian community in a small enclave in Kosovo, a stun grenade was thrown onto the balcony of a recently returned Serb family, resulting in burns to an elderly female. The immediate legacy of this attack impacted on the subsequent accounts elicited during this fieldwork trip, and again demonstrate both the fluidity and the contingency of security, as perceived and articulated in our work. Consequently, any notion that it is possible to replicate studies such as ours should be treated with a good degree of scepticism although we have done our best to produce a valid body of empirical work within these constraints. Overall, our work is framed by a good deal of contingency in that it speaks to perceptions of security within a particular time and place in the history of the country in question.

It is important to note that our positionality[3] as Western-educated, well-financed researchers was one of considerable privilege in relation to members of the various host populations, though not so much in regard to the numerous well-heeled international staff we encountered. Although we faced many risks in the field, we were also privy to numerous cultural and social benefits as a result of our economic and social capital. Contacts with the UN in particular enabled us to travel in ways that most local residents could only aspire to. The experience of being moved around in air-conditioned 4x4 vehicles and UN helicopters, together with the frequent opportunity to dine in expensive restaurants, served to compound our distance from the everyday insecurities to which members of the local population were exposed. It is important to acknowledge the ways in which our positionality has shaped the current work in terms of a contradictory mix of both distance and close social proximity. In regard to the latter, for example, extensive contact with the international and local elites in each site facilitated a unique vantage point from which to view the power practices of those tasked with administering security. In this sense, it was possible to move between a range of stakeholders, each constituted through distinctive power relations, which in turn shaped the ways that informants felt able to discuss their perceptions of security. It is also important to flag the ethnic, gender and autobiographical identities of the research team, comprising one female and one male, both of whom have South Asian heritage, and one white male with a background in the British armed forces. 'Data' is not collected like so many carrots plucked from a field, but rather should be seen as a social product generated within the context of face-to-face power relations. 'Findings' are necessarily mediated by individuals embedded in the social world whose subjectivities, whilst they should be reflexively acknowledged, can never be exorcised from the ways data is collected, analysed and written up. In this way, each of our biographies shaped data in both obvious and less obvious ways, and acknowledging this places us within what some might see as a post-positivist approach to social research.

Our approach to making sense of security in the peacekeeping context is, we hope, innovative. Our post-structural and deconstructionist inclinations have led us to engage with various disparate strands of critical literature, and this, combined with the findings of our fieldwork, has led us to believe that peacekeeping operations in their contemporary guise are far from benign activities. Indeed, they are laden with transformative intent and seek to shift subjectivity in line with a liberal-democratic view. It is for this reason that we include a brief sketch of the critical peacekeeping literature below, as it is within this growing canon that light has been thrown on the normative underpinnings of peacekeeping interventions. Whilst not related directly to the lines of enquiry pursued later in the book, nevertheless the critical element of the peacekeeping literature provides a broad context to the current work, as well as encouraging sensitivity to the political, economic and cultural impact multidimensional peacekeeping may have on its numerous recipients and their associated security subjectivities.[4]

Critical peacekeeping theory: a short introduction

In the wake of the exponential growth of complex peacekeeping operations in the post-Cold War period there has been a rich scholarly literature that has sought both to critique the wider project of peacekeeping and, less radically, to recommend how interventions can be made more effective. Peacekeeping is a multifaceted business and questions raised in these literatures, whilst largely overlooking its social face, range from the ideologies framing intervention (as we also do below) through to the ways in which operations have been and continue to be poorly resourced. These approaches have done much to further understanding of peacekeeping and the international relations framing their implementation, as well as how operations can go awry with tragic consequences for host populations and peacekeepers alike. In sum, the accomplishment of the peacekeeping literature is considerable, as commentators have successfully illuminated the countless political intricacies and moral dilemmas confronted by UN and NATO operations. Consequently, this raised awareness has percolated into the thinking of those for whom the formulation of peacekeeping doctrine is their bread and butter. Here, both soldier and civilian policymakers are faced with huge challenges that are beyond simple problem-solving approaches. After all, peacekeeping troops frequently encounter ethnic hatred or deeply entrenched conflict fuelled by the competition for raw materials. Perhaps onlookers expect too much of peacekeeping in ways that unconsciously salve the collective conscience of media-informed witnesses to these and other humanitarian catastrophes. Given that the Enlightenment vision of a peaceful world remains stubbornly elusive, their disappointment will no doubt persist. However, often-cited and somewhat depressing neo-realist prognosis of this sort has tended to narrow awareness of the everyday, human face of peacekeeping, as questions of international security are played out above and beyond those most influenced by intervention or lack thereof.

In this book, we address a series of points focused at ground level, including (1) the ways in which host populations and those who work in missions make sense of the UN or NATO presence in regard to military peacekeepers and security; and (2) the meanings attached by these individuals to security in regard to the specific presence of the UN and NATO–KFOR entities in their organizational guise. Our interrogation of these questions is then framed more widely in regard to how the everyday articulates with the geopolitical, giving rise to the notion that the Blue Helmets are key vectors of space–power exercised through their everyday security performances. How might we begin to contextualize our approach within the wider critical peacekeeping frame?

The peacekeeping literature focuses on numerous aspects, including the relative success and failure of various missions, operational and organizational issues, and rules of engagement. Other contributions have been concerned with conflict resolution alongside questions of sovereignty. This literature also deals with the transition in UN peacekeeping from traditional blue-helmet peacekeeping during the Cold War, a context in which peacekeepers attempted to 'placate' and 'refrigerate' the environment in order to facilitate conflict resolution (Richmond and Williams 2004: 33), through to current-day 'multidimensional' operations. The earliest interventions were premissed on the so-called 'holy trinity' of consent, impartiality and the minimum use of force. The second generation of peacekeeping combined traditional peacekeeping with humanitarian components and attempted to facilitate democratization, most importantly the holding of elections. Finally, third-generation peacekeeping missions tend to be framed as quasi-enforcement operations. These operations, often following Chapter VII 'peace enforcement' mandates, have provoked controversy. It is not just that accusations have been levelled at UN peacekeepers for 'going in too hard', as demonstrated in the case of Haiti, but also that peacekeeping of this and other kinds has the capacity to generate new forms of insecurity (Aoi et al. 2007).

These and other controversies led to the Brahimi Report, which called for UN peace operations to be reformed. Despite the initial optimism surrounding the report and some of its recommendations, it quickly became a topic of criticism (Bellamy and Williams 2004). Indeed, its overreliance on the 'problem-solving' or managerial approach (that seeks to stabilize and improve the effectiveness of peacekeeping within a liberal international society) proved to be its undoing. First, such an approach prevented an adequate conceptualization of peace operations within international politics, which meant that systemic structural causes of conflict were overlooked, if not ignored. Second, there were criticisms that the report did not go far enough and remained within the existing problem-solving paradigm, rather than putting forward suggestions for 'thinking anew' about peace operations. More recently, critical commentators have questioned the underlying norms, values and beliefs on which UN peace support operations are based (Paris 1997, 2001, 2002, 2003; Pugh 2004; Zanotti 2006; Chandler 2001, 2004; Richmond and Williams 2001, 2004), including those of gender (Enloe 1993, 2000; Razack 2004; Whitworth 2004) and neo-imperialism (Zisk-Martin 2004). In the main, these critiques call into question the normative role of multidimensional/ complex peacekeeping missions in the post-Cold War world, a context in which liberal democracy is generally seen as *the* panacea for 'failed states'. In this way, it is argued that peacekeeping missions have come increasingly to play a vital function as vehicles for global governance. According to Cox (1997: 60), for example, global governance is conducted by the so-called *nébuleuse*, which is understood to be 'a loose elite network of influential agencies sharing a common set of ideas ... that collectively perform the governance function'. Here, policy doctrine is initiated and executed through intergovernmental expert agencies and peacekeeping missions. An important feature of the *nébuleuse* is that 'there is no formal decision-making process; but there is a complex set of interrelated networks that evolve a common economic ideology and inject this consensual outcome into national processes of decision-making' (Cox 1997: 60–61). The sole model of development in these terms is unquestioningly believed to be 'liberal democratic capitalism' (Gill 1995: 412), which, as Cox (1997: 61) puts it, is 'a mystified structure of global governance' that 'escapes ... accountability'. In this sense, liberal democratic models have a tendency to be accepted non-consciously as morally and ethically 'right' for those regions and states that require 'civilizing'.

Peace operations are intended to protect and spread liberal democratic governance, and in so doing sustain the extant status quo. Within this dominant 'New York Orthodoxy' (Pugh 2004) of problem-solving, peace operations play an instrumental role in ensuring the construction of liberal polities, economies and societies. However, problem-solving approaches to peacekeeping are argued to be characterized by an approach that 'turns subjects of security into objects who have little to say about what "being secure" might mean to them and what security policies might be most appropriate' (Richmond and Williams 2004: 8). Similarly, in a series of articles, Paris (1997, 2001, 2002, 2003) locates peacekeeping within the broader parameters of international politics and considers whether peacekeeping practices challenge or facilitate the existing neoliberal order. Paris argues that the 'global culture' (or the international normative environment) informs the design of international peacekeeping operations and 'why and what peacekeepers do' in fundamental ways (2003: 444). He refers to the 'logic of appropriateness' that shapes and determines the boundaries of peacekeeping. Changes in peacekeeping practices therefore mirror shifts in global culture and importantly global culture determines the range of possible policies that peacekeepers are able to pursue. Paris (2003: 443) argues that,

> In short, the design and conduct of peacekeeping missions reflect not only the interests of key parties and the perceived lessons of previous operations, but also the prevailing norms of global culture, which legitimize certain kinds of peacekeeping policies and delegitimize others.

With the demise of the Cold War, which marked the triumph of liberal democracy and the 'end of history', peacekeeping operations have come to support the liberal project by maintaining traditional institutional forms of the state through facilitating the emergence of liberal democratic institutions and values. The transmission of such norms and values from the core to the periphery of the international system through peacebuilding is described by Paris as a modern version of the *mission civilisatrice* (2002: 637). He asserts that

> Peacebuilding operations embody a type of globalization that has gone largely unnoticed in recent discussions on international affairs – not a globalisation of goods and services, nor of cultural products like film and television shows, but rather, a globalisation of the very idea of what a state should look like and how it should act. (Paris 2002: 638–9)

Central to Paris's argument is that with the demise of the Cold War, the UN 'quickly and enthusiastically embraced liberal democracy' (2003: 446), which in turn has been adopted as a new standard of legitimate statehood in the post-Cold War era. Included in this normative shift are a range of other organizational actors (such as the UN, the IMF, the World Bank, USAID, OSCE and OAS), each of which promotes liberal democracy as the only legitimate form of domestic governance. In doing so, the underlying discourse transmitted by these institutions and organizations is that liberal democracy is a necessary prerequisite for achieving long-term peace and security, including development, human rights, justice and democratization.

Within the UN, this ideological commitment has been facilitated through the creation of a number of agencies to promote liberal democracy turning on the principle of periodic and 'genuine elections'. For Paris, peace agreements, the use of so-called 'experts' to guide the process of political and economic liberalization, the conditionalities imposed by international agencies and institutions, and the creation of 'proxy-governance' (in Kosovo and East Timor for example), are transmission mechanisms through which the liberal bias of these institutions is disseminated (Paris 2002: 642–5).

Rather than waiting for security to be established before sending peacekeepers to observe the 'adherence' of the peace, a number of post-1989 missions were deployed into ongoing civil conflicts with war-fighting mandates, particularly in Somalia and Bosnia. In addition, new peace support operations were deployed into post-conflict societies in order to oversee the implementation of comprehensive peace accords which often entailed large-scale reform of domestic political, military, judicial and economic institutions (Paris 2003: 449). Paris (1997: 56) also argues that, 'paradoxically, the very process of political and economic liberalization has generated destabilizing side effects in war-shattered states, hindering the consolidation of peace and in some cases even sparking renewed fighting.' The spread of these missions is not inconsiderable. Since the end of the Cold War, UN peacebuilding missions have been deployed to Namibia, Cambodia, Angola, Rwanda, Mozambique, Bosnia, Croatia, El Salvador, Nicaragua, Guatemala, Liberia, Sierra Leone, East Timor and Kosovo (Paris 2003: 450); their record at providing the foundations for sustainable peace is best described as 'mixed', not least since the attempt to transform war-shattered states into market democracies has been carried out too quickly in many instances (Paris 2004: 5).

Drawing on the work of Michael Cox (1997) and Mark Duffield (2001, 2002), Michael Pugh (2002, 2004, 2005) explores contemporary peacekeeping and humanitarianism from the perspective of critical theory, locating analysis within the broad context of world order politics. Central to Pugh's analysis is the relationship between peace support operations, humanitarianism and global governance. He argues that 'theorists of International Relations have paid little attention to how and why "peacekeeping", "peace support operations" and related "humanitarian" relief missions are significant in sustaining a particular representation of global governance norms' (Pugh 2004: 39). He further argues that by failing to examine the underlying inequities and inequalities embedded in the global system and how they contribute to conflict, peacekeeping 'can be considered as a form of riot control directed against the unruly parts of the world to uphold the liberal peace' (Pugh 2004: 41). Here the term 'liberal peace' is intended to capture the belief that liberal democratic states are inherently peaceful and stand as a model that so-called 'failed states' need to follow. Peacekeeping missions thereby re-create rather than transform the systemic inadequacies of the neoliberal order, and consequently replicate the structures and relations of power that configure core–periphery relations alongside the marginalization of large sections of the population in the south.

Although the New York Orthodoxy asserts the need and rationale for task-sharing and cooperation between the UN and regional organizations, it is asserted that 'in the context of US hegemony ... the orthodoxy has been to police the liberal peace and the US-dominated conception of the world order' (Pugh 2004: 44). For example, the use of the Security Council veto, the design of mandates, control over the 'purse-strings' and financial dominance serve to consolidate US power. Peace support operations are there to facilitate the liberal peace, and to guard against potential threats to it. The *nébuleuse*'s aid and humanitarian policies are informed by the ideals of liberal peace that simultaneously reproduce outcomes that sustain the hegemonic view of the political economy. The role of peace support operations in sustaining a particular status quo is illustrated further by Pugh in his discussion of 'humanitarianism'. Here he argues that peace support operations and humanitarianism have come to reflect, legitimize and reinforce the international order and promote globalization. For example, the discourse of humanitarianism was deployed during NATO's involvement in Kosovo in such a way as to capture the moral high ground, to legitimize an action that was not authorized by the UN Security Council (it was vetoed by Russia and China) and, therefore, technically illegal. The discourse was used to gain and maintain public support by making ethical appeals as well as to cover up inconsistencies in the NATO case (Pugh 2004: 49).

Another critical scholar, Laura Zanotti (2006), draws on the work of Michel Foucault to explore peacekeeping, democracy and normalization in the post–Cold War world. Here, the certainties and predictabilities of bipolarity have been replaced by 'potential sources of instability proliferated into a localized capillary and polymorphous "microphysics of threats"' (Zanotti 2006: 150). In response, UN peacekeeping has developed into a technique of normalization in the international arena (Zanotti 2005: 150). This so-called 'pro-democracy peacekeeping' domesticates and normalizes states that are potential threats to peace and security. She writes:

> Liberal/democratic government was increasingly included in the task of UN peacekeeping. No longer limiting its role to containing crises, the organization intervened in so-called failing states through 'complex' peace operations that, in addition to a military component, included conducting broad institutional reforms and even performing (transitionally) the functions of state administrations. (Zanotti 2006: 151)

UN peacekeeping operations have developed along two principal trajectories, those of institutional disciplinarity and governmentalization. These trajectories endeavour to modify states' behaviour and steer conduct through peacekeeping and peacebuilding. As a result, the international order is sustained through the multiplication of disciplinary and regulatory mechanisms aimed at transforming behaviour. In this task, peacekeeping has also been backed by multilateral organizations and international financial institutions (again, the *nébuleuse*) that have devised various criteria and instruments for identifying, assessing, rewarding or punishing the ways states govern their populations. Indeed, the criteria of democracy have become a key conditionality for the allocation of international aid and assistance from international donors. Zanotti (2006:152) argues that

> International organizations endeavour to tame unpredictability, cast light onto obscure borderlands and promote the transformation of abnormal states into responsible, peace-loving, predictable, 'transparent' administrations and productive members of the 'international community'.

Similarly, Chandler (2004) explores a number of the controversies concerned with the idea of liberal peace in international politics. His particular focus is on the ways that the international legal order has been reformed to allow for humanitarian interventions. Yet this has been a far from simple endeavour:

Since the end of the Cold War ... opponents of intervention, mainly non-Western states, have been sceptical of the grounds for privileging a moral justification for interventionist practices and have expressed concern that this shift could undermine their rights of sovereignty and possibly usher in a more coercive, Western-dominated, international order. (Chandler 2004: 260)

He goes on to explore how the debate had developed in regard to the creation of the International Commission on Intervention and State Sovereignty, which published a two-volume report, *The Responsibility to Protect*. Central to Chandler's concerns are the attempts to create a new framework legitimizing humanitarian intervention (the liberal peace) presented in ways that appeared to reconcile the age-old debate between humanitarian intervention and sovereignty. However, he argues, it has little to do with a moral shift in international politics from the rights of sovereignty; rather, the underlying imperatives remain those of realpolitik. Therefore the discourse of the liberal peace is being used strategically (by the USA and UK, for example, in their 'war on terror') in order to justify interventions. As Chandler asserts, 'the liberal peace thesis appear to have been fully appropriated by the Conservative "hawks" in the Washington establishment who are often seen to be guided by the principles of *realpolitik* and US power rather than any genuine desire to "refocus the discussion on the victims"' (Chandler 2004: 73). The discourse of 'prevention' and 'pre-emptive' intervention (as opposed to containment during the Cold War) is presented in moral terms that have been largely resistant to critique.

Rather than signalling the emergence of a global humanitarian conscience, the critical peacekeeping literature has attempted to tease out the ideological dimensions of peacekeeping and allied humanitarian interventions. In sum, it is argued that modern-day peacekeeping reflects a new balance of power in the post-Cold War world. This power has been, and continues to be, directed at fostering liberal subjectivities in the troubled populations of the anarchic borderlands, a process that has assumed a new urgency in the post 9/11 world where security and development have become increasingly intertwined

(Duffield 2002). Given the identification of this new balance of power, how might we begin to think through security from those perspectives that engage the social and human face of peacekeeping? It is to this topic we now turn.

Insecure spaces

Sociological, anthropological and post-structural approaches to peacekeeping remain underutilized at the expense of macro-level political science or international relations theorizing. In addition, and not unrelated to disciplines that tend to orient themselves towards the state level, is the scarcity of accounts that take the embodied experiences, beliefs and feelings of both host populations and those employed in missions as the prime point of departure with regard to how peacekeeping is made sense of 'from below', as Béatrice Pouligny (2006) describes it in her book on the subject.

As noted above, the thematic kernel of the book dealing with perceptions of security can be separated into two discrete but closely linked spheres. The first way in which security is conceived follows widespread use of the spatial metaphor in regard to the particular *forms*[5] by which accounts were conveyed. Space and place have been of interest to social scientists, who have used them to reveal the intuitive and taken-for-granted aspects of everyday life. For example, human geographers and sociologists have shown how space is able to provide individuals with a sense of belonging or identity. Space may have aesthetic and emotional dimensions as well as be shaped by political and economic relations. Space and place may be understood differently by different people and can be contested, fluid and uncertain. Importantly for our study, spatial practice (such as that of peacekeeping) shapes how space is experienced, and the extent to which it is considered secure or insecure. Whether it is the conditions of roads, the movement of peacekeepers through communities, or the switch from fixed to temporary security posts, interviews evoked a kind of security kinesis, leading us to consider how security exists in and through space. Here, security was invariably presented as physical mobility in terms of free movement between places of communality; what phenomenologists of security might describe as a kind of 'becoming through movement'.

With this in mind, we developed analyses that took space as the prime point of departure whilst also developing sensitivity to the spaces brought into being or maintained through the security practices of UN and NATO–KFOR military troops. These spaces can be seen as contingent outcomes of international institutions and their agents rooted in what we describe as the security *project*.[6] Thinking with and through space offered one way in which to explain who got security and who did not, as well as how security is experienced by peacekeepers and local people alike. Space worked at many levels: first, it shaped how people thought about, perceived and articulated security; second, it provided a lens through which to develop deeper insights into security; and, finally, it linked micro-level concerns of everyday security with broader global processes that could frame the UN and NATO as exemplary spatialized power actors. This emphasis on space called for a reappraisal of the supporting literatures upon which we drew to contextualize both empirical and theoretical concerns. In this way – and stimulated by concerns expressed in our fieldwork – we have found the critical geopolitics literature to be of conceptual and ideological value in our thinking. Of course, it is nothing new to suggest that security can be reduced to movement, as those who have endured incarceration will tell us.[7] Yet an interest in the ways in which peacekeepers actively and necessarily create and maintain spaces of security and insecurity tends to have been overlooked by scholars. These spatial processes can be noted in regard to the zones in Haiti and the enclaves in Kosovo. Here, peacekeepers' impact on space is constitutive rather than benign, and as such exacts a dialectical influence on perceptions of security.

The second dimension by which security was perceived concerned its enactment as an embodied performance that necessarily constituted an 'audience' which required securing. These performances turned on the presentation of (peacekeepers') bodies in ways that impacted on the spaces of security or insecurity perceived by host populations and international staff working in the mission. Bodies were noted to be an active, participative element of space, shaping or indeed constituting it by and through human activity, alongside feelings of safety and risk. One has only to consider the impact of a group of well-armed, male peacekeeper bodies in contrast to that of a solitary female civilian and the range of secure and insecure space to which these example give rise. The stress here is on the social contingencies shaping peacekeeper/host-population/international employee relations in and through which security performances are considered convincing or otherwise. Security, as has been suggested by some within the Critical Security Studies literature is not a 'thing', a noun that 'names', as Michael Dillon puts it, but rather a principle of formation, the practice of which is profoundly social-relational (Dillon 1996). Thus, rather then entering the field with a neat, universal language of security and insecurity to be 'tested systematically' through its imposition on interviewees, we asked individuals and small groups to interpret and convey what they understood security to be.[8] Our interest here was on the mundane, the routine and the obscure social aspects of security that give rise to the notion of 'everyday security'. In using the sensitising concept of embodied performance through space, we sought to complement the critical peacekeeping literature, which tends to lack a sociologically sophisticated understanding of human agency as it is played out socio-relationally through everyday interaction of flesh, tissue and cognition.

Taken together, spatial practices, on the one hand, and security performances, on the other, underscore the ways in which the presence of peacekeepers in the villages, towns and cities of post-conflict countries becomes inscribed into the social-relational encounter with peacekeeper audiences as well as on the physical landscape. Through linking the critical geopolitical with the ethnographic, we have attempted to address the paucity of detailed interview and ethnographic work on peacekeepers from a critical geopolitical perspective. In sum, this is a book about what peacekeepers *do* – in terms of their constitution of space – together with *how* they do it through their security performing practices. The other key message to emerge from our empirical work that stands as a cohering theme with the space–performance nexus concerns peacekeepers' role in *fuelling* insecurity in their everyday security practices. For example, the so-called force protection prerogative where military commanders' concern to protect the security of personnel in their charge over those of the host population, may render security performances as superficial in the eyes of those who feel let down by peacekeepers' lacklustre response to incidents. The relative inaction of French KFOR troops in protecting particular groups during the 2004 riots in Kosovo is a case in point that led, in turn, to the sense that these troops exacerbated insecurity through their passive stance. Finally, it is hoped that we have conducted the current research with the requisite humility and modesty given our deeply privileged flirtation with spaces of both hope and desperation. Borrowing conceptual terminology coined by the cultural and literary theorist Raymond Williams, we aspire at best to provide alternative *ways of seeing* peacekeeping, the likes of which go some way to convey particular *structures of feeling* experienced by host populations as well as international staff who both work and live in mission sites.

In this book the sensitizing concepts of performance and space are used metaphorically to stimulate an awareness of the deeply human and social experiences of security. In applying these concepts to empirical material, we are drawing on non-representational theory developed in human geography and allied disciplines, including sociology. Non-representational theory focuses on: the relational or dialogic constitution of social practice; the mundane in terms of the 'manifestations' of everyday life; the expressive, embodied, affective and ordinary subject; and, cross-cutting these spheres, the non-intentional, tacit, human agent who goes about her routine social achievements 'without knowing it' through the exercise of a 'practical intelligibility' shaped by an 'unformulated grasp of the world' (Taylor, quoted in Thrift 1996: 10; Thrift 1997: 126–8). As Nash (2000: 655–6) suggests:

> The emphasis is on practices that cannot adequately be spoken of, that words cannot capture, that texts cannot convey – on forms of experience and movement that are not only or never cognitive (together with those that can be seen) as micro-geographies of habitual practices.

Thinking with non-representational theory in ethnographically informed ways can be used to complement more traditional empiricist approaches noted in the mainstream literature on peacekeeping. As Dowler and Sharp (2001: 172) have argued more broadly:

> A broadening of the methodology of critical geopolitics ... to what might be considered as an ethnography of international relations offers exciting possibilities for understandings of the complex local embodied geographies that reconstruct the nation and the geography of international relations.

An interest in the non-representational is particularly apposite within the context of questions of security that engaged people in visibly affective, embodied and pre-discursive ways during interview and, more widely, in their everyday lives. An insightful, though somewhat opaque, critique of traditional approaches to framing security, as noted above, is to be found in the work of Dillon (1996), who has sought to expose the effects of modernist and calculative technologies that come to mirror Weber's iron cage of bureaucracy in its modern guise, as mainstream International Relations. He argues that 'what most distinguishes International Relations is the way in which it so intimately allies itself to ... closure of thought, in order to develop a highly technologised and instrumentalised account of (inter)national politics' (Dillon 1996: 7). Similarly, to focus on security as a concept, a thing, would actually be 'less likely to tell us about any particular *experience of rule* under any particular discourse of danger' (Dillon 1996: 17; emphasis added). Whilst Dillon is clear that power and control can be exercised in the name of security, he has also attempted to foreground the non-representational in his thinking through engaging with Heideggerian philosophy. Here, the focus on existentialism and phenomenology clears a path to the non-conscious, to questions of 'being', to authenticity of experience, and to 'becoming' that involves choice and agency grounded in the distinctiveness of the human condition.

Whilst these more abstract concerns signal the deeper, human aspects of security, they are notoriously difficult to demonstrate empirically. Yet, as they were recurring metaphors that emerged in our fieldwork, we have felt compelled to try and tease out space and performance in ways that articulate with less orthodox, deeper conceptions of security. Rather than treating accounts as literal utterances that speak for themselves (though they can be treated in this way), readers should note that the empirical component has been used as a *catalyst* to develop new concepts around peacekeeping. It should also be added that our two sensitizing concepts have emerged through a series of reflexive moves grounded in the researchers' intuitive sense that the space–performance nexus could play an insightful explanatory role when it came to examining security. Thus, within a few short minutes of arriving in-mission, we became aware of the spatiality of the UN or NATO–KFOR presence. These organizations and their agents of security were quickly noted in their territorializing roles, whether it was restricting movement (through space) in the form of a vehicle checkpoint, or the ritualized security performance of parading through capital cities in UN-marked tanks or jeeps. In sum, performance and space have arisen at the interface of our own experiences, those of interviewees, and finally in regard to diverse scholarly contributions that have sought to subject the invisible, the taken-for-granted and the obscured to critical enquiry.

Organization of the book

Chapter 1 sketches the political histories of Haiti, Kosovo and Liberia within the context of a number of first-hand impressions regarding the spatial feel of these post-conflict countries and the security conditions within them at the time of the fieldwork. The overall aim of this opening chapter is to provide for a sense of how historical events have given rise to particular bounded spatial territories – most obviously the example of the zone and the enclave in Haiti and Kosovo respectively.

A critical examination of both the UN and NATO is considered in Chapter 2 in ways that bring the ideological and spatial dimensions of these organizations into sharp relief. Our analyses here proceed from the observation that the UN has tended to exercise control over particular territories whilst NATO can be seen in respect of its expansionist proclivities. At the time of writing, NATO expansion has moved under the critical spotlight in hitherto unprecedented ways, drawing attention to its impulse to colonize geographical space. Both the UN and NATO converge in respect of their normative aspiration to facilitate the liberal peace in one or other ways, as noted above in the overview of the critical peacekeeping literature.

Zones and enclaves – spaces of both symbolic and material insecurity – are considered substantively in Chapter 3 through an examination of peacekeepers' spatially productive security practices. To what extent are international staff and local people able to move around either Liberia or Kosovo? Chapter 4 deals with freedom of movement, in particular UN and NATO peacekeeping troops' role in road-building together with their ability to visit remote communities.

In Chapter 5 we note how explanations for Liberia's relative security in contrast to the other two missions might be found in the spatially diffuse peacekeeping practices that have prevailed in the country. Here, concerns of the integrated mission – framed in terms of a struggle over contested space – and the threat of the ex-combatant figure failed to assume territorially bounded spaces of insecurity that in turn allowed peacekeepers to engage broader security concerns. Chapter 6 introduces the idea of performance and performativity as an alternative way in which to think about how peacekeepers 'stage' security dramas for the benefit of an audience 'in need of security'. These dramas flow from the embodied peacekeeper, replete with military equipment or 'props', who sets about choreographing security performances judged according to their capacity to deter peace spoilers.

Chapter 7 reveals the centrality of national or ethnic identity to how peacekeepers are 'imagined' as troops/men/peacekeepers of particular kinds. Here racialized and ethnicized stereotypes in circulation within missions among local people and international staff require a critical sensitivity to the colonial overtones of peacekeeping more widely. Chapter 8 develops the idea of 'gender space' through an examination of how peacekeepers who sexually abuse females and minors in PSOs do so from a position of privilege. This power is linked to their masculinity as well as to financial and potential cultural capital. To further illustrate these activities, we draw on a feminist geopolitics approach to the failure of these men to protect, together with discussion of critical men's studies in regard to the role of intra-masculine relations in these exploitative activities.

The concluding chapter picks up the theme of peacekeeping's unintended consequences as the example of recent thinking about how it is that UN and NATO missions create both security and insecurity. Our summary thoughts turn on recognizing the inevitable power that comes with peacekeeping. This understanding may be at odds with the broad assumption that at worst PSOs are benign or neutral and at best exact a positive influence on those who work and live in these and other post-conflict sites in the presence of the Blue Helmets.

ONE

From conflict to peacekeeping: Haiti, Kosovo and Liberia

What does it feel like to enter the space of a peacekeeping mission? On our fieldwork trip to Cyprus[1] in 2004, for example, it was much like arriving in any other sunny tourist destination in southern Europe. The passengers milling around the airport tended to be white European tourists busy shopping, eating and drinking. While security forces paced through different parts of the airport, nothing seemed out of the ordinary for a tourist destination. However, flying into Toussaint Louverture Airport, on the outskirts of Port-au-Prince; Robertsfield Airport some 35 miles outside of Monrovia; and Priština International Airport, a short distance away from the capital city in the province of Kosovo, were experienced as quite different from stepping off the plane in Cyprus. Yet all four places: Cyprus, Haiti, Liberia and Kosovo are post-conflict countries that play host to UN peacekeeping missions.

The airports of Haiti, Kosovo and Liberia tended to be filled with large numbers of humanitarian workers, Blue Beret peacekeepers and other internationals from around the world. In Kosovo, aged Mercedes taxis queued outside the airport. In Monrovia and Port-au-Prince, few people took taxis (or tap-taps), with most greeted by friends, colleagues or family. The ride from the airport to the city centre in Port-au-Prince is seen by many as risky, where the shortest route skims the notorious 'gang' neighbourhood of Cité Soleil. In Monrovia, the combination of storms in the rainy season and lack of street lighting can make the 45-minute journey from the airport to the city centre a treacherous one, not least since roads are in a poor state of repair.

Once inside the capital cities of all these missions one experiences the overwhelming institutional presence of the UN; unlike Nicosia in Cyprus, the UN dominates the urban spaces of Haiti, Kosovo and Liberia. White Toyota Land Cruisers branded with black lettering fill the landscape. Military surveillance equipment and vehicles, especially khaki-coloured jeeps and tanks, are regularly seen patrolling the busy streets. In Liberia and Haiti, where national public transportation is virtually non-existent, the supreme power of the UN vehicles stands in marked contrast to broken-down tap-taps and other ageing vehicles used to transport locals to and from various destinations. Uniformed soldiers and international civilian police, alongside corporate-dressed civilian workers, throng the restaurants, cafés and bars. On Sundays, international workers are seen in abundance at a number of leisure spots, including white sandy beaches in Haiti and Liberia, once a magnet for tourists in more peaceful times.

Peacekeeping mission sites are both exceptional and everyday physical, social and political spaces. On the one hand, each mission has a particular flavour or feel to it, which is dependent upon the historical and political context of the country, the number and composition of peacekeeping troops and civilian contractors, and the UN mandate in force. Missions vary in their degree of safety, a point which can be illustrated by contrasting previous UN deployments to Somalia or the current UN–AU mission in Sudan, where, at the time of writing, several peacekeepers had just been killed. UNFICYP in Cyprus differs sharply from these two examples, as it is safe and peaceful. On the other hand, given that peacekeeping missions have a great deal in common, they can also can be viewed as 'peace franchises', a point explored further in Chapter 2. For example, the UN often set up their headquarters in old hotels, and when visiting the main offices of the UN one is struck by the sheer familiarity of these buildings whether in Africa, Europe or the Americas. In some cases restaurants which cater for UN staff are mobile, moving from one mission to another, as is the case with particular Thai restaurant owners in

Liberia. The ubiquitous and much-maligned presence of 'expensive' Lebanese stores in numerous African missions underscores this sense of familiarity between geographically disparate missions.

In this chapter we provide historical information on the peacekeeping missions of Haiti (MINUSTAH), Kosovo (UNMIK, NATO–KFOR) and Liberia (UNMIL) with the aim of revealing the kinds of spaces to which they have given rise. These research sites were selected for a number of reasons. First, we wanted to have a sample of missions from the Americas, Europe and Africa. We knew that the evolution of conflicts in these regions differed from one another in ways that produced diverse perceptions of security. In Haiti, there was no official civil war, while in Liberia the conflict spanned the years 1989–2003. Kosovo had been part of a larger regional war, and then a more specific localized war in the late 1990s. In this way, each mission's experiences of security and insecurity was framed by a different trajectory of conflict. Second, we tried to select missions that were similar in both geographical size[2] and the numbers of personnel employed within them. Here, we made the assumption that the impact of the mission on different actors was likely to be similar. If we had included a mission such as that in Kashmir, for example, we would have been faced with a very small group of UN personnel with whom to work and study. Third, we wanted to research missions that were at different stages of development, but none that was either drawing down or that had been very recently established. First-hand reflections of the spatial feel of each of the sites within which fieldwork was conducted are examined below, together with an overview of the historical and political context of these countries. We also include a sense of the everyday nature of the missions in terms of security perception of both international staff who work and live in the mission and members of the host population.

All three mission sites share histories of conflict and political turbulence; yet each is unique. Commonalities, however, should not be taken as evidence that each of these countries can be labelled as inherently insecure or violent. Simplistic assumptions made about any one country's pathological trajectory or genealogy adds little to an in-depth understanding of the complex nature of conflict in each of these research sites. However, similarities across these UN and NATO–KFOR mission sites included: allegations of state incompetency; the ongoing existence of corruption and repression together with the violent activities of security forces; the active role of paramilitaries and/or criminal gangs; the dynamism of charismatic and popular leaders; widespread poverty and or/unemployment; and, finally, sharp levels of social stratification based on socio-economic status, ethnicity, 'race' and/or tribe.

Political histories and spatial feels

HAITI

Unlike many other countries in the region, Haiti gained independence early. In 1804 the first slaves rebelled against their colonial masters, an event which threatened to destabilize the dominant European order (Hallward 2004; Sheller 2000).[3] Haiti enjoyed tense relationships with its former colonial power, France, and with its long-established neighbour, the United States. By 1915, Haiti was occupied by the USA under the guise of promoting 'stability and democracy'; however, the USA helped to entrench racial divisions and hierarchies by favouring the light-skinned mulatto elites (Sangmpam 1995: 634). The USA withdrew in 1934 after growing confrontations, but was keen to see the 'right' leader in power in order to maintain interests in the region. In 1957 François 'Papa Doc' Duvalier was elected president, with US backing. Duvalier, a doctor and product of US rule, identified himself as *noiriste* (a partisan of black citizens, rather than light-skinned elites), and attempted to elevate indigenous Haitian culture as a national response to colonialism or US domination in the region (Farmer 2006: 91). After the death of Duvalier in 1971, he was succeeded by his son Jean-Claude, or 'Baby Doc', who ruled in a similar autocratic fashion.

By 1986, many Haitians felt that they had suffered from two consecutive dictatorships. A popular movement fuelled by many diasporics who had fled during the repressive Duvalier years began to gain momentum, and Jean-Bertrand Aristide, 'an ex-Salesian father and part of the grassroots Catholic movement', emerged as a potential leader (Gammage 2004: 748). With the backing of the country's elite, in 1991 a brutal coup led by the head of the army Raoul Çedras saw the ousting of President Aristide. The ensuing period evolved into a protracted period of violence against many poor Haitians. The international community began to recognize that conditions in Haiti were spiralling out of control by early 1993, when the UN adopted Resolution 841, imposing an embargo on weapons, oil and petroleum; plans for a multinational force with Canadian, US and French troops (UN Mission in Haiti: UNMIH) were initiated but never fully completed.[4] In mid-1994 the UN Security Council adopted Resolution 940, which led to the creation of a multinational force (MNF) that intended to use force to facilitate the departure of the military leadership. In March 1995, the UN assumed leadership of the mission and approximately 6,000 UN troops were deployed across Haiti. In December 1995 elections were held. Aristide returned to contest the leadership again and met with widespread support, but René Preval was elected. Aristide's party, Famni Lavalas, became increasingly associated with illegal and violent activities. The activities of some of Aristide's supporters and rival groups, widely labelled as gangs or *chimères* (ghosts), led not to the democratic ideal that was expected by many Haitians, but instead to civil violence, which became the everyday norm, especially for those living in the capital Port-au-Prince. The height of this conflict occurred over the course of one month, immediately preceding Aristide's departure from Haiti in January 2004.

Following Aristide's exit, the UN authorized the deployment of a Multinational Interim Force called the Mission in Haiti (MIH) made up of troops from the USA, Canada, France and Chile. In April 2004 the UN Security Council replaced MIH with the UN Stabilization Mission in Haiti (MINUSTAH) under Resolution 1542. This force, led by Brazil and with troops predominantly from Latin America, was to number approximately 9,000 (Dupuy 2005: 187). In 2007 the mission had 7,200 military personnel and 1,951 civilian police.[5] Along with the establishment of a UN mission, Gerard Latortue, a former UN worker, was appointed to serve as the interim prime minister. In 2006, a series of elections, monitored by MINUSTAH, saw the election of René Preval as president.

After a chaotic flight from the USA that required a stopover in Miami, we arrived in Haiti. Upon leaving the aircraft we were met by dry hot weather nudging 30 degrees Celsius. In the arrivals hall we were welcomed by our UN contact, who whisked us away in an air-conditioned white UN vehicle to a quaint hotel in Pétionville. After dropping our bags, we were taken for food and refreshments at a well-known French restaurant that is mostly frequented by wealthy locals and UN personnel. After lunch, we had just a little while to settle in before our fieldwork began the next day. Sitting out that evening on the terrace of our rooms, everything sounded peaceful and calm in the city. The view from our terrace was sheltered by lush trees and vegetation, making our hotel an oasis in the middle of the city.

Early on Monday morning we were woken by the sounds of car horns, alarms and heavy traffic in the nearby area. We were driven by our contact's driver to UN headquarters where we began interviews with UN military and civilian staff. There was no access to UN transportation for the duration of our fieldwork, necessitating the use of a rental car from a recommended company across town. Our UN driver was not sure if he was able to travel in that particular area as it was thought to be part of the notorious 'red zone' (areas off-limits for all UN staff). As it turned out, the rental car office was located near to the airport, and on the border of the neighbourhoods of Cité Militaire and Cité Soleil, areas considered to include a number of the most insecure neighbourhoods in Port-au-Prince. Eventually we made it to the rental compound, which was heavily guarded.

The experience of the secure and insecure spaces of Port-au-Prince was visceral as we moved between and within areas of danger and safety. Unfamiliarity with the city's layout was not only disorienting but encouraged us to continually ask whether we were venturing into the UN red, green or amber zones, each of which impacted on our sense of security. Whilst in Port-au-Prince, we were advised to avoid travelling after sundown, which we did. As private individuals there was little protection against any form of crime or violence as we did not carry any weapons and were unable to speak Kreyol, compounding our sense of occasional isolation and vulnerability. Though a driver was available in the daytime and early evening, we more or less stayed within the UN recommended travel zones, which meant avoiding suburbs such as Cité Soleil, Cité Militaire, Bel Air, Martissant and Carrefour. It was inadvisable to walk much of the city; consequently our perceptions of security were very much vehicle-centred. Unlike field trips to Liberia, where it was possible for us to walk in certain parts of Monrovia and in the counties, Port-au-Prince had a reputation for being a violent and dangerous city and we complied with the advice given to us by our UN contact as well as by the UN Security Office. In addition, conversations with locals confirmed for us a general public feeling of anxiety and fear about the city and the everyday dangers of robbery and kidnapping.

Exposure to the space of the city was also temporally limited to the daytime and certain 'safe' locations in the evening and night-times. In the specific case of Cité Soleil in Port-au-Prince, the stark disparities between citizens is inscribed on the urban landscape[6] and, indeed, is sharpened considerably when juxtaposed with the presence of wealthy internationals in other parts of the city. Shops are fashioned on the architectural styles of excess, mirroring boutiques in Beverley Hills, or old colonial mansions. The juxtaposition of these buildings with the corrugated iron roofs of the poorer neighbourhoods is stark. In the better-off areas, young boys and men offer to 'watch and protect' vehicles, with the expectation of a small payment upon the departure of the privileged few. The acute demand for UN employment for 'locals' on wages far beyond what the average Haitian might easily generate elsewhere underscores the absence of wider economic opportunities. Further indicators of poverty and associated inequalities take the form of sex workers touting for business late in the evening on the poorly lit streets of Pétionville.[7] They gravitate towards the numerous clubs and late-night restaurants, which in turn jostle for the custom of the wealthy – whether elite members of Haitian society or internationals enjoying a night out. Haitians endure a constellation of social and economic disadvantage, together with overcrowding that in turn generates violence. Slum areas are distinguished by: high rates of unemployment, poor sanitation and waste disposal, high levels of violence (particularly against women and children, but also in relation to the number of fatalities for men), poorly resourced schools and health facilities, and extreme poverty for most of their residents (Muggah 2005; Farmer 2006). One of Haiti's gangs' more notorious and, during the period of fieldwork, ubiquitous activities turned on their high-profile role in kidnapping. While gangs appear to be motivated by political parties and movements,[8] this violence can also be understood as financially driven.

Over three years have passed since the UN peacekeeping mission began and yet their impact on security is mixed (Muggah 2005). The threat of being kidnapped motivates many local and non-local residents to restrict their movements throughout the capital and from rural to urban. In Port-au-Prince, levels of insecurity have ebbed and flowed, in spite of the presence of UN military and security forces. Because of the number of peacekeeping missions previously established in Haiti, the history of security forces' use of violence against the general public and the more recent acts of violence committed by pro-Aristide supporters from poor neighbourhoods have resulted in a serious mistrust of the international community. The legacy of Haiti's complex history continues to resonate across this mission site and its population in numerous ways. In sum, our particular sense of this came in terms of the highly concentrated and territorially discrete slums in and around the capital city. These areas were categorized by the UN as 'red zones', both concentrations of insecurity and the focus of rigorous peace enforcement work. Their impact on the spatial feel of the fieldwork site was considerable and shaped perception of security for internationals working as part of the mission as well as the host population.

KOSOVO

The province of Kosovo's current status remains contested[9] primarily by the two major ethnic groups within its boundaries – Albanians and Serbians. Though much of Kosovo's current insecurity has resulted from years of conflict within the larger region following the fall of Communism, it is also related to Kosovo's continued state of limbo, an issue yet to be finally resolved some eight years after the UN–NATO deployment.[10] Unlike Haiti, Kosovo is not an independent country. It has been a place of conflict intermittently for many years and is situated within a region that experienced substantial instability during the early 1990s. Unrest around 'ethnic cleansing' reached a peak in 1999 when NATO bombing attempted to halt a humanitarian catastrophe. Kosovo is mythologized in both Serbian and Albanian culture, leading to competing claims over the 'rightful' inhabitants of the region. For Serbians, Kosovo has had historical significance since at least 1389, the date generally used to refer to the Ottoman defeat at Kosovo Field (Judah 2002; King and Mason 2006). It is here that the great battles against Islamic invaders in 1389 and 1448 took place, leading to the comment that 'Kosovo is to the Serbs what

Jerusalem is to the Jews' (Palmer 2002: 9/10). Serbian nationalists have used historical events such as these as evidence that Kosovo is unquestionably Serbian, framing Albanians as outsiders who have no legitimate claim to the land. Ethnic Albanians offer an equally compelling claim, casting themselves as descendants of the ancient Illyrians, locating their identity in the history of the region in earlier times than their Slav neighbours. Albanian nationalists have tended to see Kosovo as Albanian and 'argue politically for the annexation of the region into a "Greater Albania"' (Palmer 2002: 10).

At the end of World War II Marshall Tito declared the existence of socialist Yugoslavia, which included the republics of Croatia, Montenegro, Serbia, Slovenia, Bosnia-Herzegovina and Macedonia (Campbell 1998). Here, Tito attempted to transcend ethnicity through emphasizing socialist commonality. One of the by-products of this partially successful approach to state building was to freeze ethnic tensions in ways that became clear only in the years following his death. Over time Kosovo faced growing debt and unequal development; tensions began to increase among the population. Unemployment grew significantly and there was widespread concern and unrest, especially among ethnic Albanians who claimed that Serbs were dominating jobs (Nelles 2005: 3). In 1981 student riots took place at the University of Priština, where many complained of the discrimination Albanians faced in obtaining work that they were equally qualified to perform. Importantly, these riots fuelled separatist beliefs as well as repressive responses from Belgrade, and relations between Kosovar Albanians and Serbs never recovered (Pula 2004). Much of this discontent was stymied during the wars in Yugoslavia which plagued the region in the 1990s. Serbia played a significant role within the conflict, but the Kosovo issue was sidelined in the face of accounts of 'ethnic cleansing' of various groups including the many Muslims living in Bosnia (Campbell 1998; Judah 2002).[11]

In 1995 the Dayton Agreement was signed with the aim of bringing conflict in the region to an end. However, since 1987, the charismatic figure of Slobodan Milosevic had been gaining popularity, bringing with him a unique nationalism inflected with an allegiance to socialism and internationalism (King and Mason 2006). He quickly allied his rhetoric to Serbia's historical claim to the territory, and, in shifting from socialism to nationalism, began to campaign for a unification of Serbia (King and Mason 2006: 37). In February 1988 Milosevic took over as president of Serbia, and dedicated many speeches to the 'Kosovo issue'.[12] During meetings with Albanian activists, who were growing frustrated with the limits of a non-violent approach to transforming the situation, four leading activists made designs for an armed faction: the Kosovo Liberation Army (KLA) (Judah 2002).[13] On 13 October 1998, 'NATO voted to authorize air strikes if security forces were not withdrawn from Kosovo with 96 hours' (King and Mason 2006: 44). Western nations demanded major concessions from Belgrade including the opening of dialogue between the main ethnic communities, the withdrawal of paramilitary forces, and autonomy for Kosovo. On 24 March, NATO began seventy-eight days of air strikes, targeting infrastructure in both Serbia and Kosovo.[14] UN Security Council Resolution 1244 of 10 June 1999 called for the withdrawal from Kosovo of all the military, police and paramilitary forces of the Federal Republic of Yugoslavia (FRY). Eventually Milosovic capitulated. It was agreed that governing powers would be held by the UN and that a NATO force (KFOR) would provide security for the mission. At its height KFOR numbered up to 50,000 troops, though by early 2008 consisted of a much reduced 17,000 military peacekeeping force.[15] As status discussions about the future of Kosovo continued, there were mixed reactions to any timelines proposed. Anti-Serb and anti-UN rioting broke out throughout Kosovo in 2004 involving an estimated 51,000 people. There were a number of fatalities, numerous injuries to police and military officers, and many buildings important to Serbs were damaged or destroyed. By 19 March the rioting had stopped, but not before the events caused considerable upheaval for a number of 'minorities' as well as bad press for the UN and KFOR. Despite this setback, in 2006 the UN began a series of negotiations to determine Kosovo's status. The discussions led by UN Special Envoy Martti Ahtisaari, whilst attempting to forge dialogue between formerly warring parties, made little progress on the substantive issue of status. Whilst some powers have been handed back to the interim government, UNMIK and NATO retain considerable authority over civil administration responsibilities and security, respectively.

Unlike the 'tropical' destination of Haiti, Kosovo is for many months of the year crisp, cold and dark. Priština in particular is a both a hybrid and a contradictory space. Swathes of landscape speak to a somewhat dilipidated sense of the post-Communist era, but within the context of the ubiquitous UN- and NATO-branded buildings also resembles a large Western military base. In and around Priština, the open countryside is littered with disused factories, bullet-ridden and bombed-out buildings, UN offices, NATO equipment and camps, and a host of new buildings located somewhat incongrously between rubble, farmland and other physical remnants of the communist era. The spatial feel of the city immediately differs from that of Haiti's Port-au-Prince. Drivable roads, paved sidewalks and crossing lights dominate the small city centre area, despite the heavy NATO bombing campaign of 1999. UN and NATO personnel are rarely out of sight. In terms of attire and deportment the security forces, including the Kosovo Police Service (KPS), appear highly professional. In contrast to Haiti, few security guards are seen outside cafés, restaurants, hotels and bars, with the exception of the UNMIK Headquarters Building where all cars and individual visitors are thoroughly searched.

The feeling of fear and anxiety that permeates Port-au-Prince is wholly absent from Priština, which overall has the feel of a safe city, unless you are from one of the minority communities. The severity and level of crime differs sharply from that noted in Haiti, and security on the streets and on the ground in public spaces is claimed by Serbians to be worse than that of the majority Albanian population. Serbian is rarely spoken in this 'safe' city, where Albanian and English are more likely to be heard. However, the presence of 'minority' enclaves in and around the city and across Kosovo more broadly demonstrates that the integration of diverse ethnic populations remains some way off – isolation, alienation and fear continue to haunt many communities in these bounded spaces. The city of Mitrovicë/a is a good example. It is roughly split by ethnicity, with the north of the city populated by Serbs, while in the southern half Kosovar Albanians reside. The divisive feel of the city can be illustrated through a number of examples. For instance, when travelling from outside Mitrovicë/a to the Serbian sector, individuals often stop vehicles adjacent to the city border and exchange their Kosovo number plates for Cyrillic/Serbian plates. Upon exiting, they go through the reverse procedure. The divided nature of the city compounds the sense of fragile and contingent security in Kosovo. The tangibility of this security 'stand-off' or 'freeze' was reinforced by violent protests that took place in February 2008. Many Serbians, angered by Kosovo's declaration of independence, refused to cooperate and some UN police officers were injured during the violence.

Conflicts predating the current PSOs in Kosovo and Haiti converge in a number of respects. They included widespread repression of ordinary citizens by security forces, government censorship of dissent and criticism, and widespread violence in and across different communities. However, Haiti's experience of violence and conflict since its inception has had more to do with 'racial' politics than with 'ethnic' politics. While notions of 'race' have been mobilized in the competing political discourses shaping the Kosovo conflict, considerably greater attention has been given to notions of ethnic identity. There are also significant differences in the level of state infrastructure and economic development. Although Kosovo is characterized by high rates of unemployment, it does contain the foundations of various institutions such as a functioning judiciary, police and military. In part this is linked to Kosovo's history within the Eastern bloc, and its geographical location on the fringes of Europe more generally. In contrast it can be argued that Haiti cannot be so compared in respect of either institutional or infrastructural levels of development. Most importantly, UNMIK/NATO–KFOR can be considered as somewhat unique. It is one of the few missions where the UN has had administrative authority over the region, not unlike the earlier mission in East Timor. Thus, while the UN is there to advise the evolving Kosovo government, they have had a much more interventionist role in establishing Kosovo's security. The institutional dominance of UNMIK and NATO troops of UN–KFOR alongside the ethnic dimension to the conflict has helped to shape perceptions of security in distinctive ways.

During the fieldwork in September 2006, so-called revenge attacks perpetrated by Kosovar Albanians against Kosovo Serbians continued to be reported.[16] The ongoing friction between groups identified through their ethnic identities was framed by Serbian commentators as overwhelmingly 'attacks perpetrated by Albanians against Serbians'. Examples included the stoning of buses used by Serbians, the shooting of cattle owned by Serbians, and the stun-grenade attack on a recently returned Serbian family in Klina in September 2006. Despite these incidents, there appears to be widespread belief, at least on the part of Kosovar Albanians, that KFOR troops are a reassuring presence. Ethnic identity continues to exert a strong, perhaps even decisive, influence on how people think about and experience security in Kosovo. Kosovar Albanians, buttressed by NATO intervention in 1999, together with declarations by George W. Bush in 2007 that Kosovo 'needs to get independence sooner rather than later',[17] now enjoy greater security than hitherto, though Kosovo is still considered to be a 'basket case' in economic terms. The ethnic enclaves (in which live mainly Serbians, although many Roma, Ashkali and Egyptians also live in territorially bounded areas) emerged in our fieldwork as synonymous with insecurity. Like the zones of Haiti noted above, ethnically divided enclaves served as spatial metaphors for the overall troubles of the UN/NATO–KFOR mission.

LIBERIA

Liberia is located in sub-Saharan West Africa and borders Sierra Leone to the west, Guinea to the north and Côte d'Ivoire to the east. Situated in the Mano river basin, Liberia has endured conflict resulting in the death and suffering of hundreds of thousands of people, together with the displacement of many millions. It was estimated that by 1991, between one-third and half of the population (2 to 2.5 million people) were displaced, while between 15,000 and 20,000 were killed (Aboagye and Bah 2004: 1). There are numerous accounts of the fourteen-year civil war in Liberia; however, it would be impossible to encapsulate the diverse nature of this civil war, which has at its roots in ethnic rivalry, territorial dispute and religious differences (Ellis 1995; Aboagye 1999; Levitt 2005). These are overlaid with a complex combination of the quest for personal power, the limited availability of basic resources, the trade in 'blood' diamonds and 'tribal' differences. Like Haiti, Liberia has its foundations in slavery. It was founded by freed slaves, or 'free people of colour', from the USA in 1820, although it was not until 1847 that the settlers declared independence from the white slave owners (Moran 2006: 2). The indigenous population was not fully enfranchised until the 1960s, demonstrating the monopolization by the Americo-Liberians of political matters (Moran 2006: 4).

Since this time, what Levitt terms the 'settler oligarchy' has been the dominant pattern of governance. While conflict has ensued between various groups along economic, ethnic, religious and geopolitical lines, the settler elite has always managed to 'win' disputes and internal wars, at least until more recently (Boas 2001; Levitt 2005). As in Haiti and Kosovo, powerful 'elites' have consistently exercised control and power, and it is not surprising that the 'masses' grew tired of poverty and repression. Samuel Doe eventually led a coup, which resulted in the execution of former leader William Tolbert and the introduction of a new political regime: the People's Redemption Council (PRC), where Doe had full powers in government (Sesay 1996: 37). Unfortunately Doe's rule did not engender security or development and by 1989 civil war had begun. Although Doe was seen to be aligned with indigenous Liberians, he was continually seen to have favoured his own ethnic community, the Krahns. The poor treatment of non-Krahn groups under his regime fostered discontent among those groups, who were forced into exile in Côte d'Ivoire, including the figure of Charles Taylor. Taylor, another leader to market himself as a 'native' and therefore a 'true' Liberian, began to gain popularity, especially among the predominantly poor population. However, Taylor's army and allies did not remain unified and in the summer of 1990 dissension emerged (Boas 2001: 710). Prince Yormie Johnson, a one-time ally of Taylor's, broke away from Taylor's army and formed the Independent National Patriotic Front of Liberia (INPFL).

Worried about the growing tensions and the formation of even more splinter militias, the Economic Community Monitoring Group (ECOMOG), under the Economic Community of West African States (ECOWAS), organized its own investigation of Liberia in mid-1990 and dispatched troops from Nigeria, Sierra Leone, Gambia, Guinea and Ghana to impose a ceasefire, provide a secure basis for elections, stop the killing of civilians and ensure the safety of foreign nationals (Sesay 1996). In 1993 the UN established an observer mission in Liberia (UNOMIL). With the help of ECOMOG, their main achievement was to broker a peace agreement in 1995 ending six years of civil war. Nigerian peacekeepers were argued by Johnson to be providing weapons to his rivals in the ULIMO–K; ECOMOG had become a faction itself (Boas 2001: 712). ECOMOG began its final withdrawal from Liberia in October 1999, leaving behind continuing insecurity and conflict (Levitt 2005: 217). By late 2003 ECOWAS pressured Taylor and the rebels to reach a ceasefire, but Taylor asked ECOWAS to send a military force to Liberia in order to enable him to beat the rebels (Levitt 2005: 221). Fighting continued between the factions of MODEL and LURD together with the government forces. At around the same time, Taylor was indicted for war crimes by the Special Court in Sierra Leone. He attempted to have these charges lifted before accepting a peace agreement. As such, it was not until the summer of 2003 that a peace accord was finally reached. As the power of the government had diminished alongside the increasing international and American pressure for Taylor's resignation, the weakened leader accepted asylum in Nigeria. Taylor did return to Liberia, but only briefly, as he was extradited to The Hague to stand trial for war crimes.

Following the peace accord, United Nations Resolution 1509 authorized the establishment of UNMIL for an initial twelve-month period from 1 October 2003. AU troops were re-hatted with blue helmets and some 15,000 international troops were deployed to Liberia. As of March 2006 there were 15,071 troops from forty-eight different countries stationed in Liberia.[18] After Taylor's exit, Gyude Bryant was appointed chairman of the transitional government in late 2003 (McGovern 2005). The transitional government was expected to prepare for fair and peaceful democratic elections. With UNMIL troops safeguarding the peace, Liberia successfully conducted presidential elections in the autumn of 2005. Despite fears of violence in the run-up to the election, Ellen Johnson-Sirleaf, a Harvard-trained economist, won the final vote peacefully in November 2005, defeating the popular candidate, former international football player George Weah.[19] Liberia's history is not unlike that of Haiti and Kosovo. Rivalries between elite groups and different ethnic or 'racial' groups alongside government mismanagement and corruption, state repression by security forces and the emergence of different militarized opposition factions led to widespread terror, violence and war. The international community has responded differently in each mission with mixed results in terms of maintaining security.

In our two fieldwork visits to Liberia it was obvious that the general security situation was fairly good and improving with each day since the inception of the mission. This was especially evident in Monrovia, a city riddled with reminders of the fourteen-year civil war that has left a legacy of trauma in the entire region of West Africa. Bullet holes on bridges, abandoned buildings that had been sites of massacres, and heavily guarded government buildings that have been reoccupied and renamed are ubiquitous features of the Monrovian landscape. Despite these haunting reminders of the recent past, a relative air of peace prevails. At our hotel near the centre of Monrovia, the streets were bustling in the early morning and daytime. Traders and market workers – invariably women – awake at 5 a.m., carrying with them their wares and often accompanying children to places of care or education. This means long working days for most Liberians, no matter what their occupation. After 6 p.m., things become relatively quiet and the curfew of 11 p.m. for all UN staff means that most traffic disappears from the main arteries of the city. Few people are out at night, except on their way to and from night shifts or finishing their meals at the few restaurants which cater to an international clientele. With the exception of bars, restaurants and nightclubs in downtown Monrovia, most people have retired home or to temporary shelter relatively early. With electricity a scarce resource, the evenings and nights become quieter as people use candlelight; if they are lucky and have access to generators, they listen to the radio or watch television. Most Liberians and international personnel work six days a week, and Sunday is noticeably a day of rest. Many Liberians can be seen attending Christian church services on Sunday, a time when security concerns seem to be furthest from the minds of ordinary citizens.

Unlike the situation in Haiti, and to a lesser extent Kosovo, security in Liberia can be partially gauged – as we see below – by the response of the host population and internationals working in the mission. Whilst concerned about the fragility of the peace in Liberia, respondents also discussed the future in positive terms relative to those in Haiti and Serbians in Kosovo.[20] Echoing the sentiments expressed by Kosovar Albanians in regard to the work of KFOR troops, contingents of the UNMIL force were generally understood to have played an important role in bringing about and maintaining peace in the country. Moreover, the election of Ellen Johnson-Sirleaf as the first female head of an African state in January 2006 spoke volumes to the international community with regard to the tangible success of the UNMIL deployment. However, the in-depth snapshot of security taken during spring 2005, some six months prior to the election, highlighted numerous tensions in the country at a more uncertain point in Liberia's recent history.[21] Here, the gross inequalities[22] configuring Liberian society have been exacerbated within the context of the influx of millions of US dollars since UNMIL's deployment in 2003.[23] Poverty, alongside the lack of economic and social development of the country are key security issues discussed and debated across all three mission sites.

A central and widely articulated problem of particular note in Liberia is the need to repair the depleted infrastructure in the country. Roads require rebuilding in order to bring about a key indicator of security – freedom of movement. In the absence of serviceable roads, numerous communities remain isolated and at potential risk of attack by ex-combatants 'operating in the bush'. Other spatial concerns include the UN's 'integrated mission' in Liberia, which was framed as something of an ideological struggle over how to define the mission's priority: security or development? Whereas respondents in Haiti highlighted gangs and kidnapping, and those in Kosovo invoked ethnic tensions, the symbol of insecurity in Liberia is often personified by the figure of the ex-combatant. The limited success of the Disarmament, Demobilization, Reintegration and Rehabilitation (DDRR) process in the country (Nichols 2005; Paes 2005; Jennings 2007), at least until the end of the fieldwork period, framed the ways in which ex-combatants are seen. Whilst ex-combatants were noted to 'cluster menacingly' in Monrovia, a number of them were also implicated in controlling the Guthrie rubber plantation.[24] To make matters worse, the under-resourced police service remain 'accountable' to the public, and as such allegations of corruption, incompetence and inaction continue to be made by Liberian citizens. Thus, peace in Liberia at the time of fieldwork remained precarious, although the spatial concentrations of insecurity noted in Haiti and Kosovo around zones and enclaves failed to assume equivalent bounded forms in this West African country.

Conclusion

While Haiti appears to be a unique case in the Americas, Kosovo and Liberia were noted to be largely inseparable from wider conflicts in their respective regions. Economically, Liberia has more in common with the impoverished Haiti than with Kosovo, although clearly the economic situation in Kosovo remains dire. This chapter set out to provide important background information for each of the three peacekeeping missions visited during the course of the research. Key political events were outlined in order to provide an insight into the multiple factors involved in the conflict, the aftermath and the peacekeeping mission. In Haiti, we discussed the history of foreign occupation and rule, and the rise and fall of a number of harsh rulers, who used a variety of security apparatuses to enforce the submission of the people. Despite attempts at building the foundations for democracy in Haiti after the Duvalier regimes, it seems that widespread poverty and the use of violence by different armed groups from the former military to the gangs dominate everyday life for many Haitians. Crucially, the political and historical trajectory of the country has given rise to the spatially bounded slums designated by the UN as zones. Understandings of the difficulties of Kosovo turn on the history of ethnic conflict in the region that in turn plays a significant role in the continued presence of the UN and NATO. These ethnic tensions are mapped onto 'minority enclaves', the likes of which represent spatial shorthand for continued insecurity. In addition, the large numbers of peacekeepers deployed to Kosovo over a considerable period of time have had a profound effect on the ways in which Kosovars understand security. While the other republics of the former Yugoslavia have had time to develop their own national institutions, Kosovo appears to have been frozen in time. In Liberia the role of militias within the context of a fourteen-year civil war, led by two distinctively charismatic yet repressive leaders, led to a severe breakdown of society. With the emergence of so many militia groups in the context of at least sixteen ethnic clans, the lines between civilian, soldier and ethnicity have been seriously blurred. And, while the threat of war has largely vanished with the establishment of successive peacekeeping missions, the country is only slowly developing in economic and social terms. UN peacekeepers have helped to foster and maintain peace, though long-term issues of security remain. Yet, in our thinking, the military peacekeeping presence in Liberia tends to stand out from both Haiti and Kosovo in regard to its relative success; reasons for this are one of a number of findings to emerge from our fieldwork. So far as Liberia goes, the question we ask concerns how best to make sense of the peacekeeping presence in contrast to the spaces of insecurity and security to which it has given rise. In order to do this it is important to take a step back and think about the spatial and ideological dimensions of the UN and NATO – the topic of the following chapter.

TWO

Space, power and peace

If space is critical to the way security is perceived what does this mean for peacekeeping? In this chapter we delve a little deeper into the links between peacekeeping and space. First we summarize the literature that has analysed space in the post-conflict setting, before moving on to look at the example of the UN through this historical–spatial lens. This is followed by an examination of the ideologies shaping the development of the UN – an organization with the aim, as the geographer Neil Smith has put it, of 'conquering geography'. We then highlight the differences between UN and NATO engagement of space, where the former is noted to control space (as the example of UNMIK and UNTAET demonstrate), while NATO is discussed in terms of its expansionist aims allied to its transformation from military alliance to 'peace movement'. The example of Camp Bondsteel in Kosovo underscores US involvement with NATO through its geopolitical aspirations. Attention then turns to the processes by which peacekeeping missions are developed in terms of their spatial dimensions, using the idea that UN PSOs can be seen as franchising space through the production of universalized territories such as headquarters, sector and team sites. The chapter closes with a number of comments highlighting the ways that military peacekeepers can be seen to mediate the space-power embedded in the institutions of the UN and NATO.

Security and post-conflict space

Scholarly work that has attempted explicitly to spatialize security in the unique context of the conflict/post-conflict setting includes that of Corson and Turregano (2003); Falah and Newman (1995); Hyndman (2003); and Outram (1997). These contributors tend to have worked with predetermined spaces such as 'safe havens', 'safe cities', UN 'preventive zones' (Hyndman 1997; Outram 1997), the 'ground safety zone' (Corson and Turregano 2003) and 'boundaries' (Falah and Newman 1995). Whilst these spatial analyses have drawn on and elaborated institutionally created and explicitly demarcated spaces, Falah and Newman (1995: 694–8) have gone furthest in elaborating the social dynamics of their case study of the Israeli–Palestinian border in regard to both its material and cognitive dimensions. Unlike our approach to understanding security, this literature works with the traditional notion that security relates exclusively to physical well-being. Yet, something of an exception, Falah and Newman (1995) have explored the deeper humanist and phenomenological meanings brought to the concept of security in ways that resonate more closely with our attempt to engage the non-articulated dimensions of the space–security nexus.[1] While this literature provides a number of useful insights into substantive examples of how to spatialize security, it has tended not to foreground the ideological dimensions of these processes. Nor has it concentrated exclusively on the peacekeeping context in regard to the universal spatial features of PSOs. These and other concerns are now considered in ways that are intended to provide a broad context and framework for subsequent chapters.

The UN: conquering geography

While there was no mention of peacekeeping operations in the 1945 UN Charter, operations have evolved throughout the Cold War years into what has been termed an 'extraordinary art, calling for the use of military personnel not to wage war but to prevent fighting between belligerents' (Banerjee 2005: 19). Peacekeeping can be seen to have passed through four ideal-typical phases as argued by Banerjee, each of which is amenable to a spatial analysis. The first phase involved non-intervention; here force was only to be used for self-defence. Impartiality represented the cornerstone of mandates during this phase of 'the non-intervention buffer zone deployments of the Cold War era' (Banerjee 2005: 19). These traditional peacekeeping operations sought to hold or fix space in ways that were largely in agreement with belligerent parties. Typically, as remains the case of the frozen space of UNFICYP in Cyprus, the space of the buffer zone is intended to preserve a physical and psychological distance between opposing groups. Over time the UN mission has come to be seen as synonymous with this anomalous space of separation, most obviously in the divided city of Nicosia.[2] The second phase to emerge after the end of the Cold War involved peacekeepers' engagement in intra- rather than inter-state conflict against the backdrop of a resurgence in ethnic tensions. This second generation of peacekeeping was distinctive in respect of the ambiguity around 'the nature of the peace to keep', and there was invariably a humanitarian dimension that had to be attended to alongside conflict management and resolution. Given that these interventions tended to occur during a lull in peace, rather than at the termination of conflict, the space into which peacekeepers were deployed can be seen to be considerably more fluid, risky and chaotic. In part this was linked to the non-state armed actors' (lack of) regard for international norms, thereby rendering peacekeepers' role as little more than monitors largely inappropriate. The evolution of the third phase of peacekeeping was explicitly spatial as 'attempts were made to regionalize peacekeeping' in the following terms:

> The expectation was that … regional organizations were better suited to maintaining peace in their respective areas. NATO in Europe, the Commonwealth of Independent States in the Caucasus and African regional organizations in their respective regions in Africa. (Banerjee 2005: 20)

This third phase sought to conflate geographical proximity with assumed expertise and was shown to be largely flawed in its application, since many of these missions, including that of ECOMOG in Liberia, proved problematic. The final phase was signalled by an exponential growth in UN and NATO operations that began to emerge from around 1999 through the discourse of the 'new military humanism' (Chomsky 1999). The development of a series of movements to promote human security and human rights dovetailed with a moral 'right' to use force, as demonstrated most recently in the Democratic Republic of Congo (DRC) and in our examples above in Haiti where peacekeepers acting under Chapter VII mandates have been involved in combat operations[3] resulting in both peacekeeping and militia casualties. The multidimensionality of these operations is exemplified through a diversity of tasks, including

> Immediate stabilisation and protection of civilians ... supporting humanitarian assistance, organising elections, assisting the development of new political structures, engaging in security sector reform, disarming, demobilising and reintegrating former combatants and laying foundations of a lasting peace. (Eide et al. 2005: 3)

In sum, it could be argued that the spaces of concern to the UN have, over the last few decades, evolved (1) in line with the changing nature of conflict, (2) in the depth and scope of operations and how they are envisioned spatially, and (3) in the most recent of phases into spaces of moral 'bankruptcy' that require the transformative influence discussed in the introduction of the *mission civilsatrice* (Paris 2004; Razack 2004). During the UN's many years of peacekeeping, the application of the UN spatial project has evolved from one of relative fixedness through holding and observing to a situation of unknown, shifting and 'anarchic' space in regard to the nature of intra-state conflict (Duffield 2002), as we suggest above. In turn, UN peacekeeping has ranged from operations of minimal spatial impact, as illustrated in early monitoring missions, through most recently to that of a normative spatial project tied to facilitating the liberal peace.

In addition to the distinct spatial phases of UN operations, it is also interesting to consider the ideological dimensions shaping the development of the UN in the broadest sense. Here, it has been asserted that the UN was conceived to 'conquer geography' in ways that meant that 'territorial considerations were allied to the desire to see the US as a pivotal global power in the post-war period' (Smith 2003: 375). The deeper imperative to establish the UN flowed from the aspiration to create global-political and military stability 'so that economic growth could continue unhampered' (Smith 2003: 374). In this way, it is suggested that

> The UN should be read through the lens of a contested global geography. The central dilemma faced by US post-war planners was

how to design a global organization that followed broadly democratic principles and recognized certain universal rights *regardless of geography* while ensuring as best they could that this organization would work for their own nationally defined interest. (Smith 2003: 376; emphasis added)

In a more provocative sense, the term *Lebensraum*[4] has been used in ways that are intended to underscore the capitalist-expansionist aims of the USA in regard to the vehicle of the UN, 'which was to be seen as the political embodiment of the American Lebensraum, a new federalism at the global scale that opened the world to ordered political economic expansion' (Smith 2003: 411). The UN, then, as one of a number of international bodies was intended to contribute towards a framework in which the 'liberal world order could develop ... and that would increasingly render interstate wars obsolete' (Callinicos 2003: 55). Key challenges included the establishment of a unified world economy and 'free' trade that would favour American companies poised to exploit developing markets in the post-war period. According to this view, the UN was legitimated through a discourse of human rights and democracy that, over the decades, has been used by the Western powers to further their own interests (Gheciu 2005: 123). The critical perspective sketched here takes issue not only with the expansionist aims of the UN as originally devised but, more importantly, with the controlling impulse characteristic of the UN peacekeeping presence. Attempts to control particular post-conflict territories come into sharpest focus within the context of those missions that combine a military peacekeeping presence with the stewardship of the states' administrative apparatus.

Perhaps the best illustration of this is the UN administrative arm in Kosovo (UNMIK), which works alongside the military peacekeeping presence (NATO–KFOR). The responsibilities of UNMIK were to bring law and order to the UN protectorate and, more widely, to function as an interim civil administration with the longer-term aim of promoting 'substantial' autonomy and self-government leading to elections.[5] In taking the UN into 'uncharted waters', this ambitious mandate has been described as challenging, 'both conceptually and operationally' (Yannis 2004: 67). The extensive authority exercised over the province by UNMIK went to the very heart of the sovereignty question, raising concerns about the 'legitimacy and powers of the international administration' (Yannis 2004: 67–8; Gheciu 2005: 124). UNMIK was to have *complete* legislative and executive authority over Kosovo and in reality has interpreted its mandate as being 'unrestrained' by sovereignty issues pertaining to the Federal Republic of Yugoslavia. In effect, 'Yugoslavia's sovereignty over Kosovo has been suspended ... and they [Yugoslavia] were to be excluded from any administrative role in the territory' (Yannis 2004: 70). The extent to which the territory is under the control of UNMIK has attracted criticism in terms, not least of the idiosyncratic influence it exerts on the rights of individuals: 'There are only two places in Europe where citizens cannot claim their rights either locally or in court in Strasbourg: Belarus is the first, the UN state of Kosovo is the second' (Zaremba 2007: 2). The absolute control exercised over this UN protectorate where: 'judges are subordinated to the UN governor who removes them if he [*sic*] wants to and ignores verdicts when it suits him' (Zaremba 2007: 3) bequeaths a legacy to the

> thousands of people in Kosovo to whom the UN represents law-lessness and lost illusions ... from a legal point of view Kosovo is the black hole of Europe. The UN arrives to defend human rights – and at the same time deprives people of all legal means to claim these rights ... the mission has legal immunity ... UN institutions in Kosovo, including their employees and their soldiers, were placed above the law. They could not be sued, prosecuted, arrested or even interrogated by a local legal body – or any other body for that matter. Only in cases where UN staff committed a serious crime could the immunity be lifted by Kofi Annan alone. (Zaremba 2007: 2)

The power exercised by UNMIK actors is argued to turn on the attempt to create a 'liberal subjectivity'[6] and so 'discipline' the population (Gheciu 2005: 124). Here, it is suggested that in all important areas of life: 'Decisions were taken by international institutions, which were not accountable to the people of the province'[7] (Gheciu 2005: 126). The generally poor regard in which UNMIK is held by both Kosovar Albanians and Serbians signals the sense of subordination endured by these groups in regard to what is seen as the slow transfer of power to the Kosovo authorities, though this process has intensified in the light of the declaration of independence by Kosovar Albanians; the so-called UN state of 'UNMIKistan' powerfully illuminates the space–power–peacekeeping nexus.

In a similar sense, the transitional administration established by the UN in East Timor in 1999 stands as a precursor to that of UNMIK. UNTAET has been described as a development which was 'consistent with the trend towards increasing social and territorial control in interventions to remedy the breakdown of failed states' (Chopra 2000: 27). It is further argued that UNTAET represented 'another form of authoritarianism unless the transitional administrators themselves submit to a judicious separation of powers and to genuine accountability to the local people whom they serve' (Chopra 2000: 27). Given that UNTAET was seen as a 'pre-constitutional monarch in a sovereign kingdom', questions around the 'replication of Indonesian system of administration' by the UN (Chopra 2000: 31; Yannis 2004) may well single out both UNMIK and UNTAET as spaces of continuity with former authoritarian regimes. Here, the centralization of power, the impunity of the UN–international elite and the stoking up of tensions that could lead to renewed internal conflict can also be seen in the UN mission in East Timor as international decision-makers have also attempted to exert control over this space. Like UNMIK, UNTAET failed to devise a coherent and actionable exit strategy through the latter's unwillingness to consult with East Timorese representatives. Neither UNMIK nor UNTAET has exercised self-restraint (Chopra 2000: 32) in its strategies of governance, resulting in control over these contested territories and the instruments by which they are administered.

Whilst it is possible to argue that UN administrations exercise thoroughgoing control over their territories and populations, a spatially sensitive analysis of NATO brings the institution's expansionist tendencies into sharp relief. Here, it is noted that the military alliance has undoubtedly – with great success – sought to shift its institutional identity to one of 'peace movement', a point now considered with an emphasis on expansion rather than control.

NATO: expanding spaces of morality

Like the UN, NATO was also established in the post-war period, though the Treaty's stated intentions were articulated in primarily military-defensive rather than diplomatic terms, namely to 'contain'

the Soviet Union.[8] The centre of gravity of the NATO military alliance appeared to be primarily European in terms of its constituent
members and its territorial area of operations. However, unlike the
UN, which came to the fore with the emergence of the so-called intra-
state 'new war' (Kaldor 1999) that is said to require both military and
humanitarian intervention, NATO appeared – at least temporarily – to
be somewhat obsolete in the face of the 'defeat' of the Soviet Union
in 1989. In the immediate aftermath of the Cold War, the Warsaw
Pact crumbled, leaving numerous states or 'former enemies' in the
East in a state of ideological and strategic limbo. NATO sought to
capitalize on this opportunity and its expansionist proclivities became
clear as it moved ever eastwards. The 'enlargement politics' of NATO
(O'Tuathail 1998: 20) were not simply about enhancing the security
of the European bloc, but carried with them deeper aims. Here, like
the UN, the diffusion of free-market principles articulated through
the guise of pan-institutions included NATO, which 'is increasingly
becoming synonymous with a zone of peace wherein all members
ascribe to democracy, free trade, and interdependent relations' (Oas
2005: 396). Given that NATO is first and foremost a *military* alliance,
questions might be raised concerning the techniques by which it has
colonized both the security apparatus and aspects of civil society
of ten formerly socialist states. Here, it is suggested that NATO's
military nature has been partially exorcised from its identity. As Kuus
(2007: 269) has argued:

> Accession [to NATO] is normally discussed as 'more' than 'just' a
> security matter. In government rhetoric, academic research and main-
> stream media coverage alike, accession is ... the ultimate codification
> of the regions identity and values.

Rather than striking a somewhat static, defensive stance, as was
the case during the Cold War years, the alliance has successfully
undergone an 'extraordinary discursive metamorphosis' into a 'peace
movement'. NATO is promoted as 'empowering', providing for 'acceptance', 'recognition' and 'a confirmation of Westernness' (Kuus
2007: 269). Indeed, NATO has come to occupy a 'normative space
of imperial right' that turns on 'cultural belonging, moral values and
universal moral rights' (Kuus 2007: 270). To some extent the UN,
but most obviously NATO, negotiate global power relations in ways

that present force 'as being in the service of peace ... these relations rely on an ethico-political dynamic which envelops a boundless universal space of civilization' (Kuus 2007: 271).[9] In part obscured by the European resonance that frames NATO is the profound and far-reaching US success in promoting its own global interests in the alliance that outstrips the same that might be said of US engagement with the UN.[10] In these terms it is argued that in relation to the US and NATO,

> There is more at play in NATO expansion than simple geopolitical security as defined by the international relations [IR] field. Indeed ... above and beyond security for central Europe, contemporary NATO expansion is a [further] moment in the cycle of the US rise to world power. (Oas 2005: 395)

And, framed in more neutral terms: 'American policymakers want NATO to serve ... as a framework for European security and as a vehicle for supporting US strategy in the rest of the world' (Forster and Wallace 2001: 111). It is our belief that NATO has served as something of a Trojan Horse for the USA in regard to its capitalist-expansionist proclivities, a view that is underscored through a brief consideration of the bombing by NATO in 1999 where, it has been argued 'nothing less than a NATO-led solution and a NATO protectorate' would have been acceptable to the US and UK regimes[11] (Blackburn 1999: 3). It was not simply that 'the military–industrial complex (of which NATO is a key element) is associated with moral good as a key part of geopolitical subject making today' (Kuus 2007: 271), but that the UN 'option' discussed at the fateful Rambouillet negotiations, in which Serb forces occupying Kosovo would vacate the province to make way for UN peacekeepers, was disregarded so that NATO might achieve an enhanced 'strategic emplacement' in the region (Blackburn 1999: 1 of 11). In turn, KFOR, rather than being made redundant as speedily as possible has – alongside UNMIK – contributed towards the fixing of tense, inter-ethnic spaces, as we saw above. As Harvey argues more broadly (2003: 83):

> The US still hangs on to NATO in spite of its general irrelevance given the end of the Cold War, in part because it keeps European military planning and development under US command. The US supports, for example, the idea that Europe should develop its own

military rapid-response force but only on the condition that it remains under NATO command.

Kosovo represents a prime opportunity for the USA to expand its grip on global military power through the vehicle of NATO against the backdrop of the global 'war on terror'.[12]

One example of this US-expansionist imperative is Camp Bondsteel in Kosovo, a military installation that has received relatively little attention in proportion to its significance in the region. Bondsteel is, of course, just one of the estimated 8,000 US bases which encircle the planet through which the USA entrenches its global military power. Located in Urosevac, near the Macedonian border, Bondsteel is the largest 'from scratch' base built since the Vietnam era[13] and its existence is a stark reminder of US military hegemony. Set within the regional proximity of a drastically depleted Serbian military, and a host of recently 'NATOized' states in the Balkans, it is difficult to understand why such considerable resources might be poured into this extensive military installation. As one commentator describing this place has said,

> Those visiting Camp Bondsteel describe it as a journey through 100 years in time. The area surrounding the camp is extremely poor ... then Bondsteel appears on the horizon with its mass of communication satellites, antennae and menacing attack helicopters circling above. Brown & Root (the private contractor running the camp) pay Kosovo workers between $1 and $3 per hour. (Stuart 2002: 2)

KFOR troops who originally lived in bombed-out apartments in Kosovo joke that two things on earth can be seen from outer space: the Great Wall of China and Camp Bondsteel! (Stuart 2002: 3). Leaked comments in the European press have confirmed what many suspected, that the USA used the bombing of the FRY specifically to establish a base that would provide them with both proximity and fly-over rights to the Balkans to protect Caspian Sea oil interests. Camp Bondsteel provides the US with a geostrategic military foothold in the region and 'is located close to vital oil pipelines and energy corridors presently under construction, such as the US sponsored Trans-Balkan oil pipeline' (Stuart 2002: 1). In addition, it has been dubbed by some as a 'mini Guantánamo' on account of the alleged torture facilities within its many kilometres of razor wire. Camp Bondsteel's role as a key node in a web of US military bases instrumental to its 'war on terror' are brought into stark relief at the sight of 'prisoners in orange coloured overalls who are kept for an indefinite period, without trial, lawyer or verdict ... because the UN governor [of Kosovo] believes they might be terrorists (Zaremba 2007: 4). Given this 'space of exception'[14] (Agamben 1998; Gregory 2006), it is all the more surprising that the majority of scholars discuss US involvement in NATO in acritical, reverential tones, choosing to ignore the ideological foundations of the alliance, as the following demonstrates:

> What NATO does is give the US a privileged position within the expanding European security system – which is an asset not to be undervalued. President Bush's visit to the European Council in Gothenburg in June 2001 – the first by a US President – brought the transatlantic security dialogue and the intensive EU–US economic relationship closer together ... the persistence of NATO makes the US a European power and contains the development of foreign policy and defence integration among European governments within a broader Euro-Atlantic framework. (Forster and Wallace 2001: 119)

What do mainstream commentators omit from their general reverence for NATO expansion? As much as some scholars believe that the USA can be made 'a European power' through the shared security alliance of NATO, US unilateralist power will continue to trump the concerns of others, even those – with the UK as exemplary in this respect – deemed to have a 'special relationship' with the global hegemon.

The UN and NATO converge in a number of aspects of their spatial power projections. Both can be said to have emerged from US interest turning on capitalist expansionist imperatives given renewed impetus after World War II. This hegemonic-aspirational dimension is inflected with a strong normative, some might say aggressively prescriptive, disposition. Here, US global interests, for example fronted by the World Bank or the International Monetary Fund, prescribe the medicine of economic restructuring programmes. States are frequently coerced into accepting these remedies with the prospect of US trade sanctions or other disciplining techniques if they refuse (Chomsky 1991). With regard to the sheer number of peace-keepers deployed around the world, the UN can be clearly shown to have expanded significantly, though unlike NATO, might not be seen as *expansionist*, but rather, as disposed to *control* space, at times in what some might see as an authoritarian fashion as we suggested in the case of Kosovo. In sum, the US has 'placed itself at the head of collective security arrangements, using the United Nations and, even more important, military alliances such as NATO, to limit the possibility of inter-capitalist wars and to combat the influence of the Soviet Union and then China' (Harvey 2003: 53).

Most important is that both the UN and NATO operate under what can be termed the metadiscourse of (national) security[15] (Woodward 2004). This most convenient of banners legitimates or, in the case of the NATO accession countries, canonizes this spatial projection in the form of a pervasive and unquestioned militarization of everyday life (Kuus 2007). In a broad sense, it is clear that the UN and NATO can be considered through the spatial lens in ways that foreground the ideological dimensions of their impact. What might a similar approach reveal about the particular example of the UN PSO? What processes lie behind the deployment of a mission and how can these be theorized spatially?

Creating securityscapes: the UN/NATO franchise

The point at which the Blue Helmets' boots hit the ground on initial deployment comes after many months of planning. Here, military and civilian logisticians subject the country in question to a geographical gaze that is framed primarily by military cartographic principles aimed at maintaining security in post-conflict conditions. A key aspect of this process is to carve up the country into a series of different spaces, each of which is developed according to certain goals. These typically include the UN headquarters site (usually located in a hotel in the capital city, as is the case in Haiti and Liberia), the sector site (to which particular national contingents are deployed) and team sites (to which military observers are deployed). Here places are created through the formulation of discrete territorial boundaries within which particular activities take place. For example, the headquarters site represents the hub of decision-making in regard to how the mandate is to be interpreted and implemented. In discussing how 'raw space' is transformed socially, Soja (1989: 78) argues that 'Place emerges as a particular form of space, one that is created through acts of naming as well as the distinctive activities and imaginings associated with particular social spaces.' In this way, the headquarters, sector and team sites can be seen as 'delimited administrative provinces' that emerge through 'negotiated and renegotiated boundaries' (O'Tuathail and Dalby 1998: 3). For example, in the case of UNMIL, sector sites have been fashioned from novel combinations of Liberia's fifteen counties. This act of territorializing is a universal feature of all UN PSOs and can be seen as a form of spatial franchise rolled out across the entirety of UN and NATO peacekeeping missions. The military geographical activities from which these territories are derived come from a visual ordering of space that is contingent on cartographic surveys. These are projected 'across an uneven, broken (and insecure) landscape that becomes territorialized in distinct ways' (O'Tuathail and Dalby 1998:3). Irrespective of their location in West Africa or Asia, the wellspring of these spaces follows from this generic carto-graphic template, which in turn flows from the drive to shape space 'to serve tactical and military strategic purposes' (Woodward 2004: 108). The creation of the various sites, whilst shaped by pre-existing natural boundaries, supply routes, transport and communication links does, nonetheless, represent a spatial imposition on the indigenous population. The important point to note here is that whether or not local people are aware, or indeed are interested in UN sector sites, they nevertheless have a direct legacy for host populations' and international employees' 'security and danger' (O'Tuathail and Dalby 1998: 4). Is one fortunate enough to live within an area to which highly professional Blue Helmets are deployed? Alternatively could the realization that the troops sent to keep the peace are poorly resourced, inadequately trained and arrive with little real interest in the mission, serve to create a sense of insecurity? Might not peace spoilers feel more confident to operate in the latter sector sites within the proximity of those Blue Helmets for whom they have less respect? Decisions regarding the choice of sector sites to which different national contingents will be deployed emerge from a series of discussions far distant from the mission itself, for example at the DPKO in New York. These 'baseline and backroom activities' (Woodward 2004: 4) are shaped by questions of national interest; to what extent might national military commanders be reluctant for their personnel to serve in known areas of insecurity in regard perhaps to its proximity to unsafe borders or minefields, for example? As such, these negotiations concerning who is to be deployed to any one mission site, and in particular to which sector site, can be seen to turn on the 'politics of location' (O'Tuathail 2000: 386).

Knowledge of the demarcated areas or sites used to carve up territory are disseminated via maps to UN personnel and others, including the local and international employees of non-governmental organizations (NGOs). These maps work at numerous levels and at the most basic are simply descriptive and informative. Yet, given their ultimate impact on host populations and those employed by the mission, including peacekeeping contingents, can also be described as 'maps of meaning ... that are actual, social and aesthetic' (O'Tuathail and Dalby 1998: 4). They are actual since they delineate a particular 'truth' of the reconfigured territory that is beyond question; few are likely to argue that sector sites should be reconfigured or that the capital city is the natural home to the headquarters. Their social dimension is to be found in the ways they impact on the economic opportunities of those who live within the headquarters site, for example, the place where wealthy international staff are concentrated. Observations from across missions in West Africa show that Lebanese traders have capitalized on the influx of US dollars accompanying UN missions through mobilizing kin and family networks (Beuving 2006). Finally, the familiarity and status of the territories of which they are productive are couched in a universal language and thus can be seen to resonate with an unequivocal (and unquestioned) military aesthetic. Here there is likely to be considerable difference in response to a UN map detailing sector sites from an indigenous member of the host society in contrast to that of a Blue Helmet, for whom these kinds of cartographic representations are taken for granted, and not only call for particular ways of seeing, but also contribute towards feelings of security and insecurity. A local female may interpret the map as a kind of external imposition, drawing and redrawing territories in ways that are artificial and apparently arbitrary, as she has not been trained to look at landscapes through the lens of military geography. Peacekeepers who physically occupy 'on the ground' space – not unlike soldiers who discuss photographs of their 'military selves' – can be seen as directly implicated into broader geopolitical strategies (Woodward et al. 2008: 5). In this way they can be said to be vectors of space–power – invariably exercised in positive ways – the practices of which shape territories and the security experienced within them. In sum, peacekeepers' territorializing impulse should be taken seriously, not least because territory has been argued to 'provide individuals and groups with a sense of security and with a place in which they can work their own identities and destinies' (Elazar 1999: 875).

Yet, in arguing that peacekeepers might function as agents of geopolitics, it is important not to over-instrumentalize their cognisance of this role within international politics. As conscious, thinking actors, the majority of Blue Berets undoubtedly act in good faith under extremely onerous conditions (Jelusic 2007). Very often, the broader mission of peacekeepers is unclear. They are profoundly under-resourced; consequently, realistic expectations of their potential achievements could render them 'ineffective' in the eyes of the host population (MacQueen 2006: 234; Pouligny 2006; Aoi et al. 2007). They likely have a real belief that in working as humanitarian warriors, they can make a valuable, albeit limited, contribution to the lives of those emerging from conflict. It is also the case that others see UN or NATO deployments as a good opportunity to save money and improve their career prospects. Broader political struggle conducted above and beyond the immediate social universe of peacekeepers may be rather less benign. Not only is the mission itself pervaded with contradiction, for example in terms of mandates that could hamper intervention,[16] but also the machinations of distant power struggles frequently result in deployments that are exceptionally challenging, when seen from the geographical expanse of particular regions and the sparse peacekeeping presence.[17] Thus contingency, unintended consequence, thwarted geopolitical instrumentality and realpolitik underlie both the genesis and the maintenance of the peacekeeping project that is nested within broader aims evoking the territory–power nexus. More cynically, it could be suggested that the humanitarian impact of the peacekeeper dispatched to protect may be powerless to halt the slaughter of distant peoples. Nonetheless, peacekeepers, whether part of a UN or a NATO operation, have considerable power to shape the spaces of security of host populations as well as international staff working in missions. Their beneficial presence might not at first glance carry with it the ideological dimensions of peacekeeping, though clearly they are agents of international organizations able to wield significant normative influence on how 'failed states' are to be refashioned through the articulation of boots on the ground with the geopolitical.

Conclusion

Space is critical to the ways security is perceived, and in this chapter we have included a series of discussions focusing on the UN and NATO in their historical and organizational guises. The point here is that the work of the UN and NATO is informed by a particular normative view of how best to transform so-called 'failed' states into liberal democratic entities, the likes of which, it is assumed, are naturally peaceful. In order to do this, peacekeepers are actively involved in territorializing post-conflict sites in accordance with military geographical practices. In turn these practices give rise to uneven and inconsistent degrees of security, as the example of sector sites suggested. The main aim of this chapter has been to signal the importance of thinking about the links between space and security within the context of the peacekeeping enterprise. Next, we move from this sensitizing discussion to the substantive examples generated from our fieldwork, where the everyday detail of perceptions of security are revealed through their spatial dimensions as they traverse the range of geographical scales (Hyndman 2004).

THREE

Zones and enclaves

What kinds of spaces and places have preoccupied peacekeepers on the ground in Haiti and Kosovo? To what extent have their security practices helped to constitute and reconstitute these spaces in ways that have shaped perceptions of safety and well-being? Building on the previous chapter, we turn now to examine the substantive experiences of those on the ground in Haiti and Kosovo, leaving the spatial dimensions of Liberia to later chapters. Members of the host population and international staff living and working in Haiti and Kosovo are examined with a view to learning more about their experiences of space, security and insecurity. We open with a discussion of Haiti, its slums and the ways in which MINUSTAH has designated these concentrations of poverty as 'red zones'. This fashioning of place from space provides peacekeepers with a particular focus for their peace enforcement operations, which in turn perpetuates and reinforces the bounded nature of these areas. These securing activities continue to attract concern from those living within the slums and ghettoes, as well as others who have reported the displacement of insecurity into previously peaceful areas. Discussion then turns to the explanatory concept of zoning. Parallels between peacekeepers' preoccupation with spaces of insecurity are next considered in respect of Kosovo and the enclave. The argument made here within the context of primarily international staff employed in the mission is that KFOR peacekeepers' work serves to harden the division between the Serbian and Kosovar Albanian populations. The logic of security work that turns on the separation of ethnic populations is dealt with next through the process of encleaving, a form of security practice that has some resonance with that of zoning. An important question raised throughout this chapter concerns the possibility of peacekeepers taking a different approach to their work, since there is nothing inevitable about the ways in which they constitute spaces of both secure and insecure kinds in the ways discussed here. A brief conclusion follows.

From slum to zone

The city of Port-au-Prince is divided into several districts and neighbourhoods. Pétionville, a relatively wealthy suburb, is south-east of the centre; Delmas is south of the airport and east of the centre; and the relatively poor neighbourhoods of Martissant and Carrefour are to the south. In the downtown region there are many low-income areas that might be formally or informally designated as slums. The most notorious of these are located north and north-west of the city centre: Bel Air, Cité Militaire and Cité Soleil. There was widespread consensus that Cité Soleil was the most well-known and universally accepted slum area. This is partly because it has come to be seen as one of the primary sites for Lavalas supporters, *chimères* and/or criminal gangs.

What of the emergence of the slums? The slums of Haiti did not spontaneously appear on the social and physical landscapes; rather, they have emerged from a constellation of political and economic developments grounded in the country's political history, as we saw above. More specifically, the economic crisis in the 1980s resulted in a significant decline in the agricultural sector, causing waves of migration to urban areas (Kovats-Bernat 2006). The heavy influx of peasants into the city led to a rapid expansion of the slums, resulting in overpopulated conditions such as poor sanitation, high unemployment and rampant crime. Although remittances from the Haitian diaspora help sustain a significant proportion of the population, those residing in slums are the victims not only of poverty, but also of political and criminal violence. The effects of violence perpetrated by gangs in geographically distinct, zoned locations could result in entire communities being 'pseudo-quarantined'. A female European NGO worker explained that 'Since 2002 the quality of the environment we have been working in has been steadily degrading.' She added: 'There was no possibility for us to go on or to pretend that we have sustainable access to basic services without looking at the issue of violence.'

It is also important to note that the formation of the slums has taken place within the context of the UN and other international actors' presence over many years, and to this day the slums are shaped by the daily activities of MINUSTAH and its large number of military and civilian staff. Here, the slum areas of much of Port-au-Prince have been deemed a 'red zone'. This territory includes all of Cité Soleil and Cité Militaire, as well as some bordering neighbourhoods. Other safer zones, colour-coded 'yellow', 'green', 'white' or 'unmarked', have developed on the basis of regular UN security assessments. They appeal primarily to internationals, the majority of whom are able to afford the higher rents within their boundaries. Military peacekeeper operations have tended to focus on the borders of the red zones, although elite UN troops acting on intelligence have penetrated deeper into the most troubled neighbourhoods.[1] A number of both Haitian citizens and international staff commented on the gangs' attempts to control the peripheries of the neighbourhoods – these broadly mirrored the boundaries used by the UN and others to demarcate the red-zone areas. Gangs were understood to be defending and perhaps expanding this turf, or in UN parlance 'zone', through such violent methods as the drive-by shootings of rival gang members. Though the boundaries of the slums is in reality fluid, and the insecurities within them mutating over time, nevertheless these troubled communities are generally viewed by UN military peacekeepers and others as having an autonomous existence pervaded by cycles of insecurity.[2] The two slums of Cité Soleil and Cité Militaire (but also Martissant and Bel Air, which were 'rescued'[3] from the red zones) have been identified by the UN as particular zones of insecurity[4] that require military intervention and policing. More specifically, the UN has seen fit to deploy special forces into these areas in order to curb gang-related activities such as kidnapping,[5] extortion, rape and murder through forceful implementation of the Chapter VII mandate.

One of the effects of UN military peacekeepers' incursions into the red zone is to contribute towards the isolation of the slums in numerous ways. Most noteworthy has been the unintended though significant number of deaths in these areas by Blue Helmets involved in peace enforcement activities.[6] Here, slums can be seen as contested territories where Haitians could be at risk from both gang members and the Blue Helmets. How are UN operations into the slums viewed by a wide range of stakeholders? As one UN civilian male employee said:

> Since coming to Haiti I've seen a real ebb and flow of security. There is a great deal of violence involving gangs, especially around here in Cité Soleil and Cité Militaire. The gangs got a response which they probably didn't anticipate when peacekeepers have gone in and conducted some serious operations. The gangs are now looking else-where for targets but it may well be that the crackdown will lead to a worsening of the security situation.

A female Haitian staff member from an NGO in Port-au-Prince provided a graphic sense of the escalation of violence leading to the death of a civilian that was believed to be the direct product of peacekeeper operations:

> All of a sudden you get the UN coming in. There are tanks, heli-copters hovering … taking up positions in my front yard … It ended up with a girl, around my daughter's age, being killed. People were shot because the neighbourhood was not cordoned off properly. Whether or not the UN brought security … I'm just not sure.

It is clear that peacekeeping operations intended to challenge gang members did not necessarily result in an increase in local residents' security. At times, UN interventions were seen to exacerbate violence in the form of so-called 'collateral damage' as a result of crossfire. UN raids in June and July 2006 on the urban neighbourhoods of Bel Air and Cité Soleil were widely discussed. The purpose of these raids was to deter criminals from the kidnappings and abduc-tions taking place in and around Port-au-Prince. However, violent clashes sparked by UN incursions resulted in fatalities and injuries to military peacekeepers, humanitarian workers, national police officers, local residents and some 'known' gang members.[7] These operations involved a number of actors including the Haitian National Police (Police Nationale d'Haiti, PNH), UN military peacekeepers from the Brazilian, Sri Lankan and Jordanian contingents, UN civilian police and several armed individuals alleged to be members of economic and political militias or gangs. Responsibility for fatalities is disputed, with the UN claiming that it followed its mandate of 'supporting' the PNH, and in so doing avoided the 'policing' activities implicated in the deaths.[8] Yet on the Internet and in the international media, the general perception is that the UN is responsible for these deaths.[9] Many discussed the ways that MINUSTAH is often seen as failing to provide security even though Haiti has a functioning political system. As a female Haitian NGO worker said, 'MINUSTAH's presence is needed for political stabilization. We *do* have a government. We *do* have a parliament. What we *don't* have is security! We do not feel the presence of MINUSTAH' (emphasis in original interview).

Kidnapping has emerged in recent years as a key indicator of insecurity in Haiti. In the worsening conditions of the deprived neighbourhoods, it is of particularly wide concern. The overall lack of security in Haiti, symbolized by threats to individuals in the form of kidnappings that occur despite the presence of MINUSTAH have led to a questioning of the 'real' reason the Blue Helmets were deployed around the country. At the same time, however, MINUSTAH was seen by others as 'essential' to the long-term security of Haiti with kidnapping being seen as likely to decrease as security 'beds down'. More broadly, the violence pervading Haitian life could be framed in regard to its zero–sum nature,[10] adding to the sense of its deep intractability. Here, in response to broader questions about the impact of peacekeeper operations, reference was invariably made to the so-called 'rippling out' of violence. The broad view was that the borders of the red zones were seen to have become increasingly permeable in ways that loosely correlated with peacekeepers' security work in the slums. While it was clear that 'no area in Port-au-Prince was entirely secure',[11] nevertheless a recent spate of shootings in the relatively wealthy suburb of Pétionville fuelled anxiety that gang violence had a creeping quality exacerbated by peace enforcement work of the Blue Helmets. It was also noted that the south-east department of Haiti was experiencing an increase in violence, and in the thinking of a Haitian male working for an NGO 'was being carried out by people coming from Port-au-Prince'. This belief was reiterated by a UN male civilian, who said: 'Two people have been killed in the last month, and it is strongly believed that the "bandits" are coming from Port-au-Prince'. Haitian citizens living in or close to (the previously peaceful) city of Jacmel echoed these concerns in their discussion of creeping insecurity, using such metaphors as the 'cockroach effect' in regard to the spread of violence.

The general sense was that insecurity seemed to 'radiate out' from Port-au-Prince, as part consequence of UN policing and military actions in the capital. Given the belief that 'violent bandit' activities were being displaced through UN action, it was somewhat ironic to note the desire by some people for MINUSTAH to counter the rising insecurities in Jacmel 'because of their experiences of tackling the gangs in Port-au-Prince'. The security work of MINUSTAH Blue Helmets in the slums or zones can be seen as a particular response to securing space. Put in colloquial terms, and seen from the perspective of MINUSTAH-directed operations, it is possible to unpack these 'turf wars' through their processual and ideological dimensions – an activity we call zoning. At this stage questions might be asked of UN commanders' views on the possibility that their troops' attempts to counter insurgents actually contributed towards insecurity. How credible were these links in the minds of those coordinating operations? Was there any way of establishing a correlation between operations and the apparent displacement of insecurity to which they gave rise? What kinds of alternative interventions were open to peacekeepers other than those that exacerbated risk for individuals living outside of the red zone?

The impulse to distil dynamic social spaces into quantifiable, fixed territorial entities that provide for rationalized strategies of engagement is the hallmark of military-cartographic ways of engaging space, as suggested in the previous chapter. The example of zoning, which has some equivalence with the creation of various sites, is instructive in this respect. Thus slums, a term that may itself resonate with a latent derision for those who live within them, are in reality places where individuals live out their everyday lives in particularly challenging conditions. Though it is clear that grinding poverty exerts a profound influence on the opportunity structures within them, nevertheless these UN designated 'red zones' or slums are home to love, hate, singing, dancing and, ultimately for many, desperation. It is within their boundaries that children are raised, that mothers and fathers make do with the most meagre of resources and that life goes on, fuelled by the tenacious hope that things will get better. Yet, to zone, or to *do* zoning, is to reduce, to simplify, to strip down and to hollow out. The term 'red zone' is two-dimensional in this sense and captures little if anything of the positive face of human existence in these places. It is here that the potency of the techniques of security practice are realized in their productive guise, as from social complexity and dynamism emerges a two-dimensional deviance, enacted by everyone and no one in the zone as a spurious homogenization seals the fate of the inherently insecure slum-dweller.

Zoning is also infused by symbol, as in the example of Haiti and other UN missions, in the form of iconic colour-coding. In the Western imaginary at least, red spells danger and can spark awareness, suspicion and being on one's guard, with the 'war on terror' making extensive use of the risk level according to the colour red. Red also means stop; go no further. Alternatively, the amber or yellow zone in Haiti speaks to a more cautionary approach. In short, the implications of delegating particular geographical territories as zones is a practice that can compound stigma for those unfortunate enough to live within these spaces. In turn, zoning may shape conditions of wider possibilities, for to 'come from the red zone' may mean that one is barely human and a potential security risk as the baggage of demeaned territory may serve as the primary lens through which individuals are imagined. In this way, different colours may bleed into one another, as in the example of a 'bandit from the red zone' entering the 'peaceful green zone'. In so doing these demonized individuals may be seen to 'contaminate' the purity of safe spaces, largely unable to shake off their tainted identity, the roots of which might be linked in part to UN security practices.

As we saw above, it was the zone in particular that preoccupied the military aspect of the MINUSTAH presence. In effect, zones are hostile territory, and to venture within them as a member of the military peacekeeping force may be to test one's warrior resolve behind the lines.[12] The interception and elimination of gang members represents the zenith of peace enforcement, with these explicitly demarcated spaces functioning as classic counterinsurgency backdrops to military activity.[13] Replete with ramshackle constructions and tight spaces in which the warrior's reactivity is key, the ever-present possibility of actual firefights hones the peacekeeper-soldier. Resulting 'collateral damage' is a very real hazard, further heightening the risky nature for civilians of UN military peacekeepers' bold operations into the red zone. It is through these more obviously militarized social practices that the red zone is interpolated as the prime site of insecurity; a particular place where it is legitimate to hunt down and eliminate gang members in ways that may counter the experience of emasculation discussed by some in the peacekeeping role.[14] Peace spoilers' resistance to arrest and detention, perhaps even using weapons brought into the country by the UN itself, vindicates the intervention, and is a self-fulfilling reminder of the abhorrent, violent activities of the gangs to which armed response is presented as the only option.[15]

The question of corruption and nepotism, played out at the considerably more opaque political level, may compound similarly if not more damaging hindrances to establishing a sustainable peace. Yet these hidden, institutionalized activities remain largely unchallenged as they are problems above and beyond military 'solutions'. All too often, those civilian and military personnel deployed to create stability can themselves be drawn into illicit practices at worst, and at best be carried away by organizational cultures of self-interest, fuelled by fatalism about the prospects for the mission and its people.[16] Consequently, in this example, the red zones can assume a reality beyond which it is difficult to think and that, ultimately, could be seen as compounding the essentialized Haitian identity thought by some to be disposed to violence and poverty. The perception that MINUSTAH operations into the red zones served to displace violence was of considerable concern to both international and local people. Though it is clear that the transformation of post-conflict sites into demarcated territories can be a productive outcome of the UN or NATO presence, nevertheless, it is the displacement of violence that is understood to result from this clash of forces. It is difficult to demonstrate causal links between peacekeepers' strategic forays into the red zones with their apparent displacement of violence, although this pattern – in terms of policing more widely – has a well-documented universality.[17] What might be framed by some as the consequence of peace enforcement fuels the need for more aggressive interventions, as the self-reinforcing pattern of violence meeting violence is seen to justify robust peace enforcement.

The practice of zoning is derived from military ways of seeing and engaging space. These spatial practices are inclined towards a process of categorizing and responding to discrete spaces – such as the zone or slum. In this way, it is possible to show how zones did not and do not exist independently of peacekeeping operations. The central point to stress here is that the conditions of possibility generated by military–cartographic ways of engaging these particular spaces are necessarily limited and may default towards the use of force. What might it mean to think beyond these possibilities? What other kinds of security practices might UN troops get involved in? How might the resources they expend (in terms of planning, use of equipment and harm to peacekeepers themselves) be deployed in different ways? Given the great variability of peacekeeper style of intervention that encompasses a wide spectrum of reconstruction and humanitarian work, is peace enforcement 'the only option'? Posing these questions might encourage us to examine the deeper rationales underpinning spatially constitutive security practice in line with the seduction of 'proper soldiering'. Where might we look to find security practices that carry with them similar effects in terms of responding to bounded spaces of insecurity? The question is now taken up within the context of the Kosovo enclave.

Kosovo and the enclave

In Kosovo, when discussion turned to security, the enclaves in which minority groups – mainly Kosovan Serbs – lived, were invariably mentioned. Much like the slums in Haiti, the formation of enclaves should be seen as the contingent outcome of a series of social and political events turning on the ethnicized history of Kosovo. Those settlements in which Kosovo Serbians lived grew significantly as the tide turned against members of this group from around the end of 1998 onwards. KFOR troops 'rushed' to protect and make secure both the Serbian monasteries (symbolic of their presence) and Gračanica and Štrpce, well-known minority settlements.[18] In the face of Kosovo

Albanian reprisals, given considerable moral and strategic impetus by the NATO intervention against Milosevic and his forces, enclaves swelled as a relatively small number of Serbians sought safety in numbers. The riots of 2004 may have also fuelled the growth of Serbian enclaves as a new wave of 'reverse ethnic cleansing' broke out some five years into the mission.[19] Whilst Kosovo Albanians tended to stress the security of the Serb communities, tellingly a number of them also made the contradictory point that 'The presence of KFOR was necessary in and around Serbian enclaves so that they don't feel threatened anymore';[20] from whom the threat might arise was a topic left unexplored.[21] Internationals described the ways in which an 'enclave mentality' emerged whereby Serbians' perception of insecurity grew in tandem with the time spent in enclaves, isolated from members of other ethnic groups. This mind-set emerged within the context of isolation that developed as part-consequence of UNMIK's provision of 'protected transportation', as one European female working for an international organization argued:

> Let's take a Serbian or minority community that has been living in isolation for six years. Many, if not all, of them may have stayed in the enclave and have only used the protected transportation provided by the UN. Of course they don't feel safe.

The main problem according to a North American female NGO worker was that:

> These populations have lived in isolation for such a long time. They haven't experienced the changes that have been going on in the municipalities. Their limited understanding of the improvements experienced by others means that they are living in a kind of 'security limbo'.

Whilst Serbians argued that they were vulnerable to attack by Kosovar Albanians, members of the latter group and a handful of internationals suggested that 'it was not in the interests of the Serbian enclaves to be that well protected'. Rather, the 'way forward' was to have a 'dialogue with your neighbours' and 'find out if you can live together in a safe environment'.[22] This potential process of reconciliation, whilst particularly challenging in the context of Kosovo and the Balkans more widely, was nevertheless perceived to be hampered by some elements of KFOR and UNMIK strategy.[23] In respect of the well-intentioned road-building efforts of KFOR troops, it was suggested by a European male working for an international organization that 'Building roads doesn't help with multi-ethnicity in any way whatsoever, because you are linking "one bunch" with "another bunch"!' The 'problem of the enclave' could be explained by the inability of the international presence to move the reconciliation process forward with real enthusiasm and vigour. In this regard, it was argued that the first 'phase' immediately following the NATO-led bombing campaign had been in place for too long, leading to stagnation. A British male with many years' experience of working in Kosovo suggested that it was 'important that after every conflict there is a period when the lid has to be kept on. You need a different medicine for different periods.' He went on: 'It is important for KFOR to initially say "Everyone stay where you are!"' But then (realistically or not) he believed that there should have been a concerted attempt to 'open up the enclaves … if this had been done, they would not have ended up as "fixed entities"'. This view was echoed by others, including a male from a neighbouring country working for an NGO who went so far as to suggest that KFOR provided 'too much security', which fuelled the 'artificiality' of minority fears.[24] Kosovo Albanians – both males and females – argued that 'if KFOR didn't protect them they wouldn't be isolated in the enclaves!' Ultimately they would feel free to 'go to the market and shops', leading to the 'natural integration'[25] of all groups in Kosovo. Recent violent events, including riots in Belgrade and the attack on a UN border crossing in 2008, however, cast some doubt on the feasibility of reconciling Kosovo Albanians and Serbians.

Stronger views still were aired around the role of the UN in 'perpetuating and reinforcing' the distance between the groups. One international in particular discussed the absence of an explicit long-term, unifying strategy choreographing UNMIK and KFOR collaboration. The chief difficulty, it was suggested, lay in 'the KFOR peacekeeping role', which was in tension with the 'returns process'. Here, Serbs were brought back to their former homes in Kosovo from Serbia in vehicles with 'flashing blue lights'.[26] In turn, it was observed, tensions could rise in this heightened security context, meaning that KFOR would then have necessarily to intervene to pre-empt or even quell actual violence. The outcome of this cycle of events served to intensify hostility and fuel the stand-off between the Kosovar Albanian and ethnic Serbian populations. The point to stress here is that the international community tended to duck questions about the apparent fixity of ethnic division, but rather took it as a 'truth' that subsequently shaped the approaches taken to security work. The reasons for this are complex but are likely to involve a mix of pragmatism, in terms of what might be seen as realistic given the historical trajectories of these ethnic groups and the tensions between them together with, as one international suggested, an unwillingness for some of his colleagues to 'get off their backsides and really get stuck in'. In this second respect, it was argued that Kosovo is something of a 'cushy' tour for UN staff (for example, in comparison to Afghanistan) and that the longer tensions existed, the longer these privileged individuals were able to enjoy the (relative) safety of the Province, its good food, and the easy accessibility of Kosovo to such tourist destinations as Greece. It should be stressed that this alleged absence of a collective will to integrate the minority and majority populations may be found as much in the sublime and nuanced aspects of institutional culture as in the self-interest of those working within UNMIK. In sum, the 'immutability' of ethnic identity provided a convenient wellspring of current and future tension around and through which the international presence could thrive in relative comfort, though the way institutional culture develops is a matter of contingency rather than outright conspiracy.

Enclaves, or ethnically exclusive and homogenous neighbourhoods, villages and towns, are an expression of power over space, and simultaneously an expression of entrapment and refuge within a fixed space. There is nothing inherent in or organic about a group of ethnically homogenous people living together – enclaves are themselves political formations. Enclaves might be said to exist only in so far as they are allowed to attain a territorial 'truth' through time, the likes of which becomes fixed in the minds of those living in them, others providing security to them and, more generally, for distant onlookers who view them as the naturally occurring outcome of inter-ethnic tensions. Enclaves are constructed from the tangible emotional foundations of fear of revenge attacks, fostered through the dialogic link between the spatial practices of KFOR troops, and actual documented violence detailed in UN and independent incident reports. Despite the fears of

Serbians, KFOR's practices were seen to fuel a hardening of partition through military-security artefacts and social practice. Here, the presence of static guard towers, vehicle checkpoints and foot patrols compound the visceral awareness that 'one is now entering an enclave'. Intrinsic to familiarizing oneself with enclaves is the dominant belief – expressed by many in the field – that these places are home to a fearful, ethnically homogeneous community of Serbian women, men and children. This perception can be seen as a microcosm of dominant views expressed in respect of the Balkans more widely in ways that manifest themselves on cartographic representations of the province.[27] As Campbell (1998: 78) has argued,

> To frame one's narrative with a map of the former Yugoslavia would seem to be no more than an unremarkable act of description. However, maps are not simply inert records or passive reflections of the world of objects but 'refracted images contributing to dialogue in a socially constructed world' ... maps conceive, articulate and structure ... maps indicate the possibility of a particular narrative.

Undoubtedly, then, the dominant narrative of insecurity in Kosovo turns on the enclave, one element of which is linked to the KFOR military presence that is shaped by a 'symbolism or meaning that goes beyond that which is indicated by just physical presence' (Woodward 2004: 109). One mundane illustration of the KFOR presence is the abandoned guard tower in the town of Lipjan in close proximity to a Serbian enclave that speaks to both space and time. In respect of the latter, the temporal dimension, the now vacated guard tower appears somewhat incongruous. It is a reminder of what was (ethnic tension requiring a military presence of Finnish KFOR troops), and as such signals a juxtaposition of past insecurity with future security. It is also a symbol of hope since it signifies the absence of threat to the minority population over which it towers. Not unlike the red zones in Haiti, enclaves are contested spaces requiring a defensive peacekeeper presence on their periphery, though clearly are not seen to warrant aggressive intervention. Interestingly, enclaves can also be seen as militarized in ways that mirror the conditions of armed forces barracks. As Woodward (2004: 110) argues: 'Living on a patrolled, gated, fenced military base (or enclave) gives a dimension of safety. Yet this is polarized with the same landscape as a potential region of stress ... with fear of attack.'

Living within the confines of an enclave, again like that of a military installation, may also be characterized by ennui: 'which appears through ... isolation ... the exclusion of outsiders ... [and most poignantly in an enclave], the lack of [economic] opportunities' (Woodward 2004: 110).[28] Here, the distinct patterns of Serbs' movement are facilitated by KFOR activities that shape enclave dwellers' security subjectivities. Yet, it is also important to note that these security subjectivities can also be positive and play a vital role in creating a sense of community within the context of shared hardship and common identity. Enclaves, and their isolation from wider communities, can protect language and culture in ways that provide for a strong sense of belonging. Considerations of the sort that flow from a sense of compassion for an oppressed minority may also help to explain the complexity of rationales shaping the security practices of KFOR troops, as it is important to see these individuals as thinking, feeling agents who believe that the continued isolation of the minorities is in their best interest.

There is little doubt that the prospects for creating a 'multi-ethnic society' in Kosovo may be unrealistic[29] and serve as little more than rhetorical fodder directed towards an international audience.[30] However, there was some evidence to suggest that sustained and dedicated intervention by international organizations *could* produce results, as one European female NGO worker believed:[31]

> There are some people in the field who have done really great things. For example in places like Klina, good work has been done which you might not expect given the fact there was a lot of fighting and atrocities committed there.

US and Spanish KFOR troops were also discussed by a European male NGO worker, who within the context of the town of Gilan said:

> Saturday was made a 'minority day'. All the minorities can walk freely in the town on a Saturday and that is just an order. It comes slowly over many Saturdays. They eventually develop confidence, and then the Spanish troops invited all minorities into their camp and they had a nice time together.

Attempts to encourage contact across the ethnic divide was also mentioned by a European female working for a local NGO:

Some work has been done at the local level. We had a project by
UNDP to clean the Ibar river. People found out from both sides of
the divide that they actually had something in common and suddenly
'Eureka!' we found something to bring them together. You do have to
do this quietly so that there are no repercussions for those minorities
and members of the majority Albanian population who are trying to
reconcile.

Finally, the story was told of how a Serbian employee was asked
to make the journey to the 'south of the river' for the first time in
seven years to have lunch with a group of Kosovar Albanians and
internationals: 'At first she was said to be "deathly afraid", but over
the course of the lunch in which discussion was conducted in the
Serbian language, she began to relax, and even "warmed up a bit".'[32]
It was also said that just prior to embarking on her homeward journey
north, she commented that she had begun to 'enjoy the lunch' and
'liked the company of the gathered group'.[33]

Conclusion

Peacekeepers are active in creating spaces of both secure and insecure
kinds, as demonstrated here and in the previous chapter. The military
response to gang members in zones, whilst implemented with the
aim of improving security, did nonetheless result in mixed results for
those living within these spaces, as well as others who experienced
a displacement of violence. The act of zoning flows from a military
strategic rationale where particular spaces are imagined as discrete and
somewhat two-dimensional. They pay host to violent gang members,
who have necessarily to be removed by military means, thereby
promising a definitive solution to a quantifiable problem. And yet
the conditions of poverty that may give rise to criminal activities are
left largely undisturbed; rather, cycles of violence may be reinforced
as the Blue Helmets engage the sharp end of peace enforcement
activities. The points of convergence with approaches taken to the
enclaves in Kosovo turn on discretely bounded, solvable spaces of
insecurity. Again, they are framed as problems that can be tackled
by protecting one population from another. Yet, in tension with
the broader aim of facilitating integration of these groups as a key

strategy for the future stability of the province, somewhat ironically they serve to freeze and fix the conflict. In the end, the spaces and places that preoccupy peacekeepers and their security work in both Haiti and Kosovo have sidetracked these troops from the broader goals of the respective mandates, to which military responses may be less than adequate.

FOUR

Free to move?

How easy is it to get around in a post-conflict country? To what extent does the presence of peacekeepers impact on one's mobility in conditions where infrastructure may have been destroyed? In this chapter, attention is turned to freedom of movement, a universal indicator of security. Our aims are to provide both a sense of how freedom of movement was seen by members of the host population and international employees and an account of the ways that peacekeepers impacted on the ability of individuals to move, mainly using examples drawn from Liberia and Kosovo.

Traversing spaces: security, movement and roads

Questions of security invariably invoked the subject of freedom of movement in Liberia, both in the capital city of Monrovia and further afield. Concern tended to focus on the damaged infrastructure; for example, two Liberian males working for a small NGO in a town outside of Monrovia said that, 'For us, security is about the freedom to move ... security is about free movement.' These sentiments were echoed by another Liberian male, employed as a security guard for a Monrovia-based NGO, who argued that security comes from 'an environment in which people can move freely'. It was believed by a female Liberian NGO worker that military peacekeepers of the UNMIL force had 'reduced people's fear and they are now going about their business. There is not that much tension now but when we first came here there was fear amongst the community. Things have relaxed and they can move from one place to another.'

A similar view was elicited in Monrovia, where physical infrastructure and security were seen as synonymous in ways that expanded definitions from the immediate threat of weaponry. As one Liberian male taxi driver suggested:

> Security makes me think of physical geography ... ie bridges, networks, roads. Insecurity is not only about the presence of arms but about travelling. The road should be passable and bridges should be safe – that's my general sense of safety.

The condition of Liberia's roads and infrastructure emerged as a key theme, as noted when the work of peacekeepers brought Lofa county within a one-day drive of Monrovia, here in the words of a female Liberian NGO worker:

> The roads are difficult and the infrastructure is destroyed. Housing is a problem and people are very much isolated. I was in Lofa County in December and it took almost two days to get there! Now, with the road fixed by military peacekeepers of the Chinese contingent, it takes eight hours.[1]

Reference to houses that await rehabilitation, social isolation, and the time it takes to travel to particular counties underscored the significance of serviceable roads to everyday life. A Liberian male NGO worker deployed in the north-east of the country understood that UNMIL peacekeepers should be directly involved in creating security through rebuilding roads and the broader infrastructure. In this way – and perhaps reflecting the relative peace within the country such that peacekeepers were not seen 'engaging' peace spoilers but, rather, constructing and repairing roads. And yet, he said, 'There is much more to be done in terms of security. When it comes to helping us build our country, peacekeepers need to help us to rebuild the roads.'[2] Poor roads were noted to fuel the sense of insecurity inasmuch as they slowed down, or even prevented, peacekeepers' response to criminal incidents – a particular concern of those in the isolated

counties. As one international female NGO worker from outside
Monrovia put it: 'Because UNMIL is slow to respond, a lot of crimes
can be committed.' A Liberian male from the same NGO echoed
this view when he suggested that 'UNMIL peacekeepers could build
roads and tighten security.' The problem of damaged roads was also
raised by a Liberian male market trader, who observed that: 'UNMIL
peacekeepers can patrol in the city but not in other areas where the
roads are damaged. They only travel on the main roads and can't
pass through the communities. When the roads are eventually fixed,
UNMIL will be able to pass through.'[3]

The better road infrastructure within Monrovia and other con-
urbations facilitated the presence of UNMIL military peacekeepers
within the capital, where they were ubiquitous in their white, 4x4
Toyota Land Cruisers. Though the imperfect condition of the roads
resulted in bone-jarring rides in Monrovia's private fleet of yellow cabs
and minibuses, movement was relatively easy. Yet the peacekeeping
presence did not appear to be spread evenly throughout the country,
and it was argued that whether or not the Blue Helmets accessed
different counties and regions depended on their designation as
'strategic' spaces. It was entirely possible to travel for considerable
periods of time in Liberia without ever seeing peacekeepers, even
where roads were serviceable, as a North American male working for
a large UN agency argued:

> We have 15,000 peacekeepers in Liberia, but they are in the strategic
> zones of the country. Anybody who is outside of that strategic zone
> is potentially vulnerable, and I can confirm that because I have been
> into the rural areas. I have been on roads where I didn't see UN peace-
> keepers for maybe two hours – there are real people out there who liter-
> ally know no security.[4] We only have about half (800) of the number of
> police we are meant to be getting and I don't know if they are going to
> go out into the districts, and be deployed at the clan level.

However, the belief that peacekeepers should make their presence
felt in more isolated areas, including those in difficult terrain, was not
shared by all. As one Liberian male NGO worker in an eastern village
asserted: 'to expect UNMIL peacekeepers to walk in the bush is sheer
madness', not least because it was difficult to make any meaningful
progress in areas of dense undergrowth. Could peacekeepers access
remote communities using their vehicles? The response from a female

UN volunteer was that 'If your area can't be reached by car, you won't be visited. On top of that, where you have a very difficult road, peacekeepers are less likely to patrol because they are nervous that they might become "sitting ducks".'

Poor roads both limit accessibility and can leave the Blue Helmets vulnerable to attack from peace spoilers,[5] as they are unable to extricate themselves swiftly from difficult situations. Concern was expressed about the apparent absence of peacekeeper foot patrols, which tended to play to the sense of neglect felt by certain communities:

> There are areas that are inaccessible, areas of 'forgotten people'. Now the repatriation has started from the refugee camps and there are very few who don't want to go home.[6] It was reported that there were people 'running around in the bush'. If people come from areas where there are no car-accessible roads, they are unlikely to be visited by UNMIL peacekeepers as I have never heard of any foot patrols.

In addition to the inaccessibility of roads, the debilitating heat and dense bush were serious impediments to peacekeeper ability to present themselves to the isolated communities of Liberia. Many expressed a strong desire that peacekeepers should push further into remote areas, as this comment from a Liberian female resident of an isolated border town suggests: 'People would like peacekeepers to go further out into the remote areas. It is better if UNMIL can go out into the bush.' While there was an overall degree of frustration that more could be done to rebuild the damaged infrastructure in Liberia, nevertheless the sense that progress was being made in certain parts of the country was largely down to the work of military peacekeeping engineers. In the lead-up to the elections, they had repaired many hundreds of kilometres of roads in order to facilitate a good voter turn-out.

How were concerns of freedom of movement discussed in Kosovo? What role did NATO–KFOR peacekeepers play in shaping who was able to move freely and what kinds of rationales underpinned their security work in this respect?

Kosovo: ethnic identity and 'parallel travel'

In discussing the insecure minorities in Kosovo (generally a reference to Serbians), an international highlighted the ways in which freedom of movement was both localized and historicized.[7] He went on to suggest that in many ways, things had improved:

> It is far from perfect, but now Serbs move. I think they live in settle-ments rather than enclaves, or maybe you call them 'Serbian territo-ries'. There is no barbed wire around them and KFOR don't seem to provide escorts for the minorities anymore.

However, whilst it was said by a European female from an inter-national organization that Serbians were able to move relatively freely, it was also stated that this group remained unwilling to use public transportation:

> Serbs have their own channels of communication and transport, and for the most part nobody bothers them, but they wouldn't act as normal people in a normal country – they are not 'allowed' really. I know they wouldn't hop on a bus full of Albanians.[8]

International staff reported that there had been only marginal success in facilitating freedom of movement for Serbian communities, particularly those living in areas that were surrounded by members of the majority population: 'Those Serbs living in villages surrounded by Albanians would travel 50 or 60 kilometres to another Serb area rather than go to the local market', as one female European employee of an international organization noted. This observation underscores the continued sense of insecurity experienced by Serbians in ways that impact on the taken-for-granted activity of purchasing food in the local market, for example. Not unlike the parallel systems of institutions developed by Kosovar Albanians during the Milosevic era, Serbians relied where possible on their own network of roads, according to a Roma businessman:

> They have roads connecting the settlements that avoid the main roads. These back roads take you from A to B through Serbian territory and are still used today. Albanians would avoid them! After all why would they want to end up in 'enemy territory'? Why go through villages full of angry Serbs and get harassed?

Of note here is the use of the phrase 'enemy territory'; the clear sense of territorial encroachment signals the exclusivity of particular spaces in relation to ethnic identity. Different perceptions of security could give rise to anomalies highlighting tensions between international organizations' risk-aversion policies and perceptions on the ground, as this male international said:

> I look at my own Serbian staff and I have one with his own car which has Serbian registration plates.[9] He drives all over Kosovo at weekends – and he's never had a problem. The irony is that when he is working they put him in an armoured vehicle, but during the weekdays he has to be in a bullet-proof vehicle!

While parallel systems of road networks between minority and majority groups had developed, numerous members of the former group spoke of their heightened anxiety when it was necessary to move from enclaves – typically in three- or four-car impromptu convoys – to seek medical assistance, for example. How had UNMIK and KFOR responded to the problem of freedom of movement? Two main strategies to facilitate freedom of movement had been in operation since 1999. They involved, first, the provision of 'protected' transportation by UNMIK and KFOR and, second, KFOR road construction activities linking Serbian enclaves with one another. Road repair or construction was frequently carried out under the auspices of Civil–Military Cooperation (CIMIC) and could also involve funding from EU and other international organizations. It appeared to be a rather ad hoc affair, however, and was linked as much with local commanders' deployment of troops and available resources as it was to requests from members of the Serbian minority. Some of the projects were quite bold, as in the case of KFOR personnel building a road straight over a hill in order to link two Serbian settlements.

Both the transport and the road initiatives were discussed in relation to questions of security and the presence of KFOR peacekeepers, or UNMIK. Yet not all of these comments were positive. For example, concern about the use of 'protected' buses (these were noted to have cages over the windows and shielded wheels) for exclusive use by Serbians led to the following belief, conveyed by a European male working for an international organization: 'In my opinion, UNMIK have made a big mistake in their approach to freedom of movement.' He continued:

> In 1999/2000 they had this bus operated by the Danish Refugee Council, which of course is a good idea in the very beginning. But due to the interests of certain individuals in UNMIK, who have now

been fired for corruption, these buses continued to operate for *far too long* and were seen as a symbol of preferential treatment for the minorities in the eyes of the Albanians. (emphasis in interview)

This strategy to engender freedom of movement actually served to harden divisions. It was also suggested that the use of KFOR assistance with transportation was an explicitly political act, since 'Serbs request convoys to make the situation appear dramatic and KFOR runs to help them!', according to a Kosovar Albanian male shop owner. A Turkish female working in Priština remarked that 'Serbs *say* they will get attacked when they move around. There are "political" benefits for them if they act like this'[10] (emphasis in interview). Clearly the use of protected transport remained a much politicized and volatile issue that provided security in the short term, but had become institutionalized both in the social practices of those who used it and in the bureaucracies of those for whom transport provision may have provided the opportunity for corruption. Finally, a Serbian female working for an international organization told of how she negotiated a sense of paranoia around her ethnic identity, leading over time to a situation where she was able to exercise a greater personal freedom to move:

> I will never forget my feeling of personal insecurity when I started walking to work in 2001. It was so big it felt as if I had a heavy weight on my legs, which prevented me from walking faster. Over time my concerns became completely different. They didn't care who I was. For them I was just another person walking on the street. This is how I started to exercise my personal freedom of movement, and to deepen my feelings of safety.

This account, whilst relevant to the individual in question, could nonetheless have a broader applicability to members of Serbian and other minority groups for whom freedom of movement represents a daily challenge. Put differently, the limited conditions of possibility experienced by oppressed groups in Kosovo have been shaped in part by the UNMIK and NATO–KFOR strategy to provide protected transportation and build roads some seven years into the mission.

In the examples of both Liberia and Kosovo, freedom of movement emerged as a key indicator of security. Though the mission sites diverge in a number of ways, road building emerged as a common theme.

A closer look at road building from the perspective of the military strategic rationale continues our analyses of the processes by which peacekeepers constitute spaces of both secure and insecure kinds.

Roads, meanings, security

In response to a query probing the motivation behind the construction of roads linking minority enclaves with one another, we received the following email from an Italian male NATO–KFOR officer who has commanded road-building work in the province:

> Freedom of Movement (FOM) is a military requirement that is a pre-requisite to provide a safe and secure environment (SASE). Main roads are designated Lines of Communication (LOC) and Main Supply Routes (MSR). Those LOC that are essential to KFOR's mission will receive NATO common funding for road repair. This may include pot-hole repair, signalization, drainage, etc. but not a complete rehabilitation. In some cases, bridges and roads have been built by the Brigades to link minority enclaves with other areas of specific ethnicity to reduce the threat for these people (the other ethnicity throwing stones being the faintest of all when they try to visit the hospital or whatever office). This is, however, not due to any initiative of HQ KFOR, but is being done on the local level. Brigades also get engaged in road building when minorities are no subject, just to keep their engineers occupied. These roads serve economic/communication interests and are in most cases built after requests by the individual communities.

This brief insight into how freedom of movement is conceptualized and operationalized militarily is instructive for a number of reasons. First, and most obvious, is the use of military argot and its associated repertoire of acronyms through which freedom of movement is imagined and constituted. Here, the intention to create safety and security may be both simultaneously recognizable and alien to members of the host population and others who work in the mission; the common desire for freedom in the physical landscape carries with it diverse meanings. As we saw in Chapter 2, in the instance of cartographic representations of particular territories, indigenous and exogenous framings may be at some distance from one another. For example, when military peacekeepers look at roads they may well see lines of communication or supply routes. They might take

into account the extent to which bush encroaching upon the edges
of the road can provide cover for potential 'peace spoilers'; they may
relish the opportunity to travel at considerable speed on the few hard
roads in the region; and finally, for example, they could approach
slow-moving road users by foot, or aged vehicles, as little more than
obstacles hindering their security work and leisure activities. Local
people are perhaps unlikely to see the roads in quite the same way,
although there are likely to be differences between the genders in this
respect with bush perhaps compounding the sense of insecurity for
women who are at risk of sexually motivated attack. Put broadly, as
we saw in Liberia, local people drew attention to the importance of
'going about their business', or more simply experiencing the novelty
of moving where and when they wished (Masquelier 2002).

Given the potential divergence in meaning considered here, together with the overall priority given to peacekeepers' security work,
members of host populations may be subjugated to strategic military
requirements as the spaces in which they live are reconfigured according to prosaic 'supply and communication priorities'. It might
legitimately be asked, supply and communication for whom? Who
benefits and who loses in terms of security? Who makes the crucial
decisions about road repair and construction; to what extent is this
process consultative? Though engineers can contribute to security
through being 'kept busy' building roads, the criteria by which such
projects are implemented is opaque. The rationale of 'threat reduction'
is said to underpin road rehabilitation and construction activities for
members of insecure minority populations. Yet threat reduction is
implicitly conceptualized in both a spatial and temporal vacuum.
In the example of Kosovo it is in tension with the stated desire by
UNMIK to see a multi-ethnic society and represents a short-term
fix, with the explicit intention to increase spatial segregation between
Kosovar Albanians and Serbians for immediate reasons of security.

Conclusion

The term 'freedom of movement' speaks directly to security. In both
Kosovo and Liberia it emerged as a key concern. Infrastructure,
road building and repair, and the extent to which individuals are

able to go about their everyday lives play themselves out in ways that engage the military peacekeeping presence, whether it be the work of engineers or the accessibility of roads to foot and vehicle patrols. The important point to note here is that, in line with our broader argument, peacekeepers can be viewed as agents of spatial power whose practices actively configure security possibilities on the ground. Thus, conducting a foot patrol or driving over poor roads with the aim of accessing isolated communities, whilst seemingly routine, does nevertheless make a profound difference to perceptions of security. That peacekeepers go about their business according to military strategic or geographical rationales is frequently lost on the host population and others who may be employed in the missions. As peacekeeprs are visitors in post-conflict countries, the onus is on them to continue to provide explanations to the host population of what they are doing and why. Whilst mission may have a 'public relations' office, it is inappropriate for it to try to convey the more routine, everyday details of the peacekeeping presence. For this reason it is even more important that peacekeepers take every opportunity to climb out of their vehicles and simply chat with local people about what they are doing in the village or community in which they find themselves. An all too frequent occurrence is the dangerously driven UN vehicle speeding through a community in ways that compound the differences between locals and privileged occupiers who threaten the security of others. Though it is clear that a good number of peacekeepers engage with locals whenever they can, many do not, and their boots may only ever tread the floors of the compounds in which they live or the leisure sites they frequent as they stick to the spaces of the secure zone.

FIVE

Contesting and consuming: space and success in Liberia

Though land-rights issues are said to be threatening the five-year peace in Liberia at the time of writing, in comparison to both Haiti and Kosovo this West African state can be seen to have benefited most from the presence of the UN. The reasons for this are complex and touch on geopolitical, regional and local political concerns, alongside a widely held belief in the longer-term prospects for peace in Liberia. Here, a combination of contingency, luck and hope, set alongside the spatial configuring of insecurity confronting peacekeepers as they entered this West African state offer clues to prevailing conditions noted at the time of the fieldwork. Yet, whilst it is clear that the UN intervention in Liberia has undoubtedly improved the security for those working and living there, nonetheless our research revealed a struggle over how to define space: military or humanitarian? In addition, it highlighted a potentially unstable future, as the imposition of a liberal market democracy may create further insecurities and tensions set against the backdrop of the violent history of the civil war. This chapter seeks (1) to understand better the spatial dimensions of UNMIL's relative success; (2) to suggest that, whilst successful, the role of the 'integrated mission' has proved controversial and its impact on long-term security unclear; and (3) to make clear that the future is far from certain for Liberians, who are being encouraged to align themselves with the liberal peace model that turns – ultimately – on stratified patterns of mass consumption. Set against this backdrop, the main argument we make in this chapter is that the spatial sequencing of operations so central to the peacekeeping project that proceeds from military security, into 'soft security' and finally into spaces of consumption, is rooted in a modernist vision of linear progress based on a rational notion of development. By no means do these stages unfold as effortlessly as intended, as we now see.

Contesting space: the 'integrated mission'

Integrated missions are those in which the Special Representative of the Secretary-General (SRSG) is the head of both the civil and military structures.[1] In this organizational model, all UN agencies fall under the direct control of the Department of Peacekeeping Operations,[2] as is the case in the integrated mission of Liberia. Unsurprisingly, members of the host population appeared largely unaware of this integrated structure, though an intuitive sense of how it shaped their perception of security was noted and is discussed below. For our NGO respondents, the integrated mission was seen to confuse working practices through identifying space as in need of 'military' or 'hard' security rather than that provided by humanitarians. Previously discrete spheres of responsibility became spaces of struggle framed in terms conveyed by one male Liberian NGO worker 'as a sacrificing of sound humanitarianism for military ends'. The politicization of security in the country was uppermost in the minds of many in the NGO community, who felt as if the integrated mission was undermining their role in Liberia. Here, it was believed that the UN was trying to silence those NGOs drawing attention to the insecurities in the country. Not only would highlighting insecurity undermine the effectiveness of UNMIL, but in addition could derail the planned presidential elections. This sense of the injustice that NGOs were little more than 'troublemakers' (at least in the eyes of a number of the more powerful UN stakeholders) was put in the following terms by a European female NGO worker based in Monrovia:

> The unhealthy thing is how UNMIL want to downplay the insecurity in the country and infer that NGOs want to 'make trouble'. We are trying to raise important issues and the space to do that is unclear. They say to us 'why don't you people stop complaining?'

The struggle between the UN and NGOs noted in this comment and more widely was framed by the broader context of the integrated mission that sought to colonize space defined – by the military component of the UN – as requiring particular kinds of robust or defensive engagement. In this way the mission was believed to have become militarized and was discussed within the context of the hierarchy that had developed between military 'problems' of 'hard' physical security and 'softer' security concerns relating to water, food, shelter and education. Anxiety was expressed by many in the NGO community that, whilst important, physical security was allowed to eclipse other priorities. In turn this fuelled the sense of vulnerability discussed by members of the host population, who noted the greater significance given to defensive weaponry, military equipment and the 'hard stance' of UNMIL troops – symbols of security/insecurity – at the expense of services such as wells for fresh drinking water.[3] From the perspective of UNMIL, physical security could be resolved by the presence of patrolling peacekeepers, who, as we saw in Chapter 4, were only able to access a fraction of Liberia's territory.

The military view of security was limited to situations where physical violence was threatened, and again it is difficult to gauge what came first, the actual existence of 'peace spoilers' or a hard peacekeeping stance intended to deter. In these terms the security practices of a number of UNMIL contingents were seen to be largely incompatible with more obviously humanitarian activities such as those dealing with the repatriation of internally displaced persons (IDPs) to their former villages and settlements. We were told that repatriation was framed by a high military presence, involving the Blue Helmets directing (mainly) women and young people back to their villages. Local and international NGO staff felt that military peacekeepers should not be involved in this kind of work since not only was their presence necessarily short-lived (once the 'job was done' they retired to barracks or other duties) but also that it spoke to the threat, fear and memories of war, rather than peace and the future challenges of rebuilding the social as well as physical fabric of communities. The sense of urgency driving the returns process and the role therein played by military peacekeepers derived from the SRSG's aspiration, as he put it, to 'Get the IDPs home before the elections so that they can vote, this is my number one priority'[4] (quoted in Sida 2005: 12). The main criteria for the returns process turned on whether or not previously occupied villages were considered 'safe'. In turn, this judgement was based on a list of 'minimum standards', covering, most significantly, the presence or otherwise of UNMIL patrols. We were supplied with a 'checklist' of these standards replete with military terminology, and priorities that former refugee camp dwellers considered inappropriate, with the provision of schools at the bottom of the list (not least because their children had received some education in the refugee camps). In these terms it was argued by those in the NGO community that there had been a 'rush to repatriate'. This hasty process turned on the prioritizing of military security over that of humanitarian concerns or 'basic services', as we now see.[5] As a Liberian male employed by an NGO said:

> The reasons that most IDPs feel insecure is that their basic social services are not provided. In the villages and towns where they are supposed to be, for instance outside Monrovia, most of the schools have not been revitalized. If social services had been provided in the communities there would be a stronger incentive for people to go back.

A European female working for a large NGO in Monrovia put it like this:

> Within the areas that are deemed 'safe for return' there are frequently no basic services. They (IDPs) get a 'return package', including money for transport, rice and tools which does help. The problem is, some humanitarian workers were concerned about the involvement of inexperienced UNMIL troops in the process.

An unknown number of peacekeepers had directed IDPs to villages that had no infrastructure, destroyed housing and, in one case, a tainted water supply. There was no sense of 'follow through'; rather – as we note in the following chapter – great attention applied to peacekeeper 'posturing', as one Liberian NGO worker put it. Here, armed peacekeepers would direct IDPs and then retire to their vehicles. We were told of one case where peacekeepers left their post after only a few minutes, leaving a large number of IDPs carrying supplies but with no sense of where they were headed. It was clear that many IDPs wanted to return to the villages and towns from which they had been forced, but again, as this Liberian male working for an NGO in Monrovia argued, 'If services had been provided in the communities there would be a real incentive for people to go back.' The broad consensus to emerge among NGO employees, articulated here by a European female, was that

> Political and military imperatives are driving this country right now at the cost sometimes of 'sound humanitarianism'. Since the phasing out of OCHA [the Office for Coordination of Humanitarian Affairs] there has not really been a sound humanitarian arm.[6]

She saw this as both a personal and a structural issue, turning centrally on the contestation of how space and security need should be defined. She went on to say:

> I don't think Mr X is very strong as a humanitarian co-ordinator. I also think that Mr Y [the SRSG] has a very warped perception and wants to take credit for all of the humanitarian efforts and development work that is being done in this country, very little of which is actually done by UNMIL. As members of the humanitarian community we don't feel like going to an office which is both humanitarian and military. We don't feel like 'going on their grounds'.

The clash of working cultures between the military and humanitarian communities is brought into focus here within the context of a hierarchy of control. An American male working for a UN agency in Monrovia discussed the 'integrated mission' as a major issue:

> Having been to Kosovo, Burundi and Rwanda, I can say that 'integrated missions' are still work in progress, and there is still a lot to be done. One view out there is that there is a black and a blue UN, with the black being the military and the blue being the UN humanitarian agencies. There is a definite need for greater coordination and better cohesion and I think it is unfortunate that the UN has taken a decision to use the 'integrated mission' approach in Liberia. In the heart of a humanitarian crisis, this decision is not good for the UN.

Once again, the complexities over how to define a humanitarian crisis are raised, with the belief here that the ideological drive to colonize and shape space has assumed an importance within and of itself. A European female working for an NGO in Monrovia underscored the battle of ideas and definitions applied to the wider field of operations:

This mission is now *so* military! Even stuff like when they [UNMIL] circulate minutes of meetings they use the [military] approach of 'need-to-know'.[7] They try to keep everything secret. They don't see a genuine need for collaboration, unlike when we worked with OCHA which was very much a partnership. (emphasis in interview)

A Liberian male working in the field office of an international NGO said in regard to the 'integrated mission':

They have this military push from the top which doesn't lend itself to collaboration. In terms of security for local people it just means the whole complementarity thing doesn't exist, to be honest. It now is on an NGO-to-NGO level, whereas before you were there with OCHA, who would know where people were in the field [both beneficiaries and NGOs]. If you had a stronger OCHA presence here you would have much better coordination, which would have trickle-down effects into the community.

Framing and naming space as 'humanitarian' had become an altogether more precarious and ad hoc business played out at the local level rather than through a high-level coordinator (OCHA). Whilst this may have encouraged a higher level of collaboration between NGOs, losing sight of the Liberia-wide 'big picture' was believed to stymie the effectiveness of 'soft security' concerns. A further limitation of the integrated mission turned on the attempt by NGO workers to distance themselves from the UN, and in particular its military elements, for reasons of their own security. A European female working for an NGO in the north of the country invoked the ways that freedom of movement was fundamentally a political issue, since being linked to UNMIL or 'armed occupiers', as peace spoilers saw them, could threaten their safety:

We don't ride in UNMIL helicopters,[8] that is not allowed. It is ten hours by road in the dry season and two days in the rainy season to Zwedru, and that is a bit of a nightmare especially with the medical supplies. In the rainy season if one of our trucks is stuck in the road we cannot go to the UN to ask for their help. We have to manage by ourselves or use another NGO.

Here, the 'compressing' of space and time providing for rapid delivery
of aid had failed to develop, despite the presence of a (UN) transport
infrastructure (mainly Russian-built helicopters) that could play a vital
role in this humanitarian aspect of the mission. Yet, a small number
of UN contacts argued that 'humanitarians are quick to jump on our
helicopters when it kicks off!' (i.e. violence breaks out). The apparent
contradiction of humanitarians who would 'not use UN transport' for
matters of personal and organizational principle, though were quick to
use it when their own security was threatened, confirmed the belief of
some UN staff that humanitarians practised double standards. While
basic 'soft' security infrastructure required for education, housing,
electricity and sanitation tended not to be of concern to the UN
military component because it 'was not part of their mandate', at the
same time numerous contingents provided humanitarian assistance
in ways that appeared to encroach upon the role of NGOs, for whom
these activities were their stock-in-trade. The case of contingents from
South Asia that expended considerable time and resources to rehabili-
tate mosques and construct schools is a case in point. This soft/hard
engagement with space further confused the turf wars between the
NGOs and the UN Blue Helmets, who used their time and resources
in ways that marked them as both humanitarians and 'warriors'.

Most importantly, the difficulties arising from the integrated
mission were couched primarily in spatial terms and as such resonate
with broader commentaries on this approach towards UN operations
(Lewis 2005: 24) as we now see. There is broad agreement amongst
humanitarians that 'humanitarian space' is: 'The space to give and
receive humanitarian assistance and protection without being harassed
or hindered by government or belligerent forces' (Lewis 2005: 24).
For example, the International Committee of the Red Cross (ICRC)
sees the term as highlighting the 'preservation of space', whilst the
Red Crescent draws on the importance of 'creating a humanitarian
space'; other agencies, including the Overseas Development Institute,
foreground the protection of this space. The NGO Concern argues
that humanitarian space is 'a physical, geographical space that is
protected from fighting such as may be seen in situations in which
humanitarian corridors are established ... [this] *action* space is required by humanitarian organisations' (Lewis 2005: 24, citing Van
Brabant 1998; emphasis added).

There is a clear sense in which the humanitarian gaze, like that of its military counterpart, carries with it a strong geographical resonance infused by transformative intent.[9] This desire to shape the canvas of operations emerges through the distinctive language whereby the 'preservation' and 'creation' of 'action spaces' speak to an unambiguous spatially constitutive agenda. However, the terms of intervention are argued to differ sharply from those of the military, where 'core humanitarian principles are increasingly compromised by the interests of a security-dominated policy agenda' (Stoddard and Harmer 2006: 23; Duffield 2002). This shift in the broader ideological agenda of international intervention produces numerous dilemmas for humanitarian actors, including, as we noted above, disassociating themselves from the military presence through using their own transportation. As we have seen, the use of military assets, including helicopters in particular, is understood to frame staff as 'potential targets' (Stoddard and Harmer 2006: 25) in ways that have a profound impact on how humanitarian space is constituted and aid can be delivered.

It is also the case that the ideology of the integrated mission in regard to the focus on security can lead to partition and the segregation of humanitarians and peacekeepers from the vulnerable host populations that can benefit from face-to-face interaction with these individuals. In these terms, there has developed a particular form of security architecture, heavily protected compounds. High fences, razor wire and guards help to mark these bounded spaces as no-go areas for local people. Ironically, it is not just the UN military component that may end up in these 'lock-down' security enclaves, but also humanitarians, for whom direct engagement with those in need can be seriously undermined.[10] The subordination of the humanitarian space to that of the military elements of the peacekeeping mission is, overall, a political question, as the integrated mission in Liberia is argued to be

> The final step in realizing the full integration of humanitarian co-ordination under a political banner, [this] may involve humanitarian concerns becoming subservient to the political process and/or the UN neglecting immediate humanitarian needs. The coordination of humanitarian action needs ... its own humanitarian space. (Stoddard and Harmer 2006: 27, citing Van Mierop 2004)

The extent to which Liberia's integrated mission has proved positive for the overall security of the country remains unknown, though its ideologically contested dimensions are clear. Integrated missions produce hierarchies of safety that are dominated by the UN through their command of resources and bureaucracies with ideologies of 'hard' security. By contrast, NGOs can be regarded warily by the UN as 'soft' entities that may be 'out of touch' and 'unrealistic' as they fail to adopt the realist beliefs symbolized by displays of hard security as practised by the UN military component. What remains unclear is whether or not the eventual draw-down of UNMIL troops will leave a security vacuum, given the investment they have placed in the immediate physical presence of peacekeepers and military equipment within the broader context of a Chapter VII mandate that provides for robust peace enforcement. In sum, attempts to 'integrate' space – whilst clearly justified where the security risk is demonstrable – can also be self-serving. On this point, rumours were circulating in Liberia that a higher security grading of the country brought with it a greater level of financial reward in field allowance, reflecting the risk of UN personnel deployed in the mission. In turn, it was argued that the security risk was 'artificially inflated' and in these terms did not reflect danger on the ground. The extent to which Liberia can be discussed as an 'insecure space' is more complex than might first appear, given the presence of multiple actors struggling to gain legitimacy for their organizational missions. So far in these discussions we have concentrated on spatial contestation, but what of the temporal realm? What role can time and space play in thinking through the future prospects of Liberia?

Ex-combatants and peacekeepers' 'response': spaces of inaction

At the time of the fieldwork, Liberia was enduring an absence of war, or, rather, as one Liberian student put it, 'proper, deep peace'. Here, we detected a sense of anxiety and, in a more colloquial sense, 'jumpiness' regarding where the country was headed. During one interview with an international on the terrace of a large hotel, we heard the sounds of a demonstration of young men (and some women), which moved into sight from our elevated position. The interviewee began to look concerned, and his responses were affected by his monitoring of the unfolding situation as the demonstrators chanted in unison as they approached the hotel. A similar situation occurred during an interview in Monrovia, where the chanting of demonstrators in the street outside caused the office full of people in which one of the research team waited for an interview to fall into a lengthy silence, reflecting on obvious concern about what might happen next.

The sense that the country teetered on the abyss of renewed conflict was frequently conveyed. Perhaps unsurprisingly, Liberians were haunted by the possibility of violence, whether it be demonstrations that could get out of hand or, on a larger scale, the remobilization of the ex-combatant community. With these concerns uppermost in the minds of Liberians, the UNMIL intervention was broadly welcomed. Few, if any, expressed a desire to see the mission vacate the country, unlike the situation in Kosovo where UNMIK were poorly regarded, or in Haiti where the presence of peacekeepers was questioned again and again. That said, insecurity in Liberia was now discussed not so much in terms of armed violence but, rather, regarding the less serious issue of criminal activity where 'silent weapons' such as knives could be used, particularly during the hours of darkness.[11] Yet in the background lurked the demonized figure of the ex-combatant. Whilst this diverse group of so-called 'loose youth' were noted to cluster in Monrovia, the sense of spatiality they invoked were of a different order to that noted in either Haiti or Kosovo. The limited success of the DDRR process in the country (Nichols 2005; Paes 2005; Jennings 2007), at least until the end of the fieldwork period, was the background against which ex-combatants were discussed. For example, in regard to delayed payment of ex-combatant tuition fees, it was believed by a Liberian female hotel worker that

> These 'loose youth' wouldn't be a threat if there was no delay in tuition payments.[12] A row could break out between ex-combatants and others seeking revenge. In turn, people who have their studies disturbed at school could also become a threat.

More seriously, reference was made to hidden caches of arms,[13] to be reinstated by ex-combatants if DDRR failed to deliver on its financial and skill-equipping promises within the context of securing employment.[14]

The central problem was said by a male NGO worker to be the '110,000 ex-combatants that need to be reintegrated. The majority of them want more than $2 a day, because they have tasted resources far greater than that. It was suggested that 'people knew where ex-combatants were' and were best advised to 'steer clear of those areas', as their mere presence was enough to make people feel anxious. One particular problem area identified by many was that of the Guthrie Rubber Plantation, where ex-combatants lived and worked.[15] This much-cited example was seen as an additional source of concern in terms of a symbolic security 'hotspot' in the country. The role of ex-combatants in a sanctioned economic activity in the plantation signalled what was considered to be a broader UNMIL malaise concerning decisive military intervention.[16] In the words of a male Liberian bar worker:

> Don't forget the Guthrie rubber plantation which is still being run by the militia. People want action! People want results! The lack of action by UNMIL to tackle members of LURD in the plantation casts them in a bad light.

Whilst less pronounced than was the case in the other two mission sites, the presence of ex-combatants did assume something of a spatial character with regard to the perception that these men and women 'clustered' in Monrovia. However, in sharp contrast to their gang counterparts in Haiti, ex-combatants in Liberia tended not to be involved in kidnapping, rape or murder on anything like the same scale. Rather, reference to their impact on communities, as we saw above, was in relation to 'low-level' crime. Internationals were identified as targets for criminal activity, although they were not entirely blameless, in the view of several respondents, since they were noted to display their wealth 'openly' in the form of expensive mobile phones and other desirable consumables such as laptop computers.[17] Given that the majority of ex-combatants were involved in various stages of the disarmament and demobilization process at the time of fieldwork, they were 'kept busy', 'focused' and so diverted from creating insecurity. The qualitatively different nature of the insecurities to which ex-combatants gave rise called for more effective policing, rather than armed incursions into the areas within which they were seen to group.

In these terms, it was neither possible nor desirable to contain, engage or segregate ex-combatants, not least since they occupied space in different ways to gangs in Haiti. Unlike MINUSTAH there were no formal zones to patrol, and little in the way of permanent concentrations of vulnerable, enclaved citizens to protect, as noted in Kosovo.[18] Crucially, ex-combatants evoked perceptions of insecurity in the absence of any real evidence that they planned to challenge either UNMIL or, by implication, peace in Liberia, though the perception that Monrovia would be the scene of future trouble predominated. It could be said that it was the relative inaction of the Blue Helmets that contributed towards the peace. In a contradictory sense, peacekeepers were noted to have a high profile physically in terms of securing the integrated mission, whilst simultaneously refusing to engage ex-combatants in ways that would ratchet up tension. The extent to which the military component of UNMIL had consciously established this more passive stance in regard to potential peace spoilers is unclear, yet its effects were notable. Peacekeepers did not 'freeze', 'fix' or exacerbate insecurity; rather, they went about their work in less (spatially) focused ways. Their spatially constitutive security practices were largely determined by what the Blue Helmets faced when first deployed in 2003. Clearly the country and its infrastructure were broken, and there were – much like both Haiti and Kosovo – slums and other forms of bounded insecurity. Whilst some minor battles were fought with 'rogue militias', nonetheless spatial concentrations of violence targeted towards either peacekeepers or members of the host population did not feature on Liberia's physical or social landscape. It is here that the combination of factors pre-dating UNMIL and the broad sentiment that the mission could assist in the transition from war to peace infused the Blue Helmets' security work. But what of the future of Liberia? Where does the country go from here in terms of the UNMIL presence and what it stands for?

Liberal market democracy:
Liberia and the third space of consumption

Whilst ex-combatants appeared to be drawn to the capital – perhaps understandably given the opportunities in the city relative to the poorer counties (Jennings 2007: 206) – how was the pull of the city discussed? This is the contrast drawn by one male ex-combatant, who said:

I won't go back to where I came from because I have tasted life in the city and I want to keep that taste. Here in the city you have nice clothes to wear, you can find food, you can have some money in your pocket, you can listen to music and you can listen to the radio. Where I come from I can't listen to any news and the school is not operating. Shall I go back and be in darkness for ever?

In Monrovia, the growing availability of music, radio, clothes and food was itself an expression of the emerging liberal economy, the recovering health of which was driven in large part by the influx of millions of US dollars, alongside the presence of the international community. Next to 'hard' and 'soft' security', financial well-being signalled through active participation in the 'free market' may be considered as a developing 'third space'. Here, the city space of Monrovia can be said to be Janus-faced. It provides for security of certain kinds including lifestyle possibilities created through the commodified identities of the 'liberal peace'. Yet it is also a site of insecurity, as the scramble for resources intensifies and inequalities are reinforced. Given our observation that UN staff frequently invoked the security of their own possessions in response to general questions about security, it is unsurprising that the desire for goods should be stimulated amongst the host population as the consumptive ideology is transmitted far and wide. Here, international staff might be seen as symbols of hyper-consumption, signalled through their possession of expensive mobile phones and watches. When combined with large numbers of unemployed, aspirational young people (some of whom may carry the status of ex-combatant), the political–economic context of this and other missions can be seen to be shaped by a liberal con-sumerist dynamic (Pugh 2004). A swiftly developing lifestyle culture that derives its vitality from the creation of economically stratified individuals may, ultimately, stoke up future insecurities within the context of the competitive city space in a post-conflict environment where unemployment is at epidemic levels and the use of violence on a country-wide scale may be fresh in the memories of its victims as well as its perpetrators.

Overall, whilst security has assumed a spatially diffuse form in Liberia in contrast to both Haiti and Kosovo, nonetheless the panacea of economic development has some distance to run before it is able to neutralize the deep-seated historical legacy of violence in the country. During our fieldwork we observed the laboratory-like (liberal economic) conditions of Monrovia, where advertising had begun to evoke the idea of a lifestyle culture within the context of fostering consumption. As noted by the political scientist Roland Paris, Liberia was very similar to the fourteen peacebuilding operations launched between 1989 and 1999 that sought to 'transform war-shattered states into "liberal market democracies" as quickly as possible ... with mixed results' (Paris 2004: 5). The possibility that 'political and economic liberalization may increase the likelihood of renewed violence' (Paris 2004: 6) in some post-conflict states resonated with our intuitive sense that aspirations prevailing among (perhaps young, male) Liberians may not be easily met by the peacekeeping project imposed upon this country. In this thinking, attempting to facilitate the third space of mass consumerism within the context of deeper, underlying (tribal and other) tensions, alongside the broader insecurities in the region, could be read as somewhat naive and short-termist. Whether or not you can 'impose democracy' through the barrel of a gun or the shared desire for a McDonald's Big Mac is a question as yet unanswered in the case of the secure/insecure space of Liberia.

Conclusion

Liberia has not experienced the flare-ups of violence and tension which still characterize Haiti and Kosovo. Explanations for this (relative) peace can be traced in part to the relaxed stance taken by the Blue Helmets to security incidents. In Liberia there was evidence of a 'hands off' approach to ex-combatant demonstrations, unlike similar situations witnessed in both Haiti and Kosovo. The broader benevolence of the population meant that military peacekeepers were more likely to encounter allies in their everyday work; here the spaces between the occupiers and their hosts converged on the site of a shared belief in future peace largely bereft of antagonism and resentment from 'beneficiary' groups. Yet, despite the obvious progress peacekeepers have made in the country, the contest over 'humanitarian' and 'military space' preoccupied many working within the NGO community. The longer-term implications of the drive to militarize the mission and prioritize hard security over the provision of services remain unclear. To what extent does this narrow emphasis on security allow host populations to escape their past experience of conflict? At what point do individuals no longer require the presence of arms to feel safe? The threat of ex-combatants, which was frequently couched in terms of their latent ability to create insecurity and plunge the country back into conflict, also shaped perceptions of security loosely configured by the spaces within which they 'clustered' in Monrovia. Finally, traces of insecurity remained in the emerging liberal democratic institutions that provided for a burgeoning of urbanized consumerist lifestyle culture. Within the dire economic conditions of a post-conflict country, it was possible to see how the creation of wealth could raise expectations whilst denying some the possibility to live out heavily commodified identities. When we considered this economic model alongside the recent memories of widespread and protracted violence, we remained uncertain as to whether it can be the panacea that brings sustainable peace if host population expectations are not met. Ultimately, Liberia – not unlike both Haiti and Kosovo – is a contested space configured by powerful and less powerful players jostling for ideological and economic influence. The manner in which these struggles shape what it is hoped will be a linear progressive evolution from hard through soft security, and on to a functioning liberal democratic state, remains to be seen.

SIX

Performing spaces of security

Following the logic of military–geographical ways of engaging space, peacekeepers have been shown to have a contradictory and uneven impact on the security of host populations and international staff working in missions. The current chapter broadens and deepens this analysis of peacekeepers' capacity to produce spaces of both insecure and secure kinds by framing peacekeeper security work as embodied performance. Instead of thinking about space and place as pre-existing, static sites – a premiss challenged throughout this book – we argue that bodily performances themselves constitute or (re)produce space. It is at the intersection of peacekeeper bodies, space and place that audiences express perceptions of security and insecurity as they appraise the credibility of the security performance played out before them. Questions about the embodied dimensions of peacekeepers' practices are asked in the following discussion through seeing peacekeepers as enacting 'performances' of particular kinds for the benefit of an audience which is 'in need of securing'. Seeing the Blue Helmets as performing security draws attention to the staging or enactment of the (perpetually deferred) military expertise (combat effectiveness) that these troops have necessarily to convey (deterrence) if their audiences are to feel secure. In these terms, keeping the peace can be seen as a precarious business since its success lies in the realm of trust – how can peacekeepers convince their audience they will react decisively when the peace is disrupted? How credible are their security performances – will they deter potential peace spoilers? Will their bodies be up to the challenge? The metaphor of performance also underscores our conception of security as having no independent reality outside of the social relations through which 'it' is constituted and sustained. In this way we see 'security ... as a principle of formation [in our case, ritualized performance] that does things or at least permits certain things to be done' (Dillon 1996: 16). On another level, seeing peacekeepers as actors opens up new ways in which to explain the 'backstage' processes shaping what is seen by host populations and internationals. What stages are open to peacekeepers and how are they used? How are these stages read in terms of security and insecurity? To what theoretical resource might we turn in order to bring the idea of the peacekeeper performer who goes about fostering spaces of inconsistent kinds?

The sociologist Erving Goffman has provided a number of useful concepts with which to theorize social practice as performance and it is to his work that attention is now directed. Though Goffman did not explicitly apply his theoretical insights to security, we have found his contributions useful to think with in ways that provide a fresh take on how – through the drama of security – peacekeepers create spaces of both security and insecurity.

Performing social life

Goffman's approach made an important contribution to formal sociology, where analysts focus on the universal features of social relations. For example, individuals – unless living in the closed spaces of total institutions such as the prison, hospital or military – generally have open to them 'backstage' regions. More often than not, these are one's home or, in the case of a waiter discussed in Goffman's groundbreaking work *The Presentation of Self in Everyday Life* (1959), the kitchen area away from the 'frontstage region' of the restaurant and the scrutiny of the dining guests. These and numerous other regions/spaces are described by Goffman as 'interactional frames' that guide performances or how people 'act'. A waitress knows that in order to maintain her professional credibility, she must engage diners with a degree of deference as well as demonstrate mastery of handling numerous items of dining ware and cutlery. She must 'perform' the role of a waitress in ways that fit with the expectations of diners; a grumpy, unhelpful waitress who drops plates may well elicit concern or frustration from her dining audience. In this way social practice is noted to flow from a stock of tacit, mutually held expectational 'norms' shaped by the interactional roles of co-present actors – in this case the diners and the 'performing' waitress. How can we think about the ritualized frames or repertoires of security through which peacekeepers perform their work? What forms might these take? These could include: the formal 'stage' of the vehicle checkpoint or static compound checkpoint, where peacekeepers are expected to be vigilant and alert. We could also add the foot patrol or vehicle patrol, the conventions of which require the Blue Helmets to move slowly through communities, perhaps engaging local people in discussion in order to ascertain security concerns. Finally, there is the ritualistic display of security that co-opts military equipment or 'props' into the performance, such as the choreographed parading of white UN tanks through the urban space. These armoured vehicles are expected to be in good condition and reliable if they are to offer a strong deterrent to possible troublemakers. A smoke-belching dilapidated vehicle will do little to reassure the audience about the latent (or actual) potential to tackle future or current insecurities. By no means exhaustive, these examples are used to highlight the ritualized frames available to peacekeepers that follow from the franchised mission as universal features of the peacekeeping presence. Goffman also recognized that performances could be read in quite sophisticated ways and judged according to the extent to which they were considered 'genuine' or 'had depth'. Did individuals 'mean' what they performed? How convincing were they in their social interactions? With regard to peacekeeping, questions could be raised here about whether or not particular contingents took security seriously, as indicated by the demeanour and stance of their bodies, or the regularity with which they appeared in communities and engaged local populations face to face.

Before applying Goffman's work to examples drawn from our own fieldwork, it is important to understand what the audience brings to the performance, since insights into expectation of the security performance are key if perceptions of risk and safety are to be satisfactorily explained. On what kinds of tacit knowledge do members of the audience draw in order to appraise their sense of secure space or otherwise – be they the host population, NGO workers, UN civilians or others?

From performance to performativity: what is expected from peacekeepers?

By using the work of feminist scholar Judith Butler (1990), it is possible to deepen Goffman's understandings of performance through a focus on its performative capacity. That is to say, performances carry with them far-reaching effects imbued with power and authority to shape not only what the audience might expect as natural, but more importantly the conditions of possibility by which normality itself is constituted. Butler has used performativity to illustrate the way gender gets mapped onto sex through they process by which a baby female is 'girled' in ways that draw on the reiteration of particular performances of demeanour, ways of speaking and the props of gender-specific clothing. These social processes, though sometimes discussed lightheartedly in terms of how colour is used to distinguish between girls and boys (pink and blue respectively), nevertheless have the capacity to 'produce gender'. We unconsciously expect girls and boys to be different from one another – each is unthinkingly allocated a performative role that contains within it a cluster of prescriptive norms. And so it is the case with peacekeepers. They, too, have necessarily to perform according to pre-existing scripts of what audiences read as authentic enactments of security. The effects of a constantly repeated performance – for example, patrolling – is productive of identity such that peacekeepers come to embody security in and of themselves through their work. As Parker and Sedgwick put it: 'Performativity has enabled a powerful appreciation of the ways that identities are constructed iteratively through complex citational practices' (Parker and Kosofsky Sedgwick 1995: 2). The sociologist Vikki Bell makes a similar point when she notes that identity formation has social and political effects on audience and performer alike. In this way she argues that one needs to 'question how identities continue to be produced, embodied and performed, effectively, passionately and with social and political consequences' (Bell 1999: 2).

The ways in which the Blue Helmets are perceived in regard to the security they provide is to be discovered at a broader level that, in turn, feeds into audience expectation about these troops. More than that, the complex assemblage of practices that constitute the audiences' expectational norms have their own distinct political dynamics and historical trajectories and can be seen as examples of the 'performative infrastructure' (Bialasiewicz et al. 2007). It is within these infrastructures that 'meanings are produced, identities constituted, social relations established, and political and ethical outcomes made more or less possible' (Bialasiewicz et al. 2007: 2). Just as states are brought into being, or made 'real' through particular 'sovereign' acts including immigration or border controls (Weber 1998; Bialasiewicz et al. 2007: 2), so UN and NATO peacekeepers are realized through the declared aims of the organizations of which they are an integral part. Here, the emergence of a widely held understanding that 'peacekeepers provide security'[1] has its roots in the message that these (mainly) men have been deployed by global institutions with a 'responsibility to protect'. Take, for example, these extracts from UN and NATO documentation, respectively, that can be read through their productive or performative dimensions:

> Each peacekeeping operation has a specific set of mandated tasks, but all share certain common aims – to alleviate human suffering, and create conditions and build institutions for self-sustaining peace.[2]

> NATO safeguards the Allies' common values of democracy, individual liberty, the rule of law, and the peaceful resolution of disputes, and promotes these values through the Euro-Atlantic area.[3]

These statements of intent draw our attention to the activities and aspirations of the UN and NATO. But they do more than *provide* information. As key elements of the performative infrastructure, they are themselves constitutive of the security performance in ways that engage the local and the global from abstract statement through to face-to-face encounter of the peacekeeper with her or his audience. These UN and NATO statements can be said to invoke 'the ideal, the material, the linguistic and the non-linguistic' (Bialasiewicz et al.

2007: 2), which help to frame a broader web of meaning, refracting and reflecting expectations at ground/audience level. The potency of these documents' 'peace message' is largely impervious to critique – after all, who could possibly challenge the laudable goals of 'alleviating human suffering' and 'building peace and stability'? With a stated 'responsibility to protect', the UN and NATO as exemplary 'forces for good' have to hand potent discursive resources that have over time percolated into the expectations of host populations and others that work within, or in proximity to, PSOs. These statements have the capacity to 'produce certain ontological effects', the likes of which give rise to particular 'performances and how they are understood' (Bialasiewicz et al. 2007: 11) at the everyday level. Their authority is further increased because they offer hope to individuals caught up in violence with few other avenues of conflict resolution open to them. However, there may be tension between these positive (and productive) UN and NATO statements and the peacekeeper performances that follow them, as this respondent, a documentary film-maker in Haiti argues:

> There were people who thought that, as foolish as this may sound, they [the UN] would pick up the garbage in the streets, dismantle gangs, and take over traffic in the streets. But, then, this is not what they are here to do. They are quick to tell you that this is not their mandate.

Simply put, the security of the spaces constituted through peacekeepers' security performances could be at odds with the demands expressed by host populations and internationals. How can we begin to explain this mismatch between expectation and performance? Using Goffman's idea of backstage and frontstage it is possible to explain the disappointment, frustration and even anger of a significant number of individuals who felt that peacekeepers reneged on their responsibility to create and sustain spaces of security. Though not all moments of co-presence between peacekeeper and beneficiary can be described as formal security encounters (for example, off-duty troops talking to bar staff whilst having a drink can be seen as 'backstage' and choosing not to perform a formal 'out front' security act), nonetheless the importance of body positioning and Goffman's 'face-work' (facial expression) are key elements of the mutual presence of peacekeepers and those they have been deployed to protect. What can we bring into view through a focus on the backstage influences shaping the peacekeeper security drama played out for expectant audiences?

Goffman generated numerous concepts with which to account for the deeper factors shaping face-to-face interaction out-front for the discerning audience. The first of these is the so-called 'strategic secret' that configures backstage preparation for audience engagement. It is conceived of in relation to the 'intentions and capacities of a team [the Blue Helmets] which it conceals from its audience [peace spoilers] in order to prevent them from adapting effectively to the state of affairs the team is planning to bring about' (Goffman 1959: 141).

In many ways the strategic secret is the *raison d'être* of peacekeeping security practice, since the rationale underpinning performance is perforce that linked to deterrence. These strategic secrets have a particular salience for potential peace spoilers, since it is those who wish to destabilize security who are most likely to modify their social practice in the face of credible peacekeeper performance. If individuals get wind that peacekeepers will fail to engage their potential acts of insecurity, the entire peacekeeping presence is rendered useless. The second concept we draw on here is that of the 'inside' secret. This is noted to 'mark individuals as being a member of a group' (Goffman 1959: 142), and to this end differentiate the insider (peacekeeper) from the outsider (beneficiary). As Goffman (1959: 142) further states: 'Inside secrets give objective intellectual content to subjectively felt social distance.' It is in this sense that UN and NATO commanders on the ground are able to authorize measures that prioritize the safety of peacekeeping personnel over that of civilians at certain moments. Inside secrets shaped by the implications of peacekeeper commanders having their troops get injured or killed whilst on 'peace operations' feed into the social distance between Blue Helmet and audience. Whilst a number of respondents believed that peacekeepers did not 'always care', this cannot be explicitly acknowledged by peacekeepers and their commanders, who are expected to protect local populations under all circumstances. In this way, being a member of a 'force for good' meant that security performances could be read as lacking depth and authenticity by audiences holding these kinds of expectations. Aside from the strategic and team secrets that are developed away from the view of expectant audiences, how else were backstage regions interpreted? What kinds of peacekeeper backstage activity frustrated the 'beneficiary' group?

'Tourista' peacekeepers

In Haiti peacekeepers were often seen more as tourists than as professionals, enjoying a leisure industry that spoke of pleasure and privilege, a world utterly denied to the host population. In popular parlance, the MINUSTAH acronym was transformed to *tourista* (which is ironic both because it is a slight on the UN and because it rhymes with MINUSTAH); it has been used pejoratively since the beginning of the current mission (2004) by mostly Haitian residents, irrespective of race and class. Peacekeepers were commonly referred to as tourists on the (back) stage region of the restaurant, the nightclubs, discos and on the beach.[4] Though UN staff including civilians were not subject to a curfew in Haiti at the time of fieldwork, a number of bars and clubs were deemed 'out of bounds', underlining the attempt to keep peacekeepers from these tourist sites for reasons linked to their use of prostitutes and security. In the summer of 2006 a former Club Med tourist beach resort some distance from Port-au-Prince reopened to the public. This resort, which boasts white sandy beaches and can only be reached by car, has been partially renovated; the large restaurant, which used to cater to hundreds of tourists in more peaceful times, serves mostly wealthy businesspeople and MINUSTAH staff on Sundays.[5] Members of the host population demonstrated a keen awareness of the venues visited by both peacekeepers and international staff. For example a Haitian female working for a local NGO wryly stated:

> Peacekeepers are *tourista*! For example, we went to a place last week, and all you see there is 'internationals' on the beach with their short shorts and skirts; they are more tourist than anything else! They are always on the beach! Every single day you go to the beach you'll find a *tourista*!

One Haitian male NGO worker suggested that the reason why MINUSTAH has created such a poor impression among the Haitian population is precisely because of the enduring images of

MINUSTAH staff making the most of the tourist facilities. As such, and perhaps somewhat unfairly, peacekeepers tended to be perceived not as 'working' towards improving the security situation in the country but, rather, as on some kind of extended vacation. As the Haitian NGO worker went on to say:

> There are many, many things that need to be done in Haiti. A large percentage of the population do not have a sense of what MINUSTAH staff are actually achieving. That is why people here see MINUSTAH as doing very little but having a good time, being *tourista*.

A senior male member of the UN staff reiterated the bad impression MINUSTAH had aquired among the local population when he said that 'this image sometimes backfires because they see us everywhere; they see us patrolling and they see us manning checkpoints.' He continued:

> We are not able to control everything and kidnappings, killings and illegal robberies are ongoing. The population often say 'They are here, but they are not really doing their jobs.' There is a joke here in Haiti that we are not MINUSTAH, we are just *tourista* and sometimes I wonder if that is not true.

A male Haitian NGO worker from Cité Soleil also conveyed the perception that UN staff could be seen as *tourista*. In this excerpt, he links tourist status with the general sense that occupying forces are inherently unable to improve the conditions of the host country: 'Some people talk about MINUSTAH as *tourista*, yeah. I see them come to the beach.' More broadly, a Belgian male working for an NGO recalled an incident in his neighbourhood that signalled the sense of frustration engendered by the wealthy members of the international community working, or, more appropriately for a number of respondents, 'relaxing' (and earning) in their country despite the need to tackle insecurity:

> Once I was in a bank in Port-au-Prince, and the UN staff have their own line where they can take their money. I remember one guy who was very, very, upset and rude. He started shouting: 'Look at these people, they come to our country only to take all our money. They are taking a lot of dollars and we are in hunger! They are taking Haitian money.'

While this NGO worker interpreted the incident as a misreading of the honest grounds of the UN's presence in Haiti, it also demonstrates the ways in which UN staff, including military peacekeepers, might be construed in terms of their commanding levels of economic and cultural capital, a trait frequently associated with tourists.[6] To be confronted with such privilege is to underscore the stratified nature of Haitian society, where there may exist an unrealistic expectation of what the 'outsiders' can do to improve the country. At a deeper level, interviewee frustration is linked to the expectation that peacekeepers should take the role of some kind of 'sacrificial warrior' – or at least act with discretion in their off-duty time. The juxtaposition of suffering locals and peacekeepers who are enjoying themselves 'on the beach' apparently 'without a worry in the world' may be incongruous for some. Perhaps it is the case that peacekeepers should be spending their leisure time in less obviously decadent ways – for example, keeping a low profile or even carrying out voluntary work that could benefit those in whose name they have been deployed. A further explanation for the quiet anger expressed towards the *tourista* reflects the broader tendency for military personnel in particular to be conceived of within a somewhat two-dimensional identity.[7] Staging of the tourist identity provided peacekeepers with the opportunity, as Goffman would have it, to step out of character within the context of the camaraderie of military colleagues, where they could 'wind down' from what many likely experience as a tough deployment far from home. In so doing, they were at ease to perform alternative identities to those staged for the audience. However, backstage regions remain largely elusive to peacekeepers,[8] not least because their leisure pursuits tend to be conducted in public spaces such as bars and hotels. It is unrealistic to expect that they should be confined to barracks, or that peacekeepers should not be granted leisure time necessarily resulting in the blurring of back- and front-stage regions and the associated ire it evokes.

In applying theoretical insights developed by both Goffman and Butler to reveal the deeper processes by which peacekeepers create spaces of secure and insecure kinds, as perceived by respondents, we return to a key medium of the security performance: the peacekeeper body. How can the peacekeeper body be theorized as its sets about shaping spaces of security? What kinds of bodies do audiences expect to see? How do peacekeeper bodies express security and insecurity through their poise, movement and demeanour?

The peacekeeper body: performing space and security

Analyses of 'the body' present a particular challenge since 'it' is usually taken for granted (unless 'it' gets ill, for example); more often than not, bodies are 'just there' in the background of everyday life. One has only to reflect on such varied observations, referred to above, as peacekeeper incursions into the red zone (dependent on active and reactive 'warrior' bodies), the use of protected transportation by Serbians (vulnerable bodies hidden behind a steel 'skin'), national/ethnic (bodies marked by skin colour or other 'readable' characteristics organized into hierarchized status groups) and masculine identities (sexed bodies and sexual bodies, as noted in Chapter 8) of the Blue Helmets, to see that bodies play an often silent but central role in how security and social practices more widely are played out through the embodied dimension. While bodies are central to performance, they can be said to be absently present in everyday life, meaning that their impact on perceptions of security through the spoken interview is difficult to tease out. In these terms, asking direct questions about the 'role of peacekeeper bodies' in security practices is impractical since these are analytically abstract rather than everyday concerns. The few comments that directly invoked peacekeeper bodies stressed co-presence between blue helmet and audience and were conveyed as simply 'seeing peacekeepers'. Other discussions wherein respondents invoked the body included the belief that peacekeepers should be fit and well, a usually unspoken expectation that came to the fore when a UN battalion's (allegedly) high rate of HIV/AIDS infection was mentioned.[9] Of equivalent, if not greater, interest to us were the ways bodies were co-opted into the security performance that could be foregrounded through an ethnographically informed approach. By observing the host population, international staff working in the mission and the Blue Helmets themselves, we were able to build up a picture of the embodied dimensions of security practice as it configured spaces of security and insecurity. Our particular interest here developed Butler's notion of the 'expressive body' alongside Goffman's understanding that embodied performances have the capacity to 'give off' particular 'feelings'.

It has been argued that socialization needs analysing 'in terms of the partial social shaping of embodied dispositions as well as the partial internalisation of mental views and attitudes' (Schilling 1997: 746). Physical bodies are more than material artefacts composed of flesh, tissue and bone; they are also social products that are co-present in face-to-face interaction, as Goffman (1972: 169) reminds us. A focus on the body's variable social dimensions reveals how it can be expressive in both verbal and non-verbal ways, as the example of 'face-work' demonstrates in respect of the latter (Goffman 1972: 5–45). Bodies provide self and others with insights into how actors are feeling, what they desire, and so on. Yet, as noted above, bodies are also taken for granted (Nettleton and Watson 1998: 12) and their place in the world is secured through non-conscious practical achievements such as the act of unthinkingly placing one foot in front of the other in the process of walking (Merleau-Ponty 1962; Nettleton and Watson 1998: 10–12). In these terms, bodies are sites of both sedimented experience and unintentionality; quite literally individuals both *have* and *are* sentient bodies through which their world and the worlds of others are brought into being, as argued here:

> The lived body helps to constitute this world as experienced. We cannot understand the meaning and form of objects without reference to bodily powers through which we engage them – our senses, motility, language, desires. The lived body is not just one thing in the world but a way in which the world comes to be. (Nettleton and Watson 1998: 11)

How might we highlight the body's role in the UN foot patrol, vehicle patrol or static checkpoint? Are peacekeepers sitting on chairs at the vehicle checkpoint or are they standing to attention, and attentive? Do peacekeepers on foot patrol slouch in a blasé manner or do they move in carefully choreographed ways, perhaps marching in unison and maintaining a good lookout in ways that constitute safe spaces? What do they 'give off' in these performances? What kinds of tacit knowledge are invoked in their audience, which in turn are used to appraise the safety of these spaces to which peacekeepers bodies give rise? In order to address these questions it is necessary to trace the formative trajectory of those bodies that are judged in respect of security expressivity. To paraphrase Simone de Beauvoir on women, peacekeeper-soldiers are not born, they are made, and consequently shape space in distinctive ways. A key element of the making of the peacekeeper is exposure to masculinized regimes intended to transform their physical sense of self, with which audiences will have some awareness or even direct experience. These intensive processes are carried out within the total institutional context of armed forces' training establishments and have repercussions for the poise and demeanour of the militarized body, as well as its latent and actual capacities in regard to the improvement of cardiovascular systems.

Civilian bodies are transformed into military bodies according to the requirements of the military occupation in question; the bodies of infantry soldiers are shaped in different ways to those of clerks according to the military demands placed upon them. The universal practices of military socialization intended to mould embodied disposition turn on two key dimensions: first, that bodies are trained to develop a particular awareness of other bodies to which they are spatially proximate through drill and other standardized ritual; second, that these bodies are imbued with strength, agility and tenacity in the face of physical hardship (Morgan 1994; Higate 2001). Both historically and currently, the *raison d'être* of military bodies is one of strict control and discipline, through which bodies (of mainly men) might be considered interchangeable in respect of their ability to discharge 'controlled violence' (Ferguson 2004: 8). The end-product of body-focused socialization serves to materialize the institutional structure of the national armed forces of which peacekeepers are a part. As Connell has argued:

> Body reflexive practices ... are not internal to the individual. They involve social relations and symbolism: they may well involve large-scale institutions ... through body reflexive practices, more than individual lives are formed: a social world is formed. (1995: 64)

Set within the context of warrior imagery through to mundane representational practices including photographs and written texts detailing the exploits of Rambo-like figures (Higate et al. 2003), audience expectations are shaped by a performative infrastructure that speaks directly to particular idealizations of peacekeeper embodiment. Given that there is argued to be an active process of 'embodying certain cultural and historical possibilities' (Butler 1988: 520), the case of the peacekeeping soldier is particularly apposite. Thus, the majority of military male[10] peacekeepers are combat-trained and as such are presumed to conduct their embodied-security selves in specific norm-bound ways. Here, the drama of bodily synchronicity crystallized in the form of the expertly choreographed military parade and drill underscores the ways that the expressive soldierly body can be differentiated from that of its civilian counterpart. Crucially, it is in its repetition, over time, that 'this mundane and ritualized form [of the embodied soldier] can be legitimated' (Butler 1988: 526) as part of the process of encouraging people to think more productively about military bodies. In sum the audience draws on unspoken 'sedimented expectations' (Butler 1988: 524) of what peacekeeper bodies should look like, and how they should move, with direct regard to their ability to perform security (although there may be some variation in the criteria applied by respondents).

The peacekeeper–audience encounter was also noted to be contingent on the current security mood and context in ways that throw the dynamic aspects of embodiment into sharp relief, as observed through peacekeepers' corporeal adaptation to the 'security climate'. For example, in Liberia an attack on a Bangladeshi checkpoint that resulted in the theft of an AK-47 from a peacekeeper badly burned by a Molotov cocktail gave rise to shifts in embodied expressivity. In the post-attack period, the embodied dimension of Bangladeshi security practice shifted in line with heightened insecurity. In this way peacekeepers (1) stood rather than sat in their fortified space; (2) paid greater attention to their weapons stock by keeping it under surveillance through close physical proximity as well as regular turning of the head towards the equipment; (3) stood up and walked from within their checkpoint to talk to drivers rather than operating the barrier remotely whilst sitting; and (4) more broadly conveyed a reactivity by keying their embodied selves into a space shaped by fresh memories of insecurity. Quite literally, their bodies were ready for action if need be. Butler reminds us that embodied performativity is also suffused with power. In our research it was noted that militarized bodies trained in the discharge of violence, particularly when considered in the post-conflict context, can be mobilized in both positive and negative ways. In performing security, the Blue Helmets have the potential to control others in ways that confirm their mastery over both space and time as the following study of Palestinian and Israeli peacekeepers suggests in a study of peacekeepers by Deborah Heifetz-Yahav:

> It was very clear that at the macro level, Israelis controlled Palestinian bodies moving through the territorial space of the West Bank and the Gaza Strip. Indeed the definition of power was body-based in terms of the control of movement, access to bodies *vis-à-vis* roadblocks, checkpoints, house searches and other activities under the general rubric of security and security practices. (Heifetz-Yahav 2005: 8)

So it was in the cases of Haiti, Kosovo and Liberia, where in the name of security peacekeepers closed roads, searched individuals and ultimately influenced how those working and living in missions lived out their own embodied sense of self. What of the props vital for the security performance and of importance to Goffman's concerns regarding the co-presence of social actors?

Bodies, props, performance

In developing the theatrical metaphor through the dramaturgical approach, Goffman recognized that performances were enhanced in both important and less significant ways through the use of props. The waitress is still considered as such even if she is not dressed in apparel that includes a white apron over a black dress. Similarly, she may or may not be carrying a notepad and writing implement to record orders if she is confident and has an excellent memory, as do some waiting staff. Yet use of these props can add depth and credibility to the performance of the waitress, particularly those employed in a traditional establishment where the uniform takes on a greater significance within the overall 'frame of action', as Goffman would put it. Similarly, a peacekeeper dressed only in swimming shorts on the stage of the beach could assume the identity of a tourist in the eyes of some, as we have shown here. Props typical of the peacekeeper performance could include: the blue beret or blue helmet; combat fatigues; a weapon; a white, UN-branded Toyota Land Cruiser; and, more exceptionally, an armoured vehicle. An African female NGO worker in Liberia linked security with how well equipped the troops were in ways that foregrounded military props. 'When the Irish roll out the tanks that is enough. The communities see the level of troops arriving and they see how well equipped they are. The more equipment they bring, the more respect there is for security.'

In Kosovo a Bosnian male working for an NGO in Priština, said:

> KFOR is a good facilitator on account of its presence and visibility. A military's own rules and procedures send a message, for example of whether you hold a weapon like this or this [respondent simulates different defensive and offensive ways of holding a weapon] ... there are a lot of things that can be signalled. Its people can create security through being in the turret of a tank, or out on the streets.

Of particular note in Liberia were the ways in which notions of professionalism were framed in direct relation to the military equipment or the military 'prop';[11] indeed equipment was often used as *the* key criterion of security performance and, in turn, the creation of safe space. For example, it was the appearance of Swedish tanks in contrast to 'the little motorbike of the Bangladeshis' that influenced perceptions of safety and a sense of well-being. Though we might not be surprised at the ways in which 'more' and 'better' equipment lends greater legitimacy to the security performance, the highlighting of equipment resonates with the broader military spectacle informing 'spectator sport' militarism[12] (Mann 1987; Ben-Ari and Fruhstuk 2003). In a less grand although perhaps more visceral sense, images of child soldiers dwarfed by the AK-47s they are barely able to manage[13] may also touch on pre-discursive, affective realms in those who have yet to be desensitized to such sights. So far as our findings go, the status attached to weaponry was often on a par with, or indeed greater than, those sentiments directly invoking peacekeepers, seen as embodied performers of safe and insecure spaces. It was as if the props used in the performance had a life of their own, or a kind of security-autonomy whereby peacekeepers, despite their fleshy sentience, were appraised only in relation to the 'non-human' weapons and equipment they displayed. How can it be that inert, material artefacts are accorded equivalence with the peacekeeper-human? In recent years, scholars working within human geography and sociology have contributed greatly to our understanding of networks by highlighting the deep interconnectedness human agents have with one another across time and space.

A number of social scientists, many of whom have emerged from the subfield of the sociology of science and technology, have contributed to what has come to be known as actor network theory (ANT). ANT draws attention to the ways that non-material phenomena (in our case, tanks, guns and a motorbike) form a coherent whole or network (Callon 1986; Latour 1987 2005; Law and Hassard 1999; Law 1987, 1992). In examining the important role of the military prop on perceptions of peacekeeper security performances and the kinds of spaces to which they give rise, ANT encourages us to rethink the divisions between human agents and their material worlds, and in so doing throws light on the importance of the non-human elements or props of the security performance. In applying ANT to an analysis of perceptions of security performance, we suggest that both guns and peacekeepers might be conceptualized as elements within a 'patterned network of heterogeneous materials' (Latour 2005: 65). These heterogeneous networks are argued to 'lie at the heart of actor-network theory, and are ways of suggesting that society, organisations, agents and machines are all *effects* generated in patterned networks of diverse (not simply human) materials' (Law 1992: 2, emphasis added).

The network in which the peacekeepers' weapon is embedded 'is social' in that 'it' participates in the peacekeepers' social relations to such an extent that perceptions of security derive directly from the inclusion (or otherwise) of military hardware in the performance. In accounting for the status accorded to objects within ANT, it has been argued that 'There is no reason to assume *a priori* that either objects or people in general determine the character of social change or stability' (Law 1992: 3). As noted above, both peacekeepers and guns (or tanks) coexist in ordered ways that are read in terms of their performative dimensions; differences exist, however, between the various parties that might sport weaponry. Whereas peacekeeper weaponry is generally accepted to have a defensive role, arms carried by peace-spoiling militias or combatants may be read through their contrasting, offensive potential, which can lead to spaces of chaos, confusion and *dis*embodiment. More broadly, however, the nexus linking peacekeepers with their defensive weaponry can be framed through the language of ANT as 'a relatively stable network ... embodied [within] in and performed by a range of durable materials' (Law 1992: 387). The importance of props to spaces of safety was replicated across all missions visited in the course of the fieldwork, as evidenced by the manner in which 'superior military equipment' was spontaneously and unthinkingly equated with both professionalism and its unquestioned corollary, 'better security'.

Conclusion

Peacekeepers can be seen to 'act out' security in so far as the material or *actual* use of force remains perpetually deferred, in the majority of cases whilst seeking to reassure and secure an expectant audience. The security dramas played out by the Blue Helmets can be disrupted by their backstage activities in terms of both strategic decisions to protect themselves first and audiences second at certain moments, and, in a more informal sense through relaxing on the beach or in the bar. Peacekeepers' bodies are central to how security is performed. This is evident in terms of the requirement for a body that meets certain standards of able bodiness, but also in regard to its poise and choreographed movement. Expectations around peacekeeper embodiment and security work are derived in part from the knowledge that these Blue Helmet soldiers have been exposed to training intended to change their physical capacities. In this sense, peacekeeper bodies are 'read' by an active audience in ways that provide for a variation in perception of security according to certain expectations. Passive, inactive and sluggish bodies may lack credibility, whereas alert, observant and physically dynamic forms of peacekeeper embodiment are likely to engender its polar opposite – that of a reassuring presence. However, there are numerous props that can be linked to bodily performance in ways that mediate, and in some respects overwhelm, audience perception. Here, guns and tanks may be accorded privilege in the appraisal of the security performance such that peacekeepers themselves might be seen as somewhat secondary. In other words, the use of technologically advanced military equipment can inflect performances with a professionalism that coheres around the 'non-human' military hardware itself. In the final analysis it could be said that the embodied role of peacekeepers turns ultimately on preventing the disembodiment of those women, men and children that this unique soldier has been sent to secure.

SEVEN

Stereotyping performance: peacekeeping and imagined identities

As we have seen, peacekeepers' bodies represented an important medium through which the Blue Helmets produced spaces of both security and insecurity. Such security practice is performed through a physical choreography that involves movement, demeanour and adornment, with props and weapons of various kinds. Yet, it is not just the ways performances are read in terms of movement through space that figured in our fieldwork, but also the ways in which 'nationality' was constructed as an inherent element of security practice. Respondents from across the missions routinely used national identity as a means for framing what peacekeepers 'were like' and as an explanation for how they approached their security work. These constructions drew on local and global stereotypes of particular ethnic and racial groups in order to explain the different levels of security perceived and felt by respondents. Even UN civilian personnel sensitive to the differences in status, role and task between military observers and members of the contingent forces prioritized national identity as *the* central explanation for different styles of security performance. Our aim in this chapter is to interrogate critically perceptions of peacekeepers' nationality conveyed by a mix of local people, NGO employees (both indigenous and international) and UN international staff. Following this, we argue that respondent perceptions of security style owe more to stereotypes of assumed national and 'racial' trait than they do actual security practice played out on the ground.

National identity and national 'character': framing peacekeepers

Peacekeepers originate from diverse sovereign states and are deployed in multinational and multicultural contexts. National identity has long been an important and vexed issue in the context of the Blue Helmets; peacekeepers are at once citizens of the world on a humanitarian mission and foreign nationals in war-torn countries (Enloe 1993). The social anthropologist Rubinstein (1993) describes the importance in early peacekeeper observer missions of symbols such as badges, insignia and flags to the national identity of the Blue Helmets. These symbols can offer a sense of continuity between different contingents of the same nationality rotated in and out of missions, in addition to invoking the international beneficence of a rainbow alliance under the universal signifier of a blue beret. More broadly, the peacekeeping project has often been co-opted into state-level identity-making processes, as evidenced by foreign-policy pronouncements concerning the responsibility (of particular nations) 'to protect'.

In the case of Canada, for example, the deployment of peacekeeping has been seen as an important component of national identity, conveyed through humanitarian intervention played out in contexts such as Somalia. Here, the violent activities of peacekeepers led to heated discussions about the meaning and future of military intervention in the face of human rights abuses against a local man, Shidane Arone, who was brutally murdered by members of the Canadian Airborne Regiment (Razack 2004). Attempts to co-opt the symbolic potency of peacekeeping into national identity have also engaged the Netherlands, which had presented itself as 'naturally disposed' to peacekeeping until the Srebrenica massacre in Bosnia, where Dutch peacekeeping troops were perceived as failing to protect 8,000 Bosnia Serbs in 1995 (Zarkov 2002; de Leeuw 2002; Sion 2008). The shockwaves from this incident reverberated through the Dutch media for many years after the event in ways that had severe consequences for the national image of the country's military peacekeeping troops (Dudink 2002; Zarkov 2002).

Prior to these two events, however, both Canada and the Netherlands allied their geopolitical imperatives to the national character of their troops in respect of their provision of humanitarian warriors to global trouble spots. As some have argued, myths that articulate peacekeepers with state beneficence serve the purpose of nation-making and justification for maintaining a military, while at the same time framing the country in question as 'progressive' on the world stage (Razack 2004). Yet, marrying the (apparent) disposition of one's national troops to the unique role of peacekeeping is also noted as a precarious strategy. Governments change, political imperatives alter and missions go awry in both reality and public perception. The case of Canada is apposite in this respect. Over the last fifteen or so years, the nation's ideological framing of military humanitarian intervention has passed through a number of stages, as noted above, with the most recent turning on 'toughness' in respect of their presence in Afghanistan as part of the NATO force. Foregrounding the military dimension of their intervention in Afghanistan has occluded the impartial and compassionate stance taken in previous times to their security work, which in turn has cast the troops – and by implication Canada – as decisive and determined in their attempt to civilize this 'failed state'.[1] While it is clear that national troops' identity and geopolitical imperatives articulate with one another in ways that shape how peacekeepers are seen, there remains little consideration of what this might look like on the ground in ongoing missions. How did the country of origin of peacekeepers shape perceptions of security performances? What did national identity mean for the kinds of professionalism these peacekeepers were believed to be capable of in the post-conflict space?

Performing national identities

UN and NATO troops from Kosovo, Liberia and Haiti used the post-conflict space as a stage upon which to celebrate their national and military identities. Great pride was attached by these military personnel to national insignia (worn on the uniform), along with the different foods and languages they imported into the multinational context of the mission in question. On numerous occasions we were invited to national celebrations, usually involving food and alcohol, where national flags were on bold display. Documentation of 'national' performances has been noted in various UN publications, as well as photographs on the UN website for the three missions where peacekeepers are shown celebrating national holidays and performing national sports. Whilst perceptive of these national differences, at times, host populations and international audiences responded with some ambivalence to signifiers of national identity – as they saw it – played out 'over and above' the core task of providing security. It was thought by some that national contingents spent excessive periods of time organizing inter-national (contingent) football matches and fiestas or mini-carnivals. A typical response came from a former KLA commander in Kosovo, who spoke explicitly about the links between nationality and KFOR troops' security performance:

> People are generally satisfied with KFOR, but sometimes troops express their nationality more than perform their mission. Different contingents of KFOR try to bring an impression of their own nationality from their own countries ... they are less occupied with security on the ground; they don't care so much. They have international rivalries with one another.

Widespread attention to peacekeepers' nationality was apparent right across the three missions and included discussion of national identity they had 'heard about', in conjunction with that they had witnessed directly, from other geographical regions within their post-conflict countries. Here, stories of whether or not particular national troops were able to create a sense of safety according to a taken-for-granted 'disposition' to peacekeeping circulated widely at the level of what can best be described as 'rumour', 'anecdote' and 'hearsay' inflected with ethnic and national stereotypes, as we now see.

In Kosovo, for instance, views about the 'proficiency of the Finnish guys', who had experienced numerous tours of duty and were believed to have developed 'a real sensitivity to inter-ethnic tensions', captured the link between country of origin and ability to stage a compelling security drama shaped by compassion and insight. Whilst there was little real agreement on those 'peacekeepers who could be trusted to do a good job', troops from the majority world or 'developing countries' were often constructed as failing to match their 'first world' peacekeeping peers in ways that perpetuated stereotypes. Assertions frequently proceeded from a stereotypical view of one nation's troops being 'better than others'. This meant that in assessing different security performances, respondents participated in a series of acritical and unthinking judgements where they ranked troops from various national backgrounds. Although not explicitly, these perceptions relied on racialized/ethnicized ideas about soldiers from 'white' European backgrounds and from 'developing' countries in Africa and Asia, and as such co-opted distorted ideologies of race and identity. Alongside 'race' and ethnicity, respondents used nationality as the all-encompassing identity marker to convey beliefs about religion.

In the case of the mostly Muslim Bangladeshi peacekeepers, religion was often raised as an area of possible bias (and therefore weakness) in providing 'proper' security. The secular or Christian backgrounds of other peacekeepers, including the Swedes and Irish, were raised as implicit assets, rather than factors negatively affecting their abilities to provide security. Once again, stereotypical and, at times, demeaning constructions of religion and race spoke to the implicit attempt by respondents of various backgrounds and both genders to create a hierarchy of national identity. In addition, degrees of professionalism were conflated with national 'character', the apparent fixity or truth of which was rarely questioned. Summing up wider beliefs in circulation across the missions, a Kosovar Albanian female working for the Kosovo government stressed the links between country of origin and occupational competence when she noted that 'KFOR troops' professionalism depends on the country they come from.'[2] However, in contrast and somewhat exceptionally, a German male working for an international organization was reluctant to conflate national identity with how KFOR peacekeepers' security performances were seen. Rather, he looked at the broader, generic context of military operations when he reflected that, 'Whether or not they are French, German or Italian they are all military. They all have orders.'

In the lead-up to the election in Liberia in October 2005, peacekeepers of the Swedish and Irish Quick Reaction Force (QRF) contingents were constructed as consummate professionals. They were perceived primarily through ideas about their apparent polished professionalism and were discussed extensively in these terms.[3] Members of the QRF maintained a visible presence among the local population by appearing regularly on the streets of Monrovia and in outlying regions via helicopter to conduct high-profile patrols. Unlike other troops within the mission, they did not officially participate in humanitarian and reconstructive work, such as that carried out by Chinese engineers or Jordanian medics, but rather assumed a policing role responding to outbreaks of violence. As such, it is unsurprising that they were perceived as more 'warrior' than 'humanitarian' since their role shaped the kinds of security performances they enacted on a regular basis. Nevertheless, their association with notions of professionalism was influenced by implicit ideas about ethnic and racial 'superiority'. Here, respondents believed that Irish and Swedish peacekeepers were the most suitable to react to security incidents because of their perceived military competence. Echoing the observations of many, a female international heading up an NGO in Monrovia observed in relation to potential disturbances: 'I would expect them to bring out the Irish special forces. They have been particularly effective in calming things down.' The three days of rioting and burning of churches in Monrovia in October 2004 were mentioned as a particular moment when the Irish special forces (also referred to as the Rapid Reaction Force) demonstrated their apparent superiority in neutralizing insecurity. A Liberian male security officer working for an NGO in Monrovia echoed this perception: 'When you say "the Irish are coming", people know they are about to see a well-equipped QRF.' There was wide consensus that Swedish and Irish peacekeepers 'acted more professionally' and that they 'were strict and a lot more focused'. In addition, their ability to create and maintain spaces of safety was derived from direct exposure to 'competent' performances, where they were noted to 'patrol more effectively'.

Comparison of the Swedes was often made with Blue Helmets originating from the majority world, including those from Africa. These observations drew on racialized stereotypes of one nation's forces 'being better than anothers' on the (spurious) grounds of assumed national trait. Further explanation for the general respect shown for Swedish peacekeepers in particular arises from direct observation of their performances and the advanced props – discussed above – used to enhance the security drama. The fact that they had been delegated the challenging and perhaps somewhat prestigious function of QRF also shows the importance of their structural role and the sense that their performances were seen as key to preventing the escalation of violence feared by many during the early days of peace in Liberia, as noted in Chapter 5. In this way, stereotype can be seen as a further dimension of the performative infrastructure, shaping expectation in circulation at the geopolitical level about 'what kinds of peacekeepers' Swedes were seen to be in the Liberian context. Here, the unreflective perception that Swedes were routinely 'fair' and likely to treat individuals in a 'balanced and equal way' was conveyed in various ways by a range of stakeholders. Respondents' tacit, unquestioned framing of these northern European nationals directly invoked a sense of balance and neutrality, captured in the following commentary on Swedish nationalism and its links with security more widely:

> In the Swedish context, neutrality and *folkhemmet*[4] are the central dimensions of nationalism ... the strong ties between the policy of neutrality and Swedish national identity may explain why in the debate on Sweden's future security arrangement the idea of Sweden as a neutral power in world affairs still occupies an important position. (Kronsell and Svedberg 2001: 155)

The convergence between the tenets of traditional peacekeeping, as practised in early observer missions, and this understanding of Swedish national character reinforces this stereotype. That these troops originate from a social-democratic welfare state with a long track record of equality (Nyman 1999) was said to 'naturally dispose these guys' – as a male UN civilian put it – to the classic model of impartial peacekeeping. However, many of the respondents adopted uncritical views of northern European Blue Helmets, relying either on the limited exposure to a particular group of peacekeepers, or on stereotypes that circulate globally about specific nations. Discussion of the Swedes can be seen as highly racialized within the broader context of the nationalized mythology of an 'advanced', 'ultra-civilized' country that promotes itself as being 'devoted to gender equality'. Yet concern about the assimilation of immigrants into Swedish society, though far removed from the immediate peacekeeping context, does suggest other readings of the Swedish 'national character'. Indeed, these readings can be seen to be located at the polar extreme of 'fairness' and 'tolerance' in ways that invoke racism, discrimination and hostility to 'others' – usually those who have fled from conflict, including large numbers of Iraqi citizens, who are experiencing real challenges to settling in Sweden.[5]

Though Nigerian peacekeepers of the ECOMOG force were regarded as tough with an uncompromising ability to create security, it is clear that they have a mixed reputation in Liberia. There are numerous reasons for this, including the loose peacekeeping mandate worked to during the civil war. This shifted between peacekeeping and peace enforcement 'as required' and was characterized by Nigerians 'changing sides' and forming 'impromptu alliances' in order to maximize military advantage (Olonisakin 1999: 13). In terms of the Nigerians' involvement in combat, in contrast to other members of the ECOMOG force, it was suggested that:

> The absence of common doctrine among ECOMOG participants was particularly obvious in the differences between the Nigerians' and the Ghanaians' approaches to peacekeeping. Whereas the Ghanaians are trained in peacekeeping and emphasize diplomacy over enforcement, the Nigerians demonstrated a preference for a more activist, combat approach to the operation. (Taw and Grant-Thomas 1999: 66)

The key factor perceived to undermine the performance of the Nigerian peacekeepers has also been put in somewhat ironic terms, as one Liberian journalist observed: 'Monrovia residents watched their cars and refrigerators being loaded onto ships bound for Nigeria ... they thanked God that at least their houses were not being burned down' (Teh 2001: 1). While there was little disagreement among respondents about the perceived efficacy of the Swedish Blue Helmets of the QRF, a somewhat nuanced sense of professionalism emerged regarding Nigerian peacekeepers in Liberia. While Swedes were seen to be quintessentially impartial, Nigerians were constructed as 'tough'. This 'tough professional' performance in the security space was perceived as deeply contradictory in ways that engaged a particular kind of competence not seen in either Kosovo or Haiti. Discussion of Nigerian peacekeepers also tended to be based on historical rather than contemporary reflection, as we see below. When asked to comment on security within the context of military personnel of the current UNMIL force, members of the host population interviewed in Monrovia and other parts of the country often fell back on discussion of Nigerian troops of the ECOMOG force that had departed Liberia some six years earlier, though they left behind a number of UN 're-hatted' peacekeepers to serve within UNMIL. Summing up the thoughts of many, a male Liberian taxi driver recalled that 'We had the Nigerians here with ECOMOG. Our historical perception of them convinces people that they are more robust [than those of the current UNMIL force].' The belief that Nigerian ECOMOG peacekeepers were tougher or more robust was aired widely, including in a BBC report where their fighting 'prowess' (alongside other aspects of their performance) is discussed:

> The Nigerians were the hard men of the ECOMOG force. On check-point duty they were considered rude and arrogant, but when there was fighting to be done they were usually the ones who did it, even if they were not too fussy about the finer points of their peace-keeping mandate.[6]

It was repeatedly argued that the 'Nigerians were feared and respected' and that they 'set the standard' against which the current UNMIL troops were judged. A Liberian employed as a private security guard suggested that people felt unsafe against the backdrop of political instability in the immediate wake of the civil war. He wondered whether current peacekeepers of the UNMIL force would be as willing to protect Liberians as effectively as the (long-departed) Nigerian troops. This perception underscores the desire for a more aggressive peacekeeping performance, which can be explained by the prevailing mood of physical insecurity in the country during the lead-up to national elections. The theme of respect was echoed by a local Liberian male working in an advocacy organization in Monrovia who argued that in a serious ex-combatant incident 'you would prefer to have the Nigerians intervene. The ex-combatants have a great respect for Nigerians. We look at them as no-nonsense, good fighters.' Similarly, a female European NGO worker, revealing her thoughts on who was most likely to evoke confidence and 'get the job done', said that 'we have a contingent of Nigerian police here who people feel much more confident about … although I do worry that the Nigerians are better known for rushing in, firing first, and asking questions later.' A further indication of the ways in which the fighting reputations of Nigerian troops of the ECOMOG force were discussed concerned the choice of personnel for so-called impromptu 'private armies'. Here, the establishment of small teams of Nigerian troops, hired informally by expatriate workers, including British, Canadian and Lebanese nationals, was said to be 'common practice'. Their main role was to protect the property and businesses of traders, many of which had been looted during the civil war. These small 'private armies' acted autonomously from the broader UNMIL force and were billeted in close proximity to the business they were employed to secure. One British expatriate businessman (who had lived and worked in Liberia throughout the entire period of the civil war) confirmed:

> We have all [referring to other business people] hired Nigerian security. I have six Nigerian troops working for me to protect my security and property. We give them somewhere to live, air conditioning and food. Now we've all got a private army. This practice is widespread ... every Lebanese has done the same thing.

While memories of Nigerians engaging in hand-to-hand combat during the civil war were fresh in the minds of respondents in ways that spoke to a particular kind of militarily robust professional performance, the other side of their presence was also commented on. For some Liberians, the idea that Nigerians could be both peacekeepers and soldiers was problematic, because, as one young male resident of Monrovia put it, 'they didn't handle you "like a peacekeeper" – they handled people very badly.' In addition, evidence that Nigerian peacekeepers were linked to organized gangs, the drugs trade and crime in Liberia was discussed. Thus, it was not only active combat fighting that became synonymous with Nigerian troops; it was also generally believed that their behaviour as members of ECOMOG was at times far from professional, such that they helped to create insecurity. Here, instances of looting (Human Rights Watch 1993; Taw and Grant-Thomas 1999: 69; Tuck 2000), gender-based violence (Martin 2005), partiality, and allied to this, involvement in illegal commercial activities (Pitts 1999: 61) had been documented during their deployment in Liberia. Yet it was also said that Nigerian troops had developed from being aggressive, ill-disciplined fighters to acting as proficient and controlled troops when serving as early members of UNMIL. This was suggested by a journalist writing in the *International Herald Tribune*, who argued that, unlike earlier Nigerian operations of the 1990s, those involved in the initial stages of the current mission showed marked improvement. Simply put, they had become more professional:

> The Nigerian and other West African peacekeepers appear omnipresent. This time they seem disciplined, effective and well trained— unlike the soldiers in a badly conceived and badly led peacekeeping operation sent in 1995 and 1996 by Nigeria's military government. Its troops were brought ignominiously home, 1,000 of them in body bags, after earning an appalling reputation as rapists, looters and brutalizers. Today observers including the UN chief representative, the US ambassador and American officers on the ground speak highly of the Nigerian troops' proficiency.[7]

Discussion of long-departed Nigerian troops, often uppermost in the minds of many Liberians, was contrasted with the apparently 'less tough' security performances of the Bangladeshi contingent. It is to a brief consideration of their style of peacekeeping that we now turn in regard to their distinctive impact on spaces of security.

Bangladeshis in Liberia were constituted as 'humanitarian professionals' responsible for occupying and creating spaces of a different kind, albeit under the qualitatively different conditions of post-civil war Liberia. Alongside India and Pakistan, Bangladesh is a major troop contributor to UN peacekeeping missions. Indeed, these South Asian countries cast the involvement of their troops in peacekeeping operations in ambassadorial terms. This aspect of foreign policy is considered – much like the cases of Canada and the Netherlands – as a way of raising the profile of their countries and their militaries within the international community. In keeping with the ambassadorial approach taken towards operations, Bangladeshi battalions performed a particular kind of humanitarian professionalism, one element of which was to colonize space by maintaining high visibility among the local community, as well as interacting directly with 'beneficiaries' in ways that differed from the styles of peacekeeping staged by Nigerian peacekeepers. In regard to the sharing of food and providing facilities, a Monrovia-based Liberian female observed:

The Bangladeshis have done exceptionally well. They forfeited one day's food per week to give the local population a sense of security. They've opened a clinic that provides health services and they provided over 350 soccer balls to the villages where young people are. Young people can play and there is a sense of fullness – that is security!

She went on to note how members of the Bangladeshi (and Pakistani) contingents engaged with local people with the intention of 'breaking down barriers between peacekeepers and the people'. Their interaction with the local community was argued to be 'second to none' and they were invariably seen to be polite and receptive to the needs of Liberians. For many, their presence was framed as 'reassuring' and underscores the different ways in which spaces of security can be produced and maintained as a consequence of contrasting security performance noted to flow from a mix of 'essentialized' national identity, character and observable practice. As a male Liberian university student in Monrovia argued, 'unlike the Nigerians, the Bangladeshis are much better, because for them peacekeeping rules are very important: they guard you!' On one occasion a member of our research team witnessed a four-man patrol of Bangladeshis driving slowly through villages throwing sweets to local children from the back of their UN four-wheel-drive vehicles. The children heralded this encounter with smiles and cheering, as they ran alongside the vehicles, scrambling for sweets and cheering 'Banga! Banga!' Nevertheless, not all agreed that the humanitarian professionalism performed by Bangladeshis engendered security. Approaches turning on reconstruction, distribution of food and helping to dig wells were also read by some as 'lacking the military legitimacy' of the Nigerians, in contrast to some of the concerns raised in Chapter 5 about peacekeepers' involvement in humanitarian work. These alternative expectations resonated with the belief that the Blue Helmets should be 'tough' and uncompromising in ways that foreground martial qualities and physical prowess.

As African regional identity shaped the construction of Nigerian peacekeepers, stereotypical views of South Asians influenced discussion of Bangladeshis. Here differences in national identity and national character were seen to play inconsistently and perhaps dangerously with potential peace spoilers and ex-combatants. As one young male in Liberia argued: 'the combatants would fear the Nigerians most, unlike the Bangladeshis or Pakistanis, who might wave a peace flag.' We heard numerous stories of how during the early months of UNMIL 'Nigerians bailed out Bangladeshis' who 'couldn't cope' and that the latter contingent were in need of protection in ways that invoked a kind of 'feminized' professionalism where 'caring' or 'compassion' was not rated as highly as 'toughness' by respondents. Rather, effectiveness in security practice was conflated with the ability to create 'fear' among those seeking to destabilize the peace, as noted with the Nigerian contingents above. In discussing the attack on the Bangladeshi guard post (considered above with regard to its impact on the embodied dimensions of security practice), one European female NGO worker argued that 'people are laughing about that [the attack]. You can't imagine them laughing about it with a different contingent!' She believed that in her particular county there was 'little respect for the Bangladeshis', and that because they 'lacked clout', they were likely to engender an overall sense of insecurity. These perceptions – elicited from both indigenous/international NGO workers and local women and men – are derived from a colonial view of subordinate others. Given that peacekeeping might be argued to be a highly colonial activity (Agathangelou and Ling 2003; Zisk-Marten 2004) it is unsurprising that racial and ethnic identity should feature so extensively in respondent concerns. Here, 'race' appeared to overdetermine what people thought of security styles and performances and was rarely discussed in anything other than a superficial way. Underscored by the framing of Swedish peacekeepers discussed earlier, the hegemony of whiteness is hidden, while South Asians are viewed as 'lesser' individuals/men (Sinha 1995).

How can we contextualize the broader influences shaping perceptions of the 'less military performances' of Bangladeshis, commented on above? This more 'passive' style of peacekeeping was demonstrated most obviously by Indian peacekeepers in Somalia (UNOSOM II), where violence against peacekeepers, though widespread, tended not to evoke aggressive counter-attack. Indeed, whilst it would be inappropriate to conflate Bangladeshi UN peacekeepers with their Indian counterparts on account of their numerous cultural and religious differences, nevertheless considerable overlap between their styles is evident in terms of the ways that local populations might see them, as well as how they present themselves. The commander of the Bangladeshi battalion commented thus on the approach taken by India to peacekeeping: 'Peace and security in peacekeeping operations can … be achieved through mutual understanding, cultural exchanges and increased military–civilian interactions' (Krishnamsamy 2001: 39). The approach to 'making peacekeeping effective', as the commander respondent argued, was to 'reach out' to local people in ways that fostered their 'trust and respect'. Given the extent to which Bangladeshi peacekeepers in our study were noted to be actively involved in rebuilding work, the notion of 'an army of reconstruction' that downplays the military dimension was evident, again in ways that mirror the humanitarian emphasis placed on peacekeeping by Indian troops (Bullion 2001). In a broader sense, the everyday security practices of Bangladeshi peacekeepers can be directly traced to the geopolitical level, as suggested by Krishnamsamy (2001: 37), who states that

> Bangladesh views its participation in UN peacekeeping as an act of goodwill. Dhaka's overwhelming willingness to contribute is in keeping with its broad foreign policy objective, which is to cooperate with the international community for the promotion of international peace and security, justice and freedom.

It has further been argued that Bangladeshi involvement in UN operations should be about 'eliciting cooperation, the possession of interactive skills found in the appropriate attitude and discipline of the soldiers … peacekeeper–community relations in the field are key' (Krishnamsamy 2001: 41). On this very point, former UN secretary-general Kofi Annan had argued that peacekeeping operations must be able to communicate with the population: 'Explaining why they are in the country, what they expect from the people and their leaders, and what people might expect from the peacekeepers' (Bullion 2001: 42). Clearly, then, these broad political objectives find expression in particular styles of security performance that play out on the ground, as discussed by respondents. Reflections on the Bangladeshi performance were conveyed relationally in contrast to the ECOMOG legacy in ways that reflect and refract a range of peacekeeper professionalisms. In turn these were cross-cut with essentialized and national(ized) framings that underline the inseparability of national identity and security performance, the findings of which invite critical engagements of the nexus linking racialized stereotypes, ideology and power. What about those peacekeepers who were seen to favour one group over another in their security work? How was inconsistent performance tied to national identity inasmuch as partiality was perceived to undermine professionalism?

Here we come to the key issue of bias: the idea that peacekeepers could stage a security drama that favoured one group over another. Respondents across Liberia, Kosovo and Haiti were highly sensitive to more traditional notions of Blue Helmet neutrality. Religious affiliation also came into play, as part of the complex intersection of national and regional identity. In Liberia, for example, Bangladeshi and Pakistani troops were seen to favour Muslim over Christian communities or tribes. Typical of this reading of the security performance was that bias functioned to protect peacekeepers from dangerous situations in ways that chime with earlier comments of Bangladeshis' apparent 'weakness' in contrast to Nigerian troops. As one Liberian male working in a northern town put it:

> Many people think that the Bangladeshis are a weak side. We no longer place trust in them, because they were accused of being too slow and even biased in favour of 'one side' [the Mandingos] along religious lines ... the Mandingos are predominantly Muslims. This is what most people in the community perceive about the Bangladeshi contingent.

This assertion was also made by four international females working for an NGO in Monrovia. They believed that 'In terms of insecurity [and UNMIL] there is a perception of certain battalions. Some people are saying that Muslims protect Muslims more than Christians ... this is an important perception.' This apparent bias was alleged to manifest itself in 'slow response times' to incidents involving 'non-Muslims'. A local Liberian male NGO worker asked the question, 'why are they [the Bangladeshis] slow in responding?' He then noted that 'some people say they are professional soldiers but I would disagree because they favour the [Muslim] "LURD".' Allegations of bias levelled against Bangladeshi troops (contingents of whom were invariably labelled as 'Muslims') were not made about any other national contingent, even though members of the numerous African troops might also self-identify as of Muslim faith (for example, some Nigerians or Senegalese). When pushed on the source of their information on this apparent bias, respondents invariably said that this was something they heard from a friend or colleague, or that it was 'widely known'. Rumour reflected through personal prejudice undoubtedly helped to shape these perceptions in ways that engage racialized ideas of these particular men. In so doing, further 'evidence' for the hierarchy of performance entered a common understanding shared by numerous stakeholders, from Liberians – including men and women members of the host population – through to international staff.

Perceptions of bias assumed a somewhat different form in the Kosovan context, where the French were seen by Kosovar Albanians to 'favour the Serbs'. The 'inconsistencies' in their security performances, alongside the perception that they were 'pro-Serb', were also elicited from international staff working in the mission.[8] Indeed, the approach of French KFOR troops was frequently framed as 'a failure of performance', as one male Kosovar Albanian university student put it. He expanded on this perception by suggesting that 'the French' were responsible for dividing the city of Mitrovicë/a into two ethnically discrete spaces, 'with the Serbians in the north and the Kosovars in the south'. Mirroring the beliefs of other Kosovar Albanians, including those outside of Priština, a female waitress in the town of Prizren underlined her sense of unease concerning the volatile space of Mitrovicë/a when she said that, 'Overall, people are content with KFOR. But, if you asked those [Kosovar Albanians] in Mitrovica they would say that they are not happy with the French troops.'

The perception that the French failed to treat Kosovar Albanians and Serbians as equally deserving in their security needs was most strongly expressed in regard to Mitrovicë/a, where questions were raised in regard to the French troops' failure to 'protect the Kosovar Albanians in the south of the city'. Yet, despite, or perhaps because of, the strength of belief that French KFOR troops failed to act in line with a fair and balanced peacekeeping ethos, it is important to emphasize that allegations of bias came predominantly from Kosovar Albanians, underlining the influence of ethnic identity in shaping perception of national identity and allied security performance. A European female working for the OSCE argued that this apparent partiality in the work of French peacekeepers was actually a result of the stereotypical views held by the ethnically divided members of the host population rather than the poor performances of the French troops themselves. She observed: 'There are definitely biases in the local population and this is linked to how they engage with KFOR.' Other international staff also sought to explain how it was that national identity could be seen to play such a decisive role in why and how peacekeepers approached their work in line with broader sentiments concerning alleged bias. Here, a female UN worker from eastern Europe referred to historical links between Serbia and France as the key explanation for the apparent 'pro-Serb' proclivities commented on above:

> People think that French military troops help Serbians because the French have traditionally been connected with Serbia. Because of this people think that the French are not that different from the Serbians because they have the same views. People also think that the French police are 'inside' the Serbian side.

The idea that there existed a strong historical friendship between the French and the Serbs was an enduring one and was expressed in various ways; this pereption was shared by the small number of the Serbians we interviewed. In terms of French–Serbian connections, it has been argued that during negotiations for the Rambouillet Conference the French foreign minister worked hard in the Contact Group to 'get France's approach accepted. Before the opening of the conference, he insisted that Serbian sovereignty over Kosovo and the supremacy of the UN should be recognized in the text.'[9] Whilst there does seem to be a broader political context to 'bias on the ground', a member of the international staff argued that perceptions of the (alleged) bias of French KFOR troops was actually a prime instance of the inability of many – mainly Kosovar Albanians – to 'move on from 1999, a time at which they were being treated badly by Serbs'. Supporting evidence for this partiality in peacekeeping practice configured along the lines of a pro-Serb stance practised by French KFOR troops has also been found in the work of others (see Cleland Welch 2006; Donini et al. 2005). In sum, then, there seem to be good grounds for suggesting that French KFOR troops may at times have favoured one ethnic group over another, giving rise to perceptions of bias. However, the complex interlinkage of perception and stereotype allied to the political beliefs of particular ethnic groups defies simple explanation. The fact remains, however, that no matter how peacekeepers conduct their performances and shape the space of both secure and insecure (military and humanitarian) kinds, it is their national identity that is believed to determine these practices.

Conclusion

National identity was conceptualized as inseparable from embodied, stereotypical notions of ethnicity and 'race'. Although there was considerable agreement about the security styles of certain national contingents, there were also dissenting voices which challenged any archetypal version of peacekeeper seen through the lens of national identity. These representations relied heavily on views of nationality that were laden with beliefs about different peacekeepers as racialized and ethnicized groups from an idealized global North or a vilified global South. Of particular note was the identity of the respondents themselves, whose own ethnic, racial or gender identities did not shape how they framed peacekeeper security performance, whether international, local or NGO worker. It was clear that all interactions (and more abstract 'imaginings') unfolded within the context of an awareness of racial identity. This is a further reminder of the deeply colonial underpinnings of the peacekeeping project that seek to improve local populations who are 'unable to manage themselves'.

Also of particular note is that, despite the ways that Bangladeshis' performance articulated closely with the geopolitical framing of their role in peacekeeping, we noted that they also staged a more robust, military or aggressive stance at particular moments. These were largely overlooked by respondents in ways that demonstrate the potency of stereotype and racist and colonial views of particular ethnic groups. We felt quite certain that for every stereotypical perception of a particular security style linked to national identity, it was possible to find an oppositional performance. The importance of the broader context of operations – in both a historical and contemporary sense – should not, however, be disregarded. Here, set against the backdrop of the brutal fourteen-year civil war in Liberia, Nigerian troops of the ECOMOG presence were noted to shape subsequent perception of UNMIL troops, set within the context of what many experienced as a precarious peace. Continuing a key theme running through this book, we note here how the geopolitical can find expression through the everyday example of peacekeeper security performances, and how it is they are read through the dominant lens of national identity by those working and living in missions. The cases of Bangladeshi, Swedish and French troops were used here to underscore links between apparently discrete levels, from the ground to the international. By no means is this a straightforward process, given the complex interaction of perception, stereotype, imagining and actually observed performance, alongside broader geopolitical influences.

Finally, it is also important to flag the wider implications of our findings. Here, it is also possible to show how a 'non-state' or 'UN-generic' identity has failed to emerge in the face of national identity as the axis along which perceptions of security styles unfolded. In this respect, our findings notably replicate those of Ben-Ari and Elron's (2001) anthropological study of UN military peacekeepers, where it is maintained that, rather than loosening ties with the state, multinational forces may actually lead to the hardening of differences of national identity. Ben-Ari and Elron argue that 'the symbolic importance of the multi-national [identities] and aspects of peacekeeping is crucial to the way they carry out their roles' (2001: 277), a point we would underline when seen through the eyes of the various audiences consulted for the current work. It is for this reason that the military components of PSOs should be seen as at some distance from the cosmopolitan 'melting pot' model of peacekeeping that has emerged recently in some discussions of peacekeeping (though usually in the absence of primary empirical research; see Woodhouse and Ramsbotham 2005). It could also be that there are other potential explanations for respondent perceptions discussed above. In this way, the prevalence of national stereotyping and apparent dislike of peacekeepers could be seen to spring from a sense of national humiliation. This could raise the question of whether or not there is some inevitability regarding the extent to which occupying forces deployed to exert control and authority may be susceptible to some of the more negative framings we have included here as 'others' from 'foreign countries'.

EIGHT

Women, men and gender space

Peacekeeping missions are masculine spaces. The UN or NATO presence is dominated by men, with female military peacekeepers constituting less than 2 per cent of the Blue Helmet numbers overall. As a consequence of this overwhelming male presence, a not insignificant number of women and minors across UN and NATO missions experience insecurity through sexual exploitation and abuse by a small minority of male Blue Helmets, UN civilian staff and employees of NGOs. Exploitative gender relations of this kind follow earlier forms of gender-based violence perpetrated during the conflict itself. For this reason, the post-war moment may not differ from that which preceded with regard to experiences of insecurity endured by vulnerable groups, including women and minors (Cockburn and Hubic 2002; Enloe 2000; Spencer 2005).

In elaborating a key line of argument made throughout this book, the following discussion considers how the presence of large numbers of (male) peacekeepers can give rise to spaces of insecurity. Our particular focus is on the ways that individuals are noted to endure a constellation of disadvantage according to their class, ethnicity, age and – crucially for this chapter – status as females. The specific findings detailed here from Kosovo, Haiti and Liberia contribute towards a growing literature documenting the sexual exploitation of women and young people, with whom a small minority of peace-keepers abuse their position of power and privilege.

The impact of exploitative performances is disproportionate to their relatively small scale, as they undermine the wider sense of trust invested in peacekeepers who have, as noted above, a stated 'responsibility to protect' as members of 'forces for good'. It is widely expected that the Blue Helmets will overall have a positive effect on the post-conflict space – which they undoubtedly do most of the time – rather than its obverse, where masculine self-interest exacerbates the insecurity of the most vulnerable. With these points in mind, the main arguments of this chapter are that the UN (and, to a large degree, NATO) needs to foster a sense among its culturally and ethnically diverse staff (1) that gender refers to women *and* men; (2) that 'masculinity matters'; and (3) that peacekeeping spaces are gender spaces, since women and minors are likely to have suffered disproportionately during the conflict.

This chapter is organized into five sections. The first outlines the theoretical perspective framing exploitative gender relations, where we briefly sketch feminist geopolitics and critical men's studies approaches to highlighting the gender space of the post-conflict setting. The second section sketches the broader patriarchal context of the post-conflict setting against which the specific instance of peacekeepers' sexual exploitation and abuse of local women and minors is played out. The third section details substantive findings generated within the missions between 2005 and 2007 of male peacekeepers' implication in sexual exploitation and abuse (SEA) despite the declaration by former secretary-general Kofi Annan in 2004 that there would be 'zero tolerance' of these damaging social practices. The fourth section considers the ways that the UN, in particular, has attempted to 'feminize' the masculine space of the mission through such policy initiatives as the deployment of female peacekeepers, gender training and, more widely across the UN, gender mainstreaming. The final section considers the ways that 'gender' continues to be shorthand for 'woman', one consequence of which is a neglect of the role of masculinity in peacekeeping's gender relations. A brief conclusion follows.

Feminist geopolitics and gender relations

Put most simply, a feminist geopolitical approach seeks to combine the central tenets of feminist/International Relations thinking (Tickner 1997; Parpart and Zalewski 1998, 2008), critical geopolitics and political geography in ways that highlight the experiences of women within networks of power, including those of the state that can fail to protect them (Shepherd 2006). The aim of the work of particular feminists, such as Jennifer Hyndman (2004), has been to 'strengthen the connections between feminist geography and political geography' in ways that 'provide for an embodied view from which to analyze visceral conceptions of violence, security and mobility' (Hyndman 2004: 308). Of particular importance for our work is Hyndman's understanding of feminist geopolitics, which encompasses various geographical 'scales' or levels and the ways they articulate with one another, from the ground up through the transnational (UN/NATO) and on to the geopolitical. Her approach and that of others (Dalby 1990, 1991; McDowell and Sharp 1997) is valuable for analysing the security of women in peacekeeping missions since it engages questions of spatiality, embodiment and the security impact of supranational powers (or surrogate states) of the UN and NATO. Feminist geopolitics and critical geopolitics share a concern with 'the hidden and insidious workings of power through the structures of everyday life' (Dowler and Sharp 2001: 167). Here, SEA perpetrated by the Blue Helmets evokes broader questions of security within the context of highly intimate and embodied aspects of exploitative gender relations – issues of central concern to feminist geopolitics. As Dowler and Sharp argue: 'Women's bodies are inherently caught up in international relations, but often at mundane or everyday levels and so are not written into the texts of political discourse' (2001: 168).

Hyndman underlines the centrality of the embodied realm when she says that 'Feminist geopolitics ... includes embodied epistemologies and the security, or protection of people' (2004: 39). Our focus here is on the asymmetry of gendered relations between peacekeeping men and local women, which, when considered in their everyday, spatial and political complexity, is noted to reflect similar gender orders such as those documented between so-called 'sex tourists' and their 'victims' (O'Connell Davidson 1998; Enloe 2000; Higate

2007). Awareness of the spatiality of exploitation proceeds from the observation that crime is one of the key ways in which space is appropriated by dominant groups (Smith 1989), and that fear of sexual crime impacts on women's spatial behaviour in ways that 'reflect and reinforce the structure of gender relations' more widely (Pain 1997: 237). Feminist geopolitics has identified masculinity as a problem with regard both to the critical geopolitical literature and empirically, at the level of the state. In terms of the former, Hyndman engages masculinity when she and other commentators (Dowler and Sharp 2001) take the critical geopolitical theorist O'Tuathail (1996) to task for 'reproducing geopolitics as masculinist practice' through his focus on 'the history of big men' (Sharp 2000; Hyndman 2004). Given that we are interested in developing a critical awareness of men within the broader frame of gender relations, how might we conceive of masculinity?

As a concept and experience, masculinity has been problematized by scholars over the past two decades, challenging the idea that 'it' has a 'core' or 'essence' (Brod 1987; Brittan 1989; Brod and Kaufman 1994; Hearn 1996; MacInnes 1998). Masculinity can refer to a 'set of attitudes and practices culturally deemed appropriate to men' (Buchbinder 1994: vii), but more broadly could encompass 'a discourse, a power structure, a psychic economy, a history, an ideology, an identity, a behaviour, a value system, or even an aesthetic' (Middleton 1992: 152). Critical studies on men (Petersen 2003; Hearn 2004; Connell and Messerschmidt 2005) have sought to understand how and why masculinity is able to shape social relations in ways that have a tendency to favour men with regard to their exercise of power. They also show how the use of physical force and an 'aggressive heterosexuality' might be prized at particular moments, not least in military and quasi-military environments (Morgan 1987, 1992, 1994; Connell 1995; Hearn 1998; Higate et al. 2003). This critical approach has also noted the significance of the male body to masculinity (Seidler 1997); the ways that masculinity can encompass a diversity of performances particularly in the military – from masculinity to masculinities (Barrett 1996); the identification of certain authoritative performances according to the ideological conditions of what it is to 'be a man' across culture and time (Cornwall and Lindisfarne 1994; Connell 1995); and, finally, how at the broadest level masculinity is argued to be an 'integral feature of the worldwide structure of diplomatic, military and economic relations' (Connell 2008: ix). The volume of critical studies on men militates against further elaboration here, although in thinking about the impact of UN and NATO missions on women in respect of SEA, we turn to three ideal-typical categories in the third section below to highlight the role of intra-masculine relations in male peacekeepers' exploitative practices.

These ideal types consist, first, of 'hegemonic masculinities' that are framed as socially central, associated with authority and power according to the norms of what it is to be a man (or masculine performance) dominating certain times and places (Messerschmidt and Connell 2005: 846). Second, 'complicit masculinities' are understood to be 'constructed in ways that realize the patriarchal dividend [but] without the tensions or risks of being the frontline troops of patriarchy ... they are complicit in this sense'. Third, 'subordinate masculinities' or 'marginal masculinities' are seen as less powerful or influential than their hegemonic counterparts. Here, homosexuality (in heteronormative contexts) or being black (in mainly white contexts) may signal relatively low status within masculine gender hierarchies (Connell 1995). Yet it is important to recognize that masculinity as 'shorthand for power', and femininity as 'relationally subordinate', can ignore the intersectionality of other identity categories shaping gender relations (Fine and Kuriloff 2006: 259). For this reason it is important to recognize that the tenacity of the patriarchal dividend that continues to accrue to masculinity at the global level and in post-conflict contexts is multifaceted and engages racial, age, political economic and cultural factors, as well as gender (Anzaldúa 1987; Mohanty 1991). Whilst men and women experience space in different ways, it is not always in terms of a hierarchy of risk where men are 'safer' than women. At times men may feel vulnerable in those situations where intra-masculine violence is likely, whilst in other contexts women fear sexually motivated attack. Female internally displaced persons (IDPs) who have to venture from the relative security of their camps to collect firewood are at greater risk of gender-based violence, as research has shown (Shanks and Schull 2000). Though questions of risk and safety can engage men and women as both perpetrators and victims, it is important to keep sight of other dimensions of power that go beyond gender. In this way, the case of a female member of the international UN or NATO staff can be shown to be economically and culturally privileged when contrasted with a poorly educated, homeless and malnourished local man. Underlining this point, a study commissioned by MINUSTAH found that a few all-female gangs were at work in Cité Soleil and Cité Militaire. These younger women were noted to emulate the practices of conventional male gangs, brutalizing local communities and in some cases committing acts of gender-based violence (Loutis 2006: 5). Despite the difficulties of using the category 'women' as the prime explanatory field, it continues to be a strong determinant of disadvantage in many contexts including those of sexual crime (Smith 1989; Pain 1997). How might a feminist geopolitical approach, coupled with sensitivity to intra-masculine gender relations, reveal the hidden role of masculinity in perpetrating and sustaining SEA in peacekeeping missions? How can we make sense of the broader patriarchal contexts in which these kinds of activities take place?

Context: women, war and after

When societies implode, the power differentials configuring pre-conflict gender relations are reinforced, leading to a perpetuation of insecurity for women, who are put at even greater risk of gender-based violence. As Rehn and Sirleaf put it:

> Women are victims of unbelievably horrific atrocities and injustices in conflict situations; this is indisputable. As refugees, internally displaced persons, combatants, heads of households and community leaders ... women often experience violence, forced pregnancy, abduction, and sexual slavery ... [they can be] deliberately infected with HIV/AIDS or carrying a child conceived in rape ... the long term effects of conflict and militarization create a culture of violence that renders women especially vulnerable after war. (2002: vi)

The vulnerability of women in the post-conflict setting frequently forces them into exchanging sex for food and shelter. Their bodies can become commodified as part of a barter system, further isolating them from their communities and placing them at risk of unwanted pregnancy, STIs and HIV/AIDS. Though the object of

critique (Shepherd 2008) landmark UN Resolution 1325 recognizes
the unique position of women in respect of gender-based violence,
alongside the greater vulnerabilities of children prior to, during and
post-conflict. As such the resolution has helped to raise awareness
of the challenges facing these particular groups, as well as provide a
framework (of sorts) for targeted intervention. There is little doubt
that 'gender' is considerably more than the faint flicker it once was
on the radar of the international community, as the global growth in
gender-focused policy, NGOs, media reporting and academic studies
testifies. Yet, overall strategies informed by a broad feminist agenda
designed to improve the lives of women continue to have mixed
results, with mass rape and other forms of gender-based violence
ongoing in the DRC (Chiwengo 2008). In regard to findings from
the current study, it was argued by female international staff working
for a large NGO in Liberia that they had received reports of a
number of women being 'ritually killed' over economic land-rights
issues. The parlous state of the agricultural economy – most notably
in respect of the outlying communities – was discussed in explicitly
gender-relational terms:

> From a security perspective the young boys are really used to fast cash.
> They are not working and especially not farming. The easiest way to
> get [resources] is theft and attacking women. Women are frequently
> the target of theft.

She elaborated on the shifting economic opportunities shaping a
trajectory that led to a form of exploitative gendered relations – prostitution – that was not always identified as a concern from the women
in question:

> Quite a few women took on small businesses, but they are now feel-
> ing vulnerable economically … these things have contributed to the
> growth of commercial sex. This is a major issue, but they don't even
> look at it as commercial sex! Many women have become so used to
> it over the years. Half of the girls have children from a very young
> age and they actually see themselves as commodities.

The international female employee of another NGO explained how
she 'experienced great difficulty in getting the women to realize that
this [commercial sex] was a problem'. When asked about insecurity,

sexually exploited Liberian women would first discuss the 'price of rice, fuel, housing' and – unsurprisingly – voice concern that they were struggling to feed their families. They did not discuss domestic violence, rape and other forms of gender-based violence initially for reasons of both stigma and straightforward survival in respect of prioritizing food and shelter.

One of a number of concerns raised in Haiti turned on the ways that women endured a compound of insecurity, especially when kidnapped: 'Women are double victims', it was argued by a female Haitian NGO employee; 'not only are they kidnapped, but then they are violated, raped and injured.' More broadly – and not unlike Liberia – it was often difficult to encourage women to discuss or even report their experiences of gender-based violence because of stigma as well as a sense of 'hopelessness' that there was little that could be done to bring perpetrators to justice. Invoking the patriarchal context of Haiti, it was argued by a local female that 'women are also victims because the government prefers an educated man over an educated woman!'

Respondents in Kosovo discussed women's disproportionate experiences of vulnerability, repression and disadvantage in various contexts. These included sexual assault, war trauma and broader economic insecurity. In particular, concern was expressed at what was believed to be a significant 'under-reporting of domestic violence' in the cases of all ethnic groups. A female employee of a large umbrella group working for women in Kosovo stated that they had 'been virtually left out of the peace negotiations' and that women 'hardly featured anywhere on the political scene!' Other comments from Kosovo underscored the general neglect of 'gender issues', particularly in the case of ethnic groups existing on the margins of Kosovan society including the Roma, Ashkali and Egyptians, underlining the compound of disadvantage resulting from the convergence of ethnic and gender identity. Overall, we argue that the experiences of women in our three geographically disparate and culturally diverse post-conflict settings are shaped by a good degree of commonality in terms of universally experienced disadvantage, inequality and vulnerability. However, whilst it was clear that women and minors were relatively disadvantaged, evidence of women's resilience and agency can also be found, even in the face of extreme levels of gender-based violence

(Cockburn and Hubic 2002). In this way, women have also been engaged in coordinating activities to create economic independence, as we see below in the case of female traders in both Liberia and Haiti. It has been shown how women have provided legal testimonies against perpetrators and involved themselves in reconciliation work in post-conflict contexts. These observations serve to elevate women from their frequent portrayal as victims – a status that may frequently be used to oppress them, not least by failing to bring masculinity into the spotlight. Women are not always vulnerable, although, as we now see, gendered relations between men and women shaped by the deployment of many thousands of men from different national militaries may exacerbate the insecurity of those bearing the brunt of the conflict – women and minors. How does the international presence of the Blue Helmets configure gender space?

Men and masculinity: after the war

Evidence detailing peacekeepers' exchange of food or resources for sex with female minors and adults in peacekeeping missions continues to be documented (Martin 2005), both confirming and adding weight to earlier findings (Fetherston 1995, 1998; Enloe 2000; Hughes 2000; Mackay 2001; Rehn and Johnson-Sirleaf 2002; Higate and Henry 2004; Zeid 2005). Peacekeepers implicated in these activities, hailing from both developed and developing countries, have been involved in exploitative practices ranging from the routine use of young and adult women for sex to the manufacture of pornographic films with local women and girls (Martin 2005). Our work adds to these findings by highlighting a number of the specificities of exploitative gender relations played out in our three mission sites. For example, evidence generated from fieldwork with two female and two male Liberian NGO workers shows that an organized ring of men acting as pimps, including police inspectors and others 'with authority', were profiteering from local women sold for sex. These respondents believed that 'the local pimps were doing very well out of the UNMIL troops, though they would never admit it'. This was because 'peacekeepers [from a particular national contingent] are the main customers. We have seen them picking up the girls in the bars and hotel!' It was almost certainly the case that 'leisure time' activities of this particular contingent were known to their commanders, who can be seen to be complicit inasmuch as they failed to discipline troops breaching the code of conduct prohibiting exploitation of this kind. Further, it was believed that the use of local women as sex workers or prostitutes was believed to have 'damaged the morale of the whole community'. This was illustrated by a Liberian female employee of a local NGO who discussed how the town, and to a certain extent outlying villages, had become more hostile to women, who were being told by 'the elders' to 'dress "discreetly"' and to 'move around in large groups when possible'. Here it has been argued in respect of women's fear of violent crime that:

> The constraints of [possible attack] also have deeper emotional and psychological effects ... they preclude certain activities in public, space, restrict independent mobility and policy an unofficial code of 'appropriate' dress and behaviour. (Pain 1997: 234)

According to a female European working in Monrovia for a major NGO, women and a number of young people in the county were suffering higher than average incidences of STIs, unwanted pregnancy, HIV/AIDS, and higher numbers of illegitimate babies – key indicators of long-term gendered insecurity. One explanation for the increased incidence of HIV infection identified the 'high rates of HIV among these troops', as the European NGO employee stated. The often assumed direction of infection from 'prostitute to peacekeeper' is turned on its head here in ways that create long-term insecurity, as the Blue Helmets are noted to be the key vectors of HIV/AIDS infection (Martin 2005). Another complex dynamic shaping these exploitative gendered relations, identified in other contexts including IDP camps (SCFUK 2004), was that young women were often encouraged by their mothers or carers to 'go and get a peacekeeper "boyfriend"'. With this in mind, an NGO in Monrovia referred more widely to the way in which women were framed in Liberia: 'They are not viewed very highly. Parents do send them off to UNMIL to be exploited. When people use the phrase "would you do this to your daughter?" ... well, in fact they do!' In this example, complicity with exploitation of minors is configured by both poverty and gender. A Liberian female working for an NGO in the county in which organized sexual exploitation was taking place made a broader point that invoked the aggressively heterosexual dimension of masculinity: 'I find it really worrying that we give men the power to rule the country, rule the finances, control the wealth ... and yet they can't control themselves – simply because [girls] wear a tight t-shirt!' Questions might be raised here about the extent to which these kinds of masculine practice are hegemonic, with a degree of reverence displayed towards those men 'credited' with sleeping with large numbers of women, as noted in the context of sexual exploitation and abuse of minors by peacekeepers in the DRC (Higate 2004).

The UN's response to the increased documentation of SEA perpetrated by its troops was a 'zero tolerance' policy, which in Liberia had developed into a so-called 'no fraternization' rule between military peacekeepers and female members of the local population. In turn, this rule undermined the kinds of security performances troops provided for members of the host population. For example, peacekeepers would avoid stopping their vehicles to assist women at the side of the road or in villages who looked as if they were in difficulty – the rule was 'keep driving', noted one of the Blue Helmets in an informal group interview. The consensus among other peacekeepers in this group supported this precept: 'Don't stop – it could be a "set up". Keep your windows wound up, the doors locked and your foot on the gas.' This attitude was triggered by an attempt on the part of an unknown number of local women to claim compensation through false allegations of sexual abuse by peacekeepers. The reaction of the Blue Helmets to policy intended to provide security for local women turned on shifting the gender-relational dynamic in ways that spoke to self- rather than 'beneficiary' protection.

Despite the existence of a 'zero tolerance' policy and a 'no fraternization' rule, however, some national contingents continued to account for the use of large numbers of condoms (thousands per month in the case of one contingent in the north of the country), underscoring the widely held notion that 'boys will be boys'. Whilst numerous international staff voiced concern at women being exploited by peacekeepers, alongside the lax discipline and wholesale disregard for local women and minors provided with money (often for school fees in the case of young girls), food or other tradable goods in return for sex, overall Liberian respondents seemed reluctant to draw attention to these activities. Rather, it was widely argued that 'Liberians were relieved that the war was over' and that concern around SEA 'had not yet reached the level of bitterness'. It was generally agreed by international staff (along with a small number of Liberian NGO workers) that 'the overall gratitude of the Liberians tends to overshadow all of these issues' of exploitation. Yet, this view was not held by all, particularly when one ventured outside of Monrovia or beyond other larger settlements. The throwing of the Molotov cocktail at the Bangladeshi checkpoint referred to in Chapter 6 was believed to have been triggered by men's anger at UN troops 'cavorting' with local women. As a Liberian female working close to the Bangladeshi base remarked: 'It is not that surprising [the attack]. Men in the town feel that UNMIL are taking away all the girls and they feel jealous.' Noted here is the intra-masculine gender relation between Bangladeshi peacekeeper and local men, who may feel as if their access to women is being undermined. In turn, the attack on the guard post can also be read as an attempt to create a subordinate masculinity from the presence of Bangladeshi soldiers, who – whilst successful with local females – are unable to defend themselves despite being armed and trained in military skills.

As we have seen, one of a number of concerns raised in Haiti touched on the ban by UNPOL officers on providing lifts for local people. Local women seeking protection in the face of vulnerability had then to seek help from PNH officers. Yet there were reports of PNH officers themselves being involved in gender-based violence, further undermining the situation of local women. Somewhat ironically, a report published in early 2007 by the BBC showed UNPOL officers ferrying local Haitian women in their cars to and from clubs and bars notorious for prostitution.[1] Other problems raised in Haiti highlighted the failure of the UN to act decisively towards the Blue Helmet or UN civilian perpetrator of SEA. As one Haitian female working for an NGO noted: 'He just gets moved to a different mission – you know somewhere else within the UN system – and then he gets a promotion!' She went on to argue that sanctions were not brought to bear on those found guilty of sexual exploitation because 'they know the right people'. These two examples involving, first, police officers taking local women to notorious clubs and bars and, second, the failure to punish male perpetrators speak directly to complicit masculinities.

As was common across the other missions sites, the sexual exploitation and abuse carried out by military peacekeepers was seen to derive from a mix of factors including 'being away from family for too long', 'poor discipline', 'having too much time and money on [their] hands', and finally, as has been noted more widely, the acceptance by the UN and the national militaries of troop contributing countries that 'boys will be boys'. It was also observed by some in Haiti that:

> [Male] international staff always seem to look for a younger girl that they can 'employ' in their house ... that is exploitation, because he has financial power and in his home country he can never employ a teenager like that.

A female Haitian NGO worker also identified UN civilian men as maximizing their financial privilege over younger females in the mission: 'You can see young girls going with rich men or older men in order to get a phone or cell phone ... here the underlying issue is poverty.' In this example, the kudos of masculine performance is enhanced through gender relations of considerable socio-economic disparity.

Sexual exploitation and abuse of local women by military peace-keepers of the KFOR contingents was raised by representatives of three different women's organizations in Kosovo. Their direct concern was prostitution and trafficking, which has a notorious history in the region. In their dialogue with the Scandinavian force commander, they argued that 'far more should be done to stop this – especially the involvement [as brothel clients] of peacekeepers'. They reported being 'shocked' when he replied that 'men will be men' and that it was 'their job' as key players in women's organizations 'to take care of the women'. Connected to discussion in the previous chapter of national identity, their surprise was compounded by the expectation, as one of the group stated, that 'the Scandinavian force commander was not as enlightened as we thought he would be!' The assumption of the female group was that the Scandinavian was disposed towards a hegemonic masculinity turning on gender equality, rather than that complicit in the exploitation of disempowered individuals. A female Roma journalist described how she had seen 'French peace-keepers "sniffing around" young women in the new Roma housing developments' and that 'some of these developments are quite isolated and secluded' adding to the potential vulnerability of women in receipt of 'unwanted advances from these troops'. Overall, it was clear that the security of a significant number of women across the missions was compromised by the presence of many tens of thousands of male UN civilians and national military contingents, with whom asymmetrical gender relations were routinely played out. Critical and feminist geopolitical analysis draws our attention to the ways that states or, in this example, supranational entities such as the UN or NATO, may exacerbate insecurity for vulnerable individuals as a consequence of gender power relations. These are often played out within the context of intra-masculine relations that fail to challenge the sharp power disparities between privileged peacekeeper and, at times, desperate local female. What of those observations that invoked the spatial dimension more explicitly? What might a fine-grained analysis reveal about the interplay of space, security and gender?

Women and gender space

Research into women's spatialized experiences has developed in respect of 'fear of violent crime' by highlighting the role of space in the 'formation and reproduction of patriarchal structures and ideologies' (Valentine 1989, 1992; Pain 1997: 233). Observations from both Haiti and Liberia brought the spatial dimension of gendered inequality into sharp focus. Here the perceived threat of attack led to a reconfiguring of the ways in which certain times and places are negotiated (Valentine 1989). Comments concerned the limited mobility of women who faced sexual harassment and violence when travelling to and from the market to trade goods. This was particularly the case during times of darkness, either early in the morning or late at night, where the intermittent availability of electricity meant that street lights didn't work, increasing the possibility of a sexually motivated attack. Research into women's fear of violent crime has also highlighted the ways that both temporal and spatial dimensions can shape perceptions of insecurity, which 'is commonly manifested in the significance of darkness as a cue of danger and by changes in feelings of security ... between night and day' (Pain 1997: 238). In addition, women traders were often targeted as economic agents even though they might be bringing home very small sums of money at the end of each day. In the specific case of Haiti, one female living in the red zone observed: 'We experience day-to-day insecurity because we have to work in the informal sector.' She went on to say: 'We have to travel to buy produce and bandits are everywhere. They are on the buses and other public transport – we have to face this every day!' In Port-au-Prince, market trading and schools begin early in the morning, requiring the movement of women and their children during the hours of darkness. The women discussed here were exposed to insecurity as a consequence of their roles as carers and mothers, which in turn encouraged a reluctance to become involved in activities outside of the home. A Haitian female government worker pointed out that 'It is difficult to organize activities [for women] in Les Cayes due to fear of being kidnapped or attacked. I wanted to recruit some people to work [for the Ministry] but the young girls ... some of them have been violated and raped.'

Certain neighbourhoods were identified as 'bad places to live for women'. It was widely reported that 'peacekeepers took no action in these places' and that the Blue Helmets remained largely insensitive to the ways that gender limited freedom of movement. The bounded spaces of the slums tended to be viewed by peacekeepers as gender-neutral territory in ways that resonate with earlier comments regarding the imagined homogeneity of the women, men and children living within them. Whereas peacekeepers might see the slums as 'war zones', local women are likely to experience them as danger zones in a different kind of war, where they are at constant risk of gender-based violence.[2] The widespread incidence of rape by armed men in the red zones has been documented by a consultant for MINUSTAH's Gender Unit, which was intended to raise awareness of the vulnerabilities experienced by women (Loutis 2005). However, the danger of the slum space means that the only outsiders local women might come into contact with are armed MINUSTAH troops conducting military operations, who might invoke a general sense of insecurity in their operations to eliminate gang members. In a broader sense, Haiti's senior gender adviser commented in a publication in 2004 that the security situation of women had not been taken into account in the work of MINUSTAH.[3] In her reflections, Nadine Puechigerbal suggests that in humanitarian relief efforts following the floods affecting the Gonaïves region in Haiti, planners and workers sometimes failed to recognize the dangers that women faced when collecting water and food provided by international agencies. The collection points themselves were protected by MINUSTAH Blue Helmets, but safe passage could not be guaranteed once the women, weighed down with supplies, were away from them.

Towards a 'feminization' of the mission space?

The most recent high-profile attempt to transform the masculine space of the peacekeeping mission was signalled by the deployment of more than a hundred female Indian peacekeepers as armed police to Liberia in 2007. This 'force protection unit' was on its third rotation at the time of writing, and has been well received both by the international media and on the ground in Liberia itself; here the common sentiment is that 'they will be less aggressive than the male troops'. Yet these female peacekeepers are depicted in the media and on their own videos placed on YouTube as much the same as their Blue Helmet male peers: as 'hard', 'tough' and well-armed. They are shown performing physical drill and exercise in ways that also appeal to an embodied masculinity foregrounding resilience and potential fighting ability. Despite its best efforts to 'gender mainstream', UN peacekeeping remains unable to field anything like the 'critical mass' of females thought necessary to shift (military) masculine culture decisively in a direction of demonstrable benefit to females members of the host population. From a total of over 75,000 military peacekeepers deployed in all UN missions as of September 2008, only 1,606 were female. In Haiti it was argued by a female Haitian employee of an international NGO that 'the policy to recruit women had been better applied by the [UN] agencies than DPKO' and that female UNPOL officers were fewer. Other comments were made regarding the low number of women in both the Sri Lankan and the Canadian military. A European female working for a small NGO said 'it's a real shame. We should have more females. This is a good case of the UN failing to apply its own policies! For me, gender mainstreaming is just a slogan.' Several female peacekeepers were interviewed in Haiti in regard to their experiences of working in the mission more generally alongside what they considered to be the most pressing insecurities for the local population. Though it is clear that local women were at disproportionate risk of gender-based violence, kidnapping and others forms of exploitation and abuse, one of the female peacekeepers stated – to nods of agreement from the others – that they 'were not aware of any gender issues in Haiti'. Not unlike their male peers, this group did not speak either French or Kreyol and had only the most limited contact with local females. Haitian females working for a number of women's organizations expressed surprise that female peacekeepers had been deployed to Haiti, as they had only ever seen male Blue Helmets, alongside a sense of resignation that female peacekeepers remained under-utilized in respect of local women. A similar situation was found in Kosovo where Kosovo Police Service (KPS) female officers were discussed. In this instance it was argued that KPS women failed to identify issues directly pertaining to civilian women within the province. In addition, not unlike their military peacekeeping compatriots in Haiti, female police officers came to be seen as uniformed officials first and women second. Whilst we are not in a position to make any grand claims about the different ways in which female peacekeepers in their performances shaped spaces sympathetic to the specific security concerns of local women, nonetheless their low numbers alone underscore their symbolic rather than material impact on rendering space safe for vulnerable females.

Finally, gender training is organized across the missions in an effort to develop peacekeepers' sensitivity to the histories of conflict and the subsequent difficulties facing women. Training sessions were usually run by gender specialists in the Office for Gender Affairs, or by human rights officers with a remit covering gender issues. One of our research team observed a gender-awareness training workshop organized for military peacekeepers but constituted mainly by prison officers from West Africa. The profound challenges of 'teaching gender' became apparent, particularly since the time allocated to workshops of this kind are invariably limited. Instructors are put in a position of having to convince students of a feminist ideology in terms that may be alien to them, depending on the understandings of gender they import from their own cultural contexts. For some individuals, understanding gender in such a way requires them to challenge almost everything that they have been exposed to in education, at home, in the workplace – indeed across every aspect of their life. Though it was not possible to follow up the potential impact of gender training, other research conducted in the DRC on this topic has shown how military peacekeepers routinely (and understandably) prioritized concerns of health and safety, including awareness of minefields, safe driving, weapons handling and patrolling conventions, over and above concerns of gender (Higate 2004).

Concluding thoughts:
the UN, NATO and the problem of gender

For many in the UN, NATO and other powerful organizations, the word 'gender' continues to be used as a synonym for 'women'. This is surprising given the depth and breadth of scholarship that has critically examined the lives of men and women alongside the gender identities of femininity and masculinity, not least in regard to war, peace and peacekeeping itself (Cohn 1987; Enloe 1989; Hooper 2001; Tickner 2001; Kinsella 2004; Razack 2004; Whitworth 2004; Higate 2007; Sion 2008). Though the UN has commissioned work on masculinity through projects designed to co-opt men and boys into strategies for gender equality (Connell 2003), these have failed to trickle down into the everyday consciousness of UN staff. Gender remains shorthand for woman, with an equivalent, everyday language of men and masculinity yet to develop. In turn, masculinity and the (hidden) power to which it speaks are allowed to thrive in these silences in ways that set differential conditions of possibility according to one's gender (and other) identities, both within the organization and in regard to its field of operations. It is not enough to increase the number of female peacekeepers, carry out 'gender training', or more broadly attempt to 'mainstream' women. Adding more women will not magically transform masculine cultures that have remained resistant to change over decades. Until it is recognized that 'masculinity matters', change is unlikely to come about in anything but the most marginal of ways.

CONCLUSION

Locating power in peacekeeping

Ultimately, peacekeeping must be reoriented in favour not of the ends of those who carry it out, but of those who perceive it, and who live and work in the places and spaces it creates. Peacekeeping is about power – the power of peacekeepers to actively shape perceptions of security, in order to engender feelings of peace and safety. The power that peacekeepers wield has its roots in organizations driven to change space, to create the conditions in which liberal democracies can flourish; far from benign, peacekeeping is inherently political.

Ideas of space and performance have enabled us both to critique existing practices and to begin to explore what such a reorientation of peacekeeping, in favour of local ends and desires, might look like. From engendering freedom of movement, through the integrated mission and on to the diffuse peacekeeping spaces of Liberia, Blue Helmet troops were observed in their territorializing practices. Yet, as unique and highly distinct actors on the world stage, these troops had the power to create safety and a sense of frustration in their audiences through unconvincing performances. Audiences were, of themselves, not without power. They were capable of mediating peacekeeper security work through their own and shared interpretations of national identity, which – when seen through their eyes – made for biased, professional, military and humanitarian performance. A foundational aspect of power open to peacekeepers flowed from their embodied selves. Lazy or active, keen or disinterested, the peacekeeper expressive body mediated by military props carried with it the power to neutralize fear or exacerbate vulnerability in the audience. However, bodies seeking sexual satisfaction often undermined the security of those for whom exploitation by the privileged was one of the few avenues open to their survival and, often, that of their families. The predominance of national or ethnic stereotypes shaping the perception of peacekeepers as security providers evokes colonial resonances, inasmuch as ideologies of race continue to shape social relations.

Peacekeepers deal in security, and in so doing face danger and the risk of death. Women and men, both local and foreign, continue to confront or live in close proximity to violence. To make explicit comparisons, in imaginative ways, of societies with differing collective experiences of politics, ethnic identities and associated patterns of violence, is potentially very valuable. As we saw in the introduction, a summary of the critical peacekeeping literature provides a strong sense of the power inhering within the peacekeeping project as attempts are made to impose a liberal peace on post-conflict countries. Encouraging states to accept the morally authoritative model of liberal democratic statehood represents a stark illustration of the wielding of power, which when harnessed to coercive economic instruments can further entrench inequality. Adopting a different approach, a number of commentators noted for their more willing acceptance of UN peacekeeping have published the collection *Unintended Consequences of Peacekeeping Operations* (Aoi et al. 2007). At first glance, this volume promises an extensive and substantively grounded critique of peacekeeping in respect of: sexual exploitation by peacekeepers; the impact of peacekeeping economies, which can drive up rents and fuel inequality; the vested interests of troops that may enter the field motivated purely by self-interest; and finally broader questions of the UN's accountability. Yet, important though the critical and unintended perspectives on peacekeeping may be, both are found lacking. In the critical peacekeeping literature, analysis is conducted at the macro-level, and consequently is at some distance from the everyday experiences and realities of those on the ground, whether international staff employed in the mission or the host population. In regard to the unintended line of enquiry, yet again a problem-solving approach (comprehensively challenged in the foregoing critical peace-keeping literature) reappears, though in a somewhat more theoretically sophisticated guise. Running through *Unintended Consequences* is the idea that, at its core, peacekeeping is a benign activity. It is as if the unintended consequences of peacekeeping are surprising 'accidents', which once ironed out will lead to a perfect model of intervention. What, for example, of the sexual abuse and exploitation of minors by some peacekeepers in both UN and NATO missions? Clearly, when missions are initiated the intention is not that peacekeepers will further the insecurity of particular vulnerable groups through sexual exploitation. Indeed, exploitation is explicitly prohibited, and troops have a heightened awareness of these proscribed activities. In order that sexual exploitation take place then, Blue Helmets demonstrate an intentionality that is well beyond unintended consequence. They have actively to seek out individuals to abuse or exploit and may do so in a pre-emptive fashion. To suggest that these activities are mere side-effects is to reinforce the notion that peacekeeping is at its core a neutral enterprise – an assumption that our work would refute. 'Power' is a word rarely uttered by either senior or junior staff working to oversee peacekeeping operations, whether UN or NATO. Yet, for good or bad, interventions driven by political-economic agendas conducted by a mix of influential and majority-world countries is about power from on high that flows from distant places. This book has shed light on such power in what we hope is a new and engaging way. The concept of space reveals how peacekeepers carry with them the ability to shape the spaces in which post-conflict populations and international staff live and work together, and how physical proxim-ity impacts on security perception. Performance is about the power within the social relations and space between peacekeepers and their audience. Though far from absolute, nonetheless peacekeepers have within their power the ability to engender a sense of security, or con-versely a sense of fear and vulnerability. Peacekeepers are exemplary bearers of power that is played out through space and on the stage where they present themselves to a critical and reflective audience. Our message is that the power of the peacekeeping project, and of the Blue Helmets themselves, should be the subject for fresh critical reflection, in times when their presence matters more than ever.

Notes

Introduction

1. For more details, see Chapter 1 n21.
2. The term 'internationals' has been used by the journalist Linda Polman (1997) in her work on peacekeeping and also in our fieldwork as a catch-all for the ubiquitous, often well-heeled and (usually) well-intentioned 'visitor' making up the multi-national presence.
3. The term 'positionality' is intended to illuminate the ways in which social researchers are inevitably embedded into their work. Hardy et al. (2001: 534) argue that 'the value of researchers can never be eradicated from their work and no amount of methodological technique or declarations of bias can strip them of their theoretical bias presuppositions.'
4. Use of the term 'subjectivities' is intended to highlight the role of power in these particular social relations captured in the concept of 'security subjectivities'.
5. The approach we take to analysing accounts is influenced by formal sociology. Put simply, we set out to identify the universal recurring forms underlying the varying content of interaction within the context of how security was perceived. In adopting this perspective on social life, we draw on work that can be traced back to Kantian philosophy as well as the sociology of Georg Simmel. See Frisby 1981 for a discussion of Simmel's contribution to sociological thought.
6. We use the term 'security project' as a way in which to capture peacekeeping as: 'An enterprise carefully planned to achieve a particular aim' (Oxford Dictionary and Thesaurus 2001). This definition evokes the strategic, means–ends approach taken to these international interventions, the

planning of which has frequently been unable to account for the inevitable contingencies arising from such bold and complex operations.

7. Although there may be some complexity here. Do prisoners experience security or insecurity on account of their imprisonment? Perhaps the example of incarceration is one in which individuals are to endure *too* much security.

8. Our work has attracted various critical responses, among which is the idea that by failing to define security, the concept can refer to 'anything and everything'. We would counter this by stressing that respondent definitions – whatever they might be – are as valid as anything the theorist might come up with and represent an important point of analytical departure.

Chapter 1

1. We originally conducted a pilot study in Cyprus; however, we do not include the data from this research here.

2. As such, Haiti is the mission with the smallest number of military and civilian personnel at approximately 9,000, with Kosovo at 17,000 (50,000 at peak) and Liberia at over 15,000. One of the largest current missions is Lebanon with over 17,000 personnel.

3. From the outset, Haitian politics has been heavily gendered, although significantly less attention has been given to this facet of history. Women actively participated in the slave rebellion (as well as other important political activities in the period preceding), as well as in the many developments of the state for the next fifty years (see Charles 1995).

4. However, this initial deployment was prematurely halted when the majority of peacekeepers arrived at the harbour in Port-au-Prince (traumatized in the wake of troop losses in Mogadishu) to the reception of thugs from Çedras's regime. The boatload of peacekeepers quickly turned around and headed back to US shores (von Einsiedel and Malone 2006: 155).

5. See: www.minustah.org/pages/Faits-et-Chiffres; accessed 20 September 2007.

6. The ubiquity of crumbling infrastructure and highly visible shanty towns leave a visitor in little doubt of the desperate economic state of the country.

7. For a report on sexual exploitation and abuse by peacekeepers in Haiti, see www.refugeesinternational.org/content/article/detail/5315/; accessed 11 February 2008. We pick up these concerns further in Chapter 8.

8. MINUSTAH has also been accused of aligning itself with right-wing political movements in Haiti. For a further discussion of this apparent affiliation, see www.pambazuka.org/en/category/features/39640; accessed 11 February 2008.

9. Kosovo declared its independence on 19 February 2008.

10. Of course Kosovar Albanians may argue that the declaration of independence resolves the issue, yet violence perpetrated against the US and other embassies in Belgrade by Serbians, together with President Tadic's tacit approval for such actions would suggest otherwise.

11. Acts of genocide in this war and the subsequent Kosovo war involved wide-spread use of gender-based violence against both female and male citizens by all the militarized forces (Zarkov 2001; Carpenter 2003).

12. Throughout Kosovo's history, complex and shifting ideas of gender have intersected with contestation over ethnic and national belonging. Gender has been important in both neighbouring and related conflicts, as well as within Serbian and Kosovar Albanian communities. In particular, Milosevic evoked numerous gendered myths about Kosovar Albanians in order to fuel fear of the 'other'. These included the Albanian man 'as rapist' of (especially) Serbian women, and Albanian women as 'baby factories'. These 'myths' served to reinforce prejudicial beliefs of Albanians as 'primitive', 'over-sexed', 'out of control' animals who threatened the survival of the Serbian nation (Mertus 2001: 264).

13. However, others have argued that the KLA's evolution began outside of Kosovo and was introduced by émigrés living in Switzerland (Mertus 1999).

14. According to Noam Chomsky, these military operations served to intensify the ethnic cleansing perpetrated by ethnic Serbs against Kosovar Albanians, leading to an exodus of many tens of thousands of this group to Macedonia and Albania (Chomsky 1999).

15. See www.nato.int/KFOR/; accessed 25 February 2008.

16. Survey research from the 2006 Kosovo Internal Security Sector Review shows that 4 per cent of Kosovar Albanians and 20 per cent of Kosovo Serbians consider ethnic violence to be the 'greatest security threat' (Welch et al. 2006: 22, 23). In the 2006 Small Arms and Light Weapons (SALW) Survey of Kosovo in 2006, it was argued that: 'Ongoing violence in Kosovo can be attributed to a number of factors, including political and ethnic rivalries ... all of this occurs against a backdrop of high unemployment, political uncertainty regarding the territory's final status and a still developing criminal justice system.' SALW survey research also found that 'perceptions of insecurity among minority communities are magnified by a belief that even if reported, crimes will not be promptly investigated ... nor perpetrators brought to justice' and that Kosovo Serbians are 'much more likely to perceive their areas as unsafe than other ethnic groups' (Sokolova et al. 2006: iii, iv).

17. For a media account of former US President George Bush's endorsement of Kosovo independence, see http://news.bbc.co.uk/1/hi/world/europe/6741121.stm; accessed 24 Jan 2008.

18. See http://unmil.org; accessed 25 February 2008.

19. In March 2006, President Ellen Johnson-Sirleaf sent a letter formally requesting the extradition of Charles Taylor from Nigeria to face justice. While Nigerian President Olusegun Obasanjo confirmed receipt of the request, Nigeria's plans to comply with the request were not immediately clear. After representatives from Liberia and Nigeria met to discuss the issue, Nigeria announced on 25 March 2006 that it would allow Liberian authorities to arrest Taylor. It was long feared that Taylor could easily slip into hiding to escape charges of the Special Court for Sierra Leone, and by 28 March Taylor had reportedly disappeared from his Nigerian compound. He was recaptured by alert border guards at dawn on 29 March trying to

cross into Cameroon. Taylor was quickly flown to Liberia, where he was escorted onto a waiting UN helicopter to face charges for crimes against humanity in Sierra Leone (though not in Liberia). The venue for his trial was changed form Sierra Leone to The Hague, and he was flown out of Sierra Leone on 20 June 2006. Since then he has been incarcerated in The Hague and his trial continues at the time of writing.

20. Supporting evidence for our small-scale empirical component drawn from the fieldwork in Liberia is provided by the Public Opinion Survey of UN-MIL's work in Liberia (Krasno 2006) discussed briefly in the Introduction above. It should be noted that this survey is limited in numerous ways, not least that it was commissioned by the UN's Department of Peacekeeping Operations Best Practices Section, a stakeholder with a vested interest in garnering a favourable response to the mission presence. In addition, on closer scrutiny, the survey design is weak in that at least 7 of its 24 questions are framed in ways that are more likely to elicit a positive rather than negative response. One example is question 3 of the survey, which asks: 'How would you rate the work of UN Peacekeepers in making you feel safer?' Whilst respondents are offered choices ranging from 'very good' through to 'poor', nevertheless a more rigorous approach to establishing how peacekeepers 'made people feel' would be to ask an open question, rather than one loaded with the word 'safer'; other questions asked in the survey are framed in similar, directed ways.

21. However, as late as August 2007, the fifteenth progress report of the Secretary-General on the United Nations Mission in Liberia states: 'Liberia has become a generally stable country in a volatile subregion. Yet, the prevailing peace is very fragile and Liberia is still susceptible to lawlessness. The most immediate threats to sustained peace and stability in Liberia ... include ... violent criminal activities ... the limited capacity of the security sector ... the weak justice system ... the proliferation of disaffected groups such as unemployed ex-combatants ... economic insecurity ... ethnic and social cleavages ... and the perception by some that the opposition political parties are not genuinely pursuing national reconciliation.' See www.unmil. org/documents/sgreports/sg15pr.pdf, p. 4; accessed 8 January 2008.

22. It is worth noting that the inequalities go well beyond those linked to economic well-being. As Sida (2005: 6) states: 'Liberia is one of five countries in the world that does not make the Human Development Index. It has appalling rates of infant mortality, maternal mortality, deaths from easily preventable diseases, endemic malaria and cholera and so on.'

23. In ways that mirror comments derived from other peacekeeping missions, complaints of the wealth brought by the UN were widespread and served to underscore the relative poverty of Liberians. This newly arrived wealth was not believed to be redistributed in any meaningful way by the UN, belying the expectations of many that this was an explicit aim of the intervention.

24. The Guthrie Rubber Plantation was occupied by ex-combatants expressing grievances at the failure of the DDRR programme to deliver on its financial promises. It had become synonymous in the minds of some participants with the perception of underlying insecurity in the months leading up to the 2006 elections.

Chapter 2

1. Empirical material in the form of interview transcripts (for example) does not naturally lend itself to immediate insights into the abstract conceptions of space and security. However, the non-verbal dimensions of face-to-face interviews conveyed a great deal about the ways that the security–space nexus impinges on affect, as well as on the embodied realm. It is important to make this point, since so much of what is written about security in the mainstream disciplines of IR and Security Studies works with a narrow, Cartesian model of agency. This theoretically impoverished approach invariably frames actors as rational beings seeking to maximize their security well-being, and in so doing neglects both the rich and contradictory nature of the embodied and emotional dimensions of the human condition. In using the concepts of performance and performativity, this analysis is extended in Chapter 6–9 in ways that highlight the significance of the non-verbal elements of interaction between peacekeepers and their audiences.

2. Nicosia is the capital city of Cyprus, but is divided between the Republic of Cyprus and northern Cyprus. During pilot fieldwork in 2004 in Cyprus, it was clear that the UN presence was generally framed in regard to the buffer zone or green zone cleaving the city of Nicosia into two very distinct spaces characterized by economic underdevelopment in the north (the 'Turkish side'), and European levels of development in the south (the 'Greek side').

3. However, there is a considerable history to peacekeepers' involvement in combat such as the case of the 20,000 troops deployed to the newly independent Congo between 1960 and 1964 (Pugh 2004: 43).

4. This German term refers to 'territory which a state or nation believes is needed for its natural development' (Oxford Dictionary 2001). Yet this term is provocative given the attempt by Hitler to seize large parts of Europe by force and is closely associated with the expansionist aims of Nazism.

5. It should be noted that the UN and NATO–KFOR are two of a number of international organizations in Kosovo. The Organization for Co-operation and Security in Kosovo (OSCE) is the other principal security actor.

6. It is worth quoting Gheciu in full as his comments, whilst directly pertaining to Kosovo, have considerably wider applicability to strategies of global governance of which PSOs are a key element. He argues that: 'One of the constitutive norms of Kantian liberalism is a norm of disciplined subjectivity; liberal selves are actors who are committed to the struggle to discipline the irrational, violent sides of themselves, and to govern their lives in accordance with the universal moral precepts revealed by reason' (2005: 124).

7. Gheciu goes on to argue that the formulation of a series of 'benchmarks' to be achieved by Kosovars 'were formulated behind closed doors … without consultation with the Provincial Institutions of Self Government, leading Kosovars to argue that they have been unfairly marginalized from the decision making process' (2005: 136). See also Karadjis 2005 on the point of benchmark 'standards' in the case of Kosovo.

8. See Schmidt et al. 2001 for a comprehensive, albeit mainstream-conservative series of essays dealing with the history of NATO.

9. A key plank in NATO enlargement has been the argument that the organization will help to 'spread democracy', an assertion refuted by Reiter (2001) based on 'a study of the empirical record'.

10. It is important to note that the US relationship with the UN has been somewhat antagonistic over the years (Gregory 2004: 324). Overt hostility characterized the US–UN relationship during the Reagan years, and most recently under G.W. Bush – particularly given UN concerns about the 2003 invasion of Iraq – has resulted in a further deterioration of relations. In the extremist thinking of the Project for a New America, it has been argued that even NATO might also be seen as 'too constraining' and that 'ad-hoc coalitions might be built on a case-by-case basis' (Harvey 2003: 79).

11. On 25 February – i.e. a month before the NATO bombing began – the *New York Times* revealed that US Secretary of State Madeleine Albright was anxious to get the Kosovo crisis out of the way before NATO's fiftieth anniversary celebrations on 22 April, when the Alliance was due to take on its new colours. See Eric Rouleau, http://mondediplo.com/1999/12/04rouleau; accessed 15 January 2008.

12. It should be noted, however, that the framing of this 'war' is beginning to change. For example, the British government has rarely used the phrase 'war on terror' since Gordon Brown became prime minister in 2007. The preferred terminology currently draws on imagery related to 'a struggle for the soul'. See: http://news.bbc.co.uk/1/hi/uk_politics/6924843.stm; accessed 29 January 2008.

13. See: www.nato.int/kfor/chronicle/1999/chronicle_199901/p12.htm; accessed 29 January 2008.

14. The phrase 'space of exception' has been developed from the work of Giorgio Agamben by a number of commentators including the critical human geographer Derek Gregory. The similarities between Camp Bondsteel (located in the UN province of Kosovo), and Guantánamo Bay, also situated in a territory of 'ambiguous sovereignty', are striking. As Gregory (2006) argues: 'Guantánamo Bay depends on the mobilization of two contradictory legal geographies, one that places the prison outside the United States to allow the indefinite detention of its captives, and another that places the prison within the United States in order to permit their "coercive interrogation".' See: www.blackwell-synergy.com/doi/abs/10.1111/j.0435-3684.2006.00230.x; accessed 29 January 2008.

15. Who gets to secure particular spaces? We pose this question because it could be argued that those deemed as 'peace spoilers', 'combatants' or 'militia' may in the experiences of some *also* provide security to the communities in which they operate. The creation of security is by no means the exclusive preserve of peacekeepers or, indeed, any of those organizations deployed to troubled regions.

16. See Dallaire 2003 for a detailed exposition of the mandate limitations implicated in the Rwanda genocide.

17. The deployment of 16,700 troops to the vast land mass of the Democratic Republic of Congo (a country one-quarter the size of the United States) is a case in point.

Chapter 3

1. Whilst the UN refused to confirm or deny the presence of special forces in the country, a number of people were confident that these specially trained individuals worked as part of the MINUSTAH military component. These beliefs may have come from the widely acknowledged presence of US special forces in the country in the mid-1990s.

2. For more insight into the understanding of the mandate and the security 'success' in Haiti, see www.globalpolicy.org/security/issues/haiti/2005/0526missionmandate.htm, accessed 21 February 2008; and Don Bohning, 'Haiti: UN Mission Unable to Establish Order', *Miami Herald*, 26 May 2005.

3. For a report on the danger of the red zones, including the incidence of rape see www.reliefweb.int/rw/rwb.nsf/db900sid/egua-79bqy4?OpenDocument; accessed 11 February 2008.

4. The zones are designated informally by the UN as follows: 'The calm green zones, the potentially unstable yellow zones, and the more dangerous red zones. For further explanation, see www.boston.com/news/world/latinamerica/articles/2006/02/02/security_shortage_seen_before_haiti_vote/; accessed 11 February 2008.

5. During the fieldwork trip in late 2006, a particularly disturbing case of kidnapping involved the capture of a 20-year-old female student from an impoverished family. Though the family managed to pay US$500 to the kidnappers, several days later the girl's bullet-riddled body was found in a ravine. In their presumed effort to further foment terror, the gang had engaged in the grisly act of gouging out her eyes.

6. For a report on the problem of civilians casualties as a result of UN incursions in slum areas, see for example: www.guardian.co.uk/world/2007/apr/01/sandrajordan.theobserver; accessed 15 January 2008.

7. For reports on civilian casualities and the role of the UN see http://news.bbc.co.uk/1/hi/world/americas/4306493.stm; and www.economist.com/world/la/displaystory.cfm?story_id=e1_qdrrsgv&cfid=11691819&cftoken=b5e251121915b78b-07dd522f-b27c-bb00-0127426a965cdf9c; both accessed 11 February 2008.

8. For a report on how peacekeepers have been blamed for casualties see www.independent.co.uk/news/world/americas/peacekeepers-accused-after-killings-in-haiti-500570.html; accessed 11 February 2008.

9. For an example of peacekeeper casualties in Haiti see www.nytimes.com/2006/01/24/international/americas/24haiti.html?_r=1&scp=1&sq=haiti+24+january+2006&st=nyt&oref=slogin; for a report on those caught in the crossfire see http://observer.guardian.co.uk/world/story/0,,2047451,00.html; both accessed 11 February 2008.

10. By this we mean that the violence was perceived to have an irreducible quality where efforts to limit it resulted in its displacement to formally 'peaceful' areas.

11. There is always the danger that a study such as ours may unintentionally reify the concept under scrutiny, not least in the ways that it encourages interviewees to place it centre stage in their accounts. Here, the notion that 'no area in Port-au-Prince was entirely secure' points to the difficulties,

and indeed the impossibility, of seeking 'total' security, no matter what the geographical context may be.

12. In contrast to the literature dealing with the experience of frustration at the absence of 'proper soldiering' by those troops deployed on traditional peacekeeping duties, these kinds of counter-insurgency operations may elicit more favourable responses from those individuals trained specifically as combat soldiers.

13. For a discussion of the hazards these activities pose for UN military peacekeepers, some of whom have been killed during these operations see www.nytimes.com/2006/01/24/international/americas/24haiti.html; accessed 15 January 2008.

14. See Razack 2004 and Whitworth 2004 for discussions on peacekeeper military masculinities, together with how the 'desire' for combat soldiering is expressed by many male military peacekeepers. In line with the work of Robert Connell (1995) it might be said that these kinds of operations provide peacekeeper-soldiers with the opportunity to engage a hegemonic rather than subordinate masculinity in regard to demonstrating and enacting their warrior prowess.

15. See: www.ijdh.org/articles/article_recent_news_1–15–07.html; accessed 11 February 2008.

16. Anecdotal evidence drawn from the three missions discussed in the current volume, and more widely in respect of the Democratic Republic of Congo and Sierra Leone, point to the prevalence of fatalism expressed by internationals in regard to local people's ability to live together peacefully. On the point of self-interest, see for example: http://news.bbc.co.uk/1/hi/world/south_asia/7075866.stm in respect of the sexual abuse of local females by Sri Lankan peacekeepers.

17. Use of the concept 'zoning' may be seen to develop the ecological approach to urban spaces pioneered by the Chicago School of sociology. Our contribution is to identify the UN presence as directly implicated in the process of displacement of violence in ways that underscore the fluidity, dynamism and permeability of spaces (or zones) characterized by 'social problems'. More recently, and in regard to the use of Anti-Social Behaviour Orders (ASBOs) in the UK context, it was found that: 'In many areas dispersal orders generated displacement effects, shifting problems to neighbouring areas, sometimes merely for the duration of the order. One neighbouring "displacement zone" saw crime, notably criminal damage, increase by 83% compared with the previous year' (Crawford and Lister 2007).

18. Personal communication with Colonel Anthony Welch, January 2008.

19. In the previous and current chapter, we have focused exclusively on the Serbian enclaves in Kosovo. However, Kosovan society is constituted by a number of ethnic groups including Ashkalis, Roma and Egyptians, many of whom live within enclaves, or territorially defined communities of shared ethnicity.

20. Those Kosovar Albanians who chose to engage with the sensitive topic of Serbian insecurity tended to reflect on the violence in a matter-of-fact way. They neither condemned nor welcomed it, but rather saw it as an inevitable consequence of the historical tensions between the two major populations.

21. In contrast to the general disdain with which UNMIK was held by the majority of respondents from across the ethnic divide, KFOR was generally seen in a positive light as acting to secure the province (Welch et al. 2006: 21).

22. Perceptions of security are extremely volatile, localized and subject to swift change, not least on account of broader political developments. For example, in December 2007 it was observed that 'Circumstances on the ground remain unstable, and the longer uncertainty status lasts, the more agitated the region around Kosovo will become and the more a sense of developing security crisis will grow.' See www.crisisgroup.org/home/index. cfm?id=3225&l=1&gclid=CLLzlfqn5pACFQJEM AodgyewOg; accessed 8 January 2007. This more sober reflection on instability could be seen to render aspirations for greater integration as potentially naive particularly in light of the declaration of independence by Kosovar Albanians in February 2008.

23. More broadly, KFOR is relatively well regarded by Kosovar Albanians, and rather less so by Kosovo Serbians, although the latter group do see them 'as the only force capable of providing physical protection' (Sokolova et al. 2006: 47).

24. Yet, it is important to underscore the cumulative impact of minor instances of insecurity: 'Although the security situation has improved significantly ... small scale incidents ... have a psychological impact. As noted by Kai Eide ... "minority communities – and especially the Kosovo Serbs – suffer from more than a perceived insecurity. It is indeed a mixture of reality and perception' (Welch et al. 2006: 21).

25. The context of these discussions turns on the contested concept of 'integration'. What does 'it' look like and when do we know that 'it' has arrived?

26. The process of returning Kosovo Serbians continues to be controversial and has been handled by both KFOR and the Kosovo Police Service (KPS). In respect of the latter, it is observed that 'Displaced Serbs returning to visit their enclaves expressed positive views regarding KPS's professionalism in escorting their convoys' (Welch et al. 2006: 21).

27. That UN cartographers have systematically 'mapped' enclaves represents a further technique of formalization of these troubled spaces. See also: http://news.bbc.co.uk/1/hi/world/europe/7252033. stm#map; accessed 22 February 2008. The 'ethnic breakdown map' of Kosovo has featured in nearly all of the BBC's recent stories on the province, underscoring the limited ways this territory is represented.

28. Many different reports already cited outline the stressful economic situation for those living in and outside the enclaves in Kosovo. However, the limited mobility of enclave residents makes employment opportunities in the larger towns and cities that much more inaccessible.

29. These aspirations should be seen against the backdrop of evidence from 'key informants' in the SALW survey, which found that: 'Each household in Kosovo has a weapon' or that 'there are two weapons for every household in Kosovo' (Sokolova 2006: 9). Seen in this way, the potential for further violence in the territory is considerable.

30. Numerous informal discussions with international and local people considered that 'talk of multiethnicity by UNMIK' was destined for their

'bosses in New York and Washington', rather than the mixed communities of Kosovo itself.

31. For example, the international organization 'has also been involved in a variety of Kosovo-wide tolerance-building training programmes, such as inter-community workshops, aimed at leading the citizens of Kosovo, both Serbs and Albanians, to change the ways in which they define members of other ethnic groups' (Gheciu 2005: 132). These activities should be seen as at the polar extreme of dedicated attempts to segregate the majority from minority populations by NATO–KFOR.

32. It should be noted that the ways in which non-Kosovo Serbians articulated integration was shaped by a deeply normative element. Here, there was a strong sense in which 'they' (Kosovo Serbians) should integrate with 'us' (Kosovar Albanians). There is nothing intrinsic in the ratio of 1.5 million Kosovar Albanians to around 100,000 Kosovo Serbians that says the onus should be on the minority group to integrate into the majority population, although this 'direction of integration' is often assumed in the context of discussions on assimilation and integration more widely.

33. This somewhat anecdotal story touches on the broader canvas of reconciliation, which has been described as 'An approach to post-conflict development in ethnically divided societies ... [it] can be understood as the transformation of relationships and it can take place at all levels of society' (Blagojevic 2007: 555). In our view, attempts to reintegrate at the lowest of everyday levels (as this example demonstrates) have greater potential than generally recognized by the international community, which, it could be said, may feel that it has progressed inter-ethnic relations in Kosovo as far as it is able.

Chapter 4

1. Notable contingents of military peacekeepers had worked hard to fix the roads in preparation for the upcoming elections. However, the use of clay rather than tarmac (for efficiency and more extensive coverage of repair) means that the roads are likely to deteriorate during successive rainy seasons.

2. In other research in Liberia on security, the desire for road building was also expressed. As one individual said: 'If UNMIL had put the time and energy into ... road building ... where their heavy logistics gives them a natural advantage ... they might have got closer to their stabilisation goal than merely duplicating humanitarian services' (Sida 2005:21).

3. The question of whether or not peacekeepers would patrol the more isolated counties and regions of Liberia if the roads were repaired is far from clear. Other factors such as 'force protection' may impinge on their choice to visit isolated communities.

4. It was suggested by some that large numbers of Liberians living in the border and remote regions remained wholly unaware of the presence of UNMIL in their country.

5. Background to the term 'peace spoiler' is outlined in the *Report of the Panel on United Nations Peace Operations*: 'As the United Nations soon discovered,

local parties sign peace accords for a variety of reasons, not all of them favourable to peace. "Spoilers" – groups (including signatories) who renege on their commitments or otherwise seek to undermine a peace accord by violence ... The United Nations must be prepared to deal effectively with spoilers if it expects to achieve a consistent record of success in peacekeeping or peace-building in situations of intrastate/transnational conflict.' See www.un.org/peace/reports/peace_operations/docs/part2.htm; accessed 11 February 2008.

6. Sida (2005: 11) notes that there have been high rates of 'spontaneous returns' by IDPs to their villages.

7. As Sokolova et al. (2006: 39) reports: 'Perceptions of community safety vary across Kosovo ... Shterpce/Strpce was considered to be particularly dangerous by its inhabitants ... there has been a history of violence directed against Kosovo-Serbs in this community.'

8. As a Kosovo Serbian female observed in other research: 'I should be able to move freely, to get in the bus or taxi and go wherever I want to. Unfortunately this doesn't exist here. There is still no trust between Albanians and Serbs in this part of Kosovo' (Welch et al. 2006: 21).

9. Welch et al. (2006: 21) report that 'Early on in its mission UNMIK attempted to address the issue of freedom of movement by issuing a Kosovo-wide license plate designed to provide anonymity to vehicles travelling in Kosovo – but the Serbian government's unwillingness to accept the plate and resistance of Serbian communities in Kosovo to use the plate has hampered this initiative.'

10. Whether or not members of the Serbian minority were 'genuine victims' represented the topic of much debate among Kosovar Albanians and others.

Chapter 5

1. The roots of the concept of the integrated mission can be traced to the Brahimi report in which the idea of the 'integrated mission emerged as a strong theme' (Sida 2005: 6).

2. In respect of Liberia: 'The SRSG is tasked with the coordination of all UN activities in Liberia, meaning that the traditional separation of the humanitarian and military political/military wings of the UN has been overturned.' (Sida 2005: 7).

3. In Chapter 7 we note the desire among some respondents for 'hard security' provided by the former Liberian troop contingent of the ECOMOG force. This chapter touches on the expressed need for softer security so underlining the complexity noted in any one mission where consensus on such issues is likely to remain elusive.

4. See Sida 2005: 11–12 for a case study of IDPs that support many of the comments made in our study.

5. As noted by Sida: 'The confusion of roles between humanitarian agencies and the military is widespread ... military contingents have engaged in basic health care and food distribution ... at the same time as using force

to control unrest ... on the other hand NGO's ... have become involved in work traditionally the province of the military such as demobilisation of adult combatants' (2005: 2).

6. As Sida also notes: 'From conversations with a number of the individuals involved and observers of the process over time it appears that relations between OCHA in Liberia and the senior management became strained ... in some cases (OCHA) were seen as inflexible and obstructive' (2005: 8).

7. The Humanitarian Common Service of the UN (HCS) which replaced OCHA is argued to have a 'military style culture [based on a] ... command and control, need to know basis' (Sida 2005: 9).

8. Sida states that: 'The use of military assets by NGOs is widespread in Liberia, in particular the use of military helicopters to travel around the country (although many NGOs have chosen not to use UNMIL transport)' (2005: 13).

9. Lischer (2007: 99) makes the point that '"Humanitarian soldiers" cannot create stability or meet local humanitarian needs', thereby supporting the wariness humanitarian NGOs have expressed towards the delivery of assistance by military personnel.

10. Thanks to Mark Duffield for drawing out the importance of an emerging security architecture in post-conflict sites where 'security providers' are becoming ever more distant from their 'beneficiaries'. Although, at the time of writing, a second humanitarian aid worker has been shot and killed by the Taliban in Afghanistan, underscoring the insecure conditions of some fields of operation.

11. A number of interviewees found themselves in a quandary regarding the use of generators to power lights, or for other purposes. On the one hand, lights may provide a degree of security, whilst on the other they may single out those who use them as relatively wealthy and a potential target for criminals.

12. See Jennings 2007 for more detail on ex-combatants entitlement to tuition fees.

13. As Nichols states: 'The large number of participants in the DDRR programme would be little cause for alarm, were it not for the apparent lack of corresponding weapons: only 27,804 for 102,193 ex-combatants' (2005: 121).

14. Jennings argues: 'More troubling, many ex-combatants expressed feelings of frustration, verging on bitterness, over what they claimed were unfulfilled promises by the international community and the lack of change in their personal situations. Many identified a lack of jobs as their primary grievance' (2007: 206).

15. The Guthrie Rubber Plantation was occupied by ex-combatants expressing grievances at the failure of the DDRR programme to deliver on its financial promises. It had become synonymous in the minds of some participants with the perception of underlying insecurity in the months leading up to the 2006 elections.

16. The Rubber Plantation was 'repossessed' by UNMIL 'on behalf of the Liberian people' in August 2006. For a further discussion see the UN's report: www.un.org/Depts/dpko/missions/unmil/pr96.pdf; accessed 8 January 2008.

17. A number of stories were in circulation about the boldness with which some internationals displayed their wealth, particularly in and around Mamba Point, where a number of robberies had taken place just prior to the fieldwork.

18. But it should be noted that there are slum areas in Monrovia that have garnered the attention of UN and Liberian government authorities; however, there is nothing like the type of organized campaign against violent crime in these neighbourhoods that exists in the context of Haiti.

Chapter 6

1. The increased awareness of male peacekeepers' involvement in the sexual exploitation of women and girls across the range of missions demonstrates that an unknown but significant number of the Blue Helmets exacerbate insecurity. The general response to their abusive activities has been frustration and outright anger in ways that suggest that expectations of peacekeepers is somewhat unique. Would the routine use of prostitutes by non-peacekeeping troops evoke such widespread concern? See Chapter 8 in this respect.

2. See: www.un.org/Depts/dpko/dpko/info/page3.htm; accessed 22 February 2008.

3. See: www.nato.int/; accessed 22 February 2008.

4. Access to a number of 'private beaches' in mission sites may cost many dollars. For example, in Liberia local entrepreneurs added a 'beach charge' to the bill for food (if one chose to eat). Drinks including Coca Cola and 7–Up were charged at US$20 or more. Individuals wishing to attend the Club Med resort in Haiti were charged between $15 and $20 entrance fee. Local beaches close to the city centres were used by locals, but the majority of the beaches referred to here were some distance away from the urban core and thus required transport. As such they were almost exclusively aimed at international workers and businesspeople.

5. For a report on the visible discrepancy between tourists and locals in the small town of Labadee, see www.nytimes.com/2007/02/16/world/americas/16haiti.html; accessed 22 February 2008.

6 See Professor Dumas' account of peacekeeping economies for more insight into the negative impact of peacekeepers on the local population: www.stwr.net/content/view/139/37/; accessed 22 February 2008.

7. The soldier identity tends to overwhelm all other identity possibilities, such as those of father or brother. Indicative of this perception is the British, US and perhaps more widespread tabloid press's frequent reporting of the 'off-duty' lives of military personnel, for example in relation to their amorous exploits with colleagues. These stories reflect in part a sense of intrigue that professional men and women are 'just like' mere civilians, for whom such exploits would be unlikely to sell newspapers in quite the same volume.

8. The definition of a backstage region for Goffman (1959) turns directly on its exclusiveness. Readers will recall the possible frisson of anxiety or excitement involved in seeing one's schoolteacher shopping in the local super-

market, or, even more intriguing, knocking on the school staffroom door to see teachers relaxing backstage between lessons. In this second example, the desire to look into the room in order to see teachers out of character can be overwhelming, and flows from the natural curiosity of human agents to look beyond the formal performances routinely presented to them.

9. HIV/AIDS raises the question more widely of national security in the face of 'failing bodies' where relatively large number of troops have tested positive for the disease in particular domestic militaries (Tripoldi and Patel 2002; Heinecken 2003)

10. It is important to note here that the soldier's body is almost always assumed to be male. Because of the low numbers of female military peacekeepers in all of the missions, respondents had minimal contact with military women and as such did not comment on differently gendered bodies (see Chapter 8).

11. Props are used to 'further the action' and are understood as any object that gives the scenery, actors, or performance space specific period, place or character. The crucial point here is that a prop must 'read well', in that it should look real to the audience. See Macgowan and Melnitz 1955.

12. That military machinery should serve as a reference point for security is epitomized in the air show, the tattoo, and the iconic drama of the military parade in the former Soviet Union, for example, representations of which include countless rows of ballistic missiles and their transporters.

13. A UN male civilian in Liberia talked informally of the disturbing sight of the child-soldier bearing AK-47s and other weaponry. The incongruous juxtaposition of the 'innocent child' with her or his 'instrument of killing' demonstrates how particular 'props' can overpower the ways in which this and related performances (and identities) are framed.

Chapter 7

1. See http://thetyee.ca/Views/2006/05/19/OutOfAfghanistan/; accessed 30 October 2008.

2. For a report which scrutinizes some of the 'bad' and 'incompetent' behaviour of NATO troops in Kosovo, see http://edition.cnn.com/2000/WORLD/europe/01/25/kosovo.investigation/; accessed 8 January 2008.

3. For a discussion of Ireland's view of its role in peace support operations, see Sreenan 2006.

4. The concept of *folkhemmet* is often used to refer to the 'Swedish middle way': a political system that attempted to steer a considered course between capitalism and communism. Its resonance with 'fairness' and 'equitability' is clear and may have seeped into the ways that members of the sample made sense of Swedish peacekeepers' security practices.

5. See: www.weeklystandard.com/Utilities/printer_preview.asp?idArticle= 5271; accessed 30 October 2008.

6. BBC, 'The Perils of Liberian Peacekeeping', 4 August 2003, http://news. bbc.co.uk/2/hi/africa/3113009.stm; accessed 17 December 2007.

7. See *International Herald Tribune*, 'Peacekeeping and Diplomacy. Why

Liberia is a Turning Point for Africa'. www.iht.com/articles/2003/09/05/edpower_ed3_.php; accessed 17 Dec 07.

8. For a discussion of France's image in Kosovo, see http://iwpr.net/?p=bcr&s=f&o=247784&apc_state=henibcr2000; accessed 8 January 2008.

9. See the journalist Eric Rouleau in the French newspaper *Le Monde*, December 1999.

Chapter 8

1. www.bbc.co.uk/pressoffice/pressreleases/stories/2006/11_november/30/un.shtml; accessed 20 September 2007.

2. See Amnesty International Country Report for Haiti, which shows high figures for violence against women in particular: www.amnestyusa.org/annualreport.php?id=ar&yr=2007&c=HTI; accessed 20 September 2007.

3. www.genderandsecurity.org/Enloe.pdf; accessed 20 September 2007.

References

Aboagye, F.B. (1999) *ECOMOG: A Sub-regional Experience in Conflict Resolution, Management and Peacekeeping in Liberia.* Accra: SEDCO.

Aboagye, F.B., and Bah, M.S. (2004) *Liberia at a Crossroads: A Preliminary Look at the United Nations Mission in Liberia (UNMIL) and the Protection of Civilian*, ISS Paper 95. Pretoria: Institute for Security Studies.

Agamben, G. (1998) *Homo Sacer: Sovereign Power and Bare Life.* Stanford: Stanford University Press.

Agathangelou, A., and Ling, L.H.M. (2003) 'Desire Industries: Sex Trafficking, UN Peacekeeping and the Neo-liberal World Order', *Brown Journal of World Affairs* 10(1): 133–48.

Anzaldúa, G. (1987) *Borderlands: The New Mestiza.* San Francisco: Spinster/Aunt Lute Press.

Aoi, C., de Coning, C., and Thakur, R. (eds) (2007) *Unintended Consequences of Peacekeeping Operations.* Tokyo: United Nations University Press.

Banerjee, D. (2005) 'Current Trends in UN Peacekeeping: A Perspective from Asia', *International Peacekeeping* 12(1): 18–33.

Barrett, F. (1996) 'The Organizational Construction of Hegemonic Masculinity: The Case of the US Navy', *Gender, Work and Organization* 3(3): 129–42.

Bell, V. (1999) 'Performativity and Belonging: An Introduction', in V. Bell (ed.), *Performativity and Belonging.* London: Sage.

Bellamy, A., and Williams, P. (2004) 'Conclusion: What Future for Peace Operations? Brahimi and Beyond', *Security Dialogue* 11(1), Spring: 183–212.

Ben-Ari, E., and Elron, E.R. (2001) 'Blue Helmets and White Armor: Multi-Nationalism and Multiculturalism among UN Peacekeeping Forces', *City and Society* 13(2): 271–302.

Ben-Ari, E., and Fruhstuk, S. (2003) 'The Celebration of Violence: A Live Fire

Demonstration Carried Out by Japan's Contemporary Military', *American Ethnologist* 30(4): 540–55.

Beuving, J. (2006) 'Lebanese Traders in Cotonou: A Socio-Cultural Analysis of Economic Mobility and Capital Accumulation', *Africa* 76: 324–51.

Bialasiewicz, L., Campbell, D., Elden, S., Graham, S., Jeffrey, J., and Williams, A.J. (2007) 'Performing Security: The Imaginative Geographies of Current US Strategy', *Political Geography* 26(4): 405–22.

Blackburn, R. (1999) 'Kosovo: The War of NATO Expansion', *New Left Review*, 1/235.

Blagojevic, B. (2007) 'Peacebuilding in Ethnically Divided Societies', *Peace Review: A Journal of Social Justice* 19(4): 555–62.

Bøas, M. (2001) 'Liberia and Sierra Leone – Dead Ringers? The Logic of Neo-patrimonial Rule', *Third World Quarterly* 22(5): 697–723.

Brittan, A. (1989) *Masculinity and Power*. Oxford: Blackwell.

Brod, H. (1987) *The Making of Masculinities*. London: Allen & Unwin.

Brod, H., and Kaufman, M. (eds) (1994) *Theorizing Masculinities*: London: Sage.

Buchbinder, D. (1994) *Masculinities and Identities*. Melbourne: Melbourne University Press.

Bullion A. (2001) 'India in Sierra Leone: A Case of Muscular Peacekeeping?', *International Peacekeeping* 8(4) Winter: 77–91.

Butler, J. (1988) 'Performative Acts and Gender Constitution: An Essay in Phenomenology and Feminist Theory', *Theatre Journal* 40(4): 519–31.

Butler, J. (1990) *Gender Trouble: Feminism and the Subversion of Identity*. New York: Routledge.

Callinicos, A. (2003) *The New Mandarins of American Power*. Cambridge: Polity Press.

Callon, M. (1986) 'The Case of the Electric Vehicle', in M. Callon, D. Law and A. Rip (eds), *Mapping the Dynamics of Science and Technology*, 19–34. London: Macmillan.

Campbell, D. (1998) *National Deconstruction: Violence, Identity and Justice in Bosnia*. Minneapolis: Minnesota University Press.

Carpenter, C. (2003) '"Women and Children First": Gender, Norms and Humanitarian Evacuation in the Balkans 1991–1995', *International Organization* 57(4): 661–94.

Chandler, D. (2001) 'The People-Centred Approach to Peace Operations: The New UN Agenda', *International Peacekeeping* 8(1): 1–19.

Chandler, D. (2004) 'The Responsibility to Protect? Enforcing the Liberal Peace', *International Peacekeeping* 11(1): 59–81.

Charles, C. (1995) 'Gender and Politics in Contemporary Haiti: The Duvalierist State, Transnationalism, and the Emergence of New Feminism (1980–1990)', *Feminist Studies* 21(1): 135–64.

Chimengo, N. (2008) 'When Wounds and Corpses Fail to Speak: Narratives of Violence and Rape in the Congo (DRC)', *Comparative Studies of South Asia, Africa and the Middle East* 28(1): 78–92.

Chomsky, N. (1991) *Deterring Democracy*. London: Verso.

Chomsky, N. (1999) *The New Military Humanism: Lessons from Kosovo*. London:

Pluto Press.

Chopra, J. (2000) 'The UN's Kingdom of East Timor', *Survival* 42(3): 27–39.

Cleland-Welch, A. (2006) 'Achieving Human Security after Intra-State Conflict: The Lessons of Kosovo', *Journal of Contemporary European Studies* 14(2): 221–39.

Cockburn, C., and Hubic, M. (2002) 'Gender and the Peacekeeping Military: A View from Bosnian Women's Organizations', in C. Cockburn and D. Zarkov (eds), *The Postwar Moment: Militaries, Masculinities and International Peacekeeping*, 103–21. London: Lawrence & Wishart.

Cohn, C. (1987) 'Sex and Death in the Rational World of Defense Intellectuals', *Signs* 14(4): 687–718.

Connell, B., and Messerschmidt, J.W. (2005) 'Hegemonic Masculinity: Rethinking the Concept', *Gender and Society* 19(6): 829–59.

Connell, R.W. (1995) *Masculinities*. Cambridge: Polity Press.

Connell, R.W. (2003) 'The Role of Men and Boys in Achieving Gender Equality', presented to UNDP Expert Group Meeting on The Role of Men and Boys in Achieving Gender Equality, Brasilia.

Connell, R.W. (2008) 'Preface: The Man Question, Gender and Global Power', in J. Parpart and M. Zalewski (eds), *Rethinking the Man Question*. London: Zed Books.

Cornwall, A., and Lindisfarne, N. (1994) *Dislocating Masculinity: Comparative Ethnographies*. London: Routledge.

Corson, M.W., and Turregano, C.G. (2003) 'Spaces of Unintended Consequences: The Ground Safety Zone in Kosovo', *GeoJournal* 57(4): 273–82.

Cox, R. (ed.) (1997) *The New Realism. Perspectives on Multilateralism and World Order*. London: Macmillan, and Tokyo: United Nations University Press.

Crawford, A., and Lister, S. (2007) *The Use and Impact of Disposal Orders: Sticking Plasters and Wake-up Calls*. Bristol: Policy Press.

Dalby, S. (1990) *Creating the Second Cold War: The Discourse of Politics*. New York: Guilford Press.

Dalby, S. (1991) 'Critical Geopolitics: Difference, Discourse and Dissent', *Environment and Planning* 9: 261–83.

Dallaire, R. (2003) *Shake Hands with the Devil*. Canada: Random House.

de Leeuw, M. (2002) 'A Gentlemen's Agreement: Srebenica in the Context of Dutch War History', in C. Cockburn and D. Zarkov (eds), *The Postwar Moment: Militaries, Masculinities and International Peacekeeping*, 162–82. London: Lawrence & Wishart.

Dillon, M. (1996) *Politics of Security: Towards a Political Philosophy of Continental Thought*. London: Routledge.

Donini, A., Minear, L., Smillie, T., van Baarda, A.C., and Welch, A.C. (2005) *Mapping the Security Environment: Understanding the Perceptions of Local Communities, Peace Support Operations and Assistance Agencies*, report commissioned by the UK NGO–Military Contact Group. Medford MA: Feinstein International Famine Center and Tufts University.

Dowler, L., and Sharp, J. (2001) 'A Feminist Geopolitics?', *Space and Polity* 5(3): 165–76.

Dudink, Stefan (2002) 'The Unheroic Men of a Moral Nation: Masculinity and

Nation in Modern Dutch History', in C. Cockburn and D. Zarkov (eds), *The Postwar Moment: Militaries, Masculinities and International Peacekeeping*, 146–51. London: Lawrence & Wishart.

Duffield, M. (2001) *Global Governance and the New Wars: The Merging of Development and Security*. London: Zed Books.

Duffield, M. (2002) 'War as a Network Enterprise: The New Security Terrain and Its Implications', *Cultural Values* 6: 153–65.

Dupuy, A. (2005) 'From Jean-Bertrande Aristide to Gerard Latortue: The Unending Crisis of Democratization in Haiti', *Journal of Latin American Anthropology* 10(1): 186–205.

Eide, E.B., Kaspersen, A.J., Kent, R., and von Hippel, K. (2005) *Report on Integrated Missions: Practical Perspectives and Recommendations*. New York: United Nations ECHA Core Group.

Elazar, D.J. (1999) 'Political Science, Geography, and the Spatial Dimension of Politics', *Political Geography* 18: 875–86.

Ellis, S. (1995) 'Liberia 1989–1994: A Study of Ethnic and Spiritual Violence', *African Affairs* 94: 165–97.

Enloe, C. (1989) *Bananas, Beaches, and Bases: Making Feminist Sense of International Relations*. Berkeley: University of California Press.

Enloe, C. (1993) *The Morning After: Sexual Politics after the Cold War*. Berkeley: University of California Press.

Enloe, C. (2000) *Maneuvers: The International Politics of Militarizing Women's Lives*. Berkeley: University of California Press.

Enloe, C. (2007) *Globalization and Militarism: Feminists Make the Link*. London: Rowman & Littlefield.

Falah, G., and Newman, D. (1995) 'The Spatial Manifestation of Threat: Israelis and Palestinians Seek a "Good" Border', *Political Geography* 14(8): 689–706.

Farmer, P. (2006) *The Uses of Haiti*. Monroe ME: Common Courage Press.

Ferguson, H. (2004) 'The Sublime and the Subliminal: Modern Identities and the Experience of Combat', *Theory, Culture and Society* 21(3): 1–34.

Fetherston, A.B (1995) 'UN Peacekeepers and Cultures of Violence', *Cultural Survival Quarterly*, Spring: 19–23.

Fetherston, A.B. (1998) 'Voices from Warzones: Implications for Training UN Peacekeepers', in E. Moxon-Browne (ed.), *A Future for Peacekeeping?*, 67–79. London: Macmillan.

Fine, M., and Kuriloff, P. (2006) 'Forging and Performing Masculine Identities within Social Spaces: Boys and Men Negotiating the Crucible of Dominant Cultural Representations at the Intersection of Class, Race, Ethnicity, and Sexuality', *Men & Masculinities* 8: 257–61.

Forster, A., and Wallace, W. (2001) 'What is NATO For?', *Survival* 43(4): 107–22.

Frisby, D. (1981) *Sociological Impressionism: Reassessment of Georg Simmel's Social Theory*. London: Ashgate.

Gammage, S. (2004) 'Exercising Exit, Voice and Loyalty: A Gender Perspective on Transnationalism in Haiti', *Development and Change* 35(4): 743–71.

Gheciu, A. (2005) 'International Norms, Power and the Politics of International

Administration: The Kosovo Case', *Geopolitics* 10: 121–46.

Ghosh A. (1994) 'The Global Reservation: Notes toward an Ethnography of International Peacekeeping', *Cultural Anthropology* 9(3): 412–22.

Gill, S. (1995) 'Globalisation, Market Civilisation, and Disciplinary Neoliberalism', *Millennium* 23(3): 399–423.

Goffman, E. (1959) *The Presentation of Self in Everyday Life*. New York: Doubleday.

Goffman, E. (1972) *The Individual as a Unit. Relations in Public: Microstudies of the Public Order*. London: Allen Lane.

Gregory, D. (2004) *The Colonial Present*. London: Blackwell.

Gregory, D. (2006) 'The Black Flag: Guantánamo Bay and the Space of Exception', *Geografiska Annaler, Series B: Human Geography* 88(4): 405–27.

Hallward, P. (2004) 'Option Zero in Haiti', *New Left Review* 27, May–June: 47.

Hardy, C., Phillips, N., and Clegg, S. (2001) 'Reflexivity in Organization and Management Theory: A Study of the Production of the Research "Subject"', *Human Relations* 54(5): 534–47.

Harvey, D. (2003) *The New Imperialism*. Oxford: Oxford University Press.

Hearn, J. (1996) 'Is Masculinity Dead? A Critique of the Concept Masculinity/Masculinities', in M. Mac an Ghaill (ed.), *Understanding Masculinities*, 202–17. Buckingham: Open University Press.

Hearn, J. (1998) *The Violences of Men: How Men Talk About and How Agencies Respond to Men's Violence to Women*. London: Sage.

Hearn, J. (2004) 'Troubled Masculinities in Social Policy Discourses: Young Men', in J. Popay, J. Hearn and J. Edwards (eds), *Men, Gender Division and Welfare*. London: Routledge.

Heifetz-Yahav, D. (2005) 'Choreographing Otherness: Ethnochoreology and Peacekeeping Research', paper presented at the First International Congress of Qualitative Inquiry, Urbana, May.

Heinecken, L. (2003) 'Facing a Merciless Enemy: HIV/AIDS and the South African Armed Forces', *Armed Forces and Society* 29(2): 281–300.

Higate, P. (2001) 'Tough Bodies and Rough Sleeping: Embodying Homelessness Amongst Ex-servicemen', *Housing, Theory and Society* (3)1: 97–108.

Higate, P (ed.) (2003) *Military Masculinities: Identity and the State*. Westport CT: Praeger.

Higate, P. (2004) *Gender Relations and Peacekeeping in Democratic Republic of Congo and Sierra Leone*. Pretoria: Institute for Security Studies.

Higate, P. (2007) 'Peacekeepers, Masculinities and Sexual Exploitation', *Men & Masculinities* 10(1): 99–119.

Higate, P.R., and Henry, M. (2004) 'Engendering (In)security in Peace Support Operations', *Security Dialogue* 35(4): 481–98.

Hoffman, D. (2003) 'Frontline Anthropology: Research in a Time of War', *Anthropology Today* 19(3): 9–12.

Hooper, C. (2001) *Manly States: Masculinities, International Relations and Gender Politics*. Columbia: Columbia University Press.

Hughes, D. (2000) 'The Natasha Trade: The Transnational Shadow Market of Trafficking in Women', *Journal of International Affairs* 53(2): 625–51.

Human Rights Watch (1993) *Liberia: Waging War to Keep the Peace; the ECOMOG*

Intervention and Human Rights. New York: Human Rights Watch.

Hyndman, J. (1997) 'Border Crossings', *Antipode* 29: 149–76.

Hyndman, J. (2003) 'Preventive, Palliative, or Punitive? Safe Spaces in Bosnia-Herzegovina, Somalia, and Sri Lanka', *Journal of Refugee Studies* 14: 167–85.

Hyndman, J. (2004) 'Mind the Gap: Bridging Feminist and Political Geography through Geopolitics', *Political Geography* 23: 307–22.

Jelusic, L. (2007) 'Motivation for Peace Operations', *International Review of Sociology* 17(1): 73–85.

Jennings, K.M. (2007) 'The Struggle to Satisfy: DDR through the Eyes of Ex-combatants in Liberia', *International Peacekeeping* 14(2): 204–18.

Judah, T. (2002) *Kosovo: War and Revenge*, New Haven: Yale University Press.

Kaldor, M. (1999) *New and Old Wars: Organized Violence in a Global Era*. Cambridge: Polity Press.

Karadjis, M. (2005) 'Dilemmas in Kosova: Benign Peacekeeping or Destructive Occupation?', *Development* 48(3): 126–33.

King, I., and Mason, W. (2006) *Peace at Any Price: How the World Failed Kosovo*, London: Hurst.

Kinsella, H. (2004) 'Securing the Civilian: Sex and Gender in the Laws of War', in M. Barnett and B. Duvall (eds), *Power and Global Governance*. Cambridge: Cambridge University Press.

Kovats-Bernat, C. (2006) 'Factional Terror, Paramilitarism and Civil War in Haiti: The View from Port-au-Prince, 1994–2004', *Anthropologica* 48(1): 117–39.

Krasno, J. (2006): *Public Opinion Survey of UNMIL's Work in Liberia*. New York: United Nations, Peacekeeping Best Practices Section.

Krishnamsamy, K. (2001) 'Building a Partnership for Peace in Intrastate Wars: India's Peacekeeping Style in Somalia (1993–1995)', in *Low-Intensity Conflict & Law Enforcement* 10(1): 27–46.

Kronsell, A., and Svedberg, E. (2001) 'The Duty to Protect: Gender in the Swedish Practice of Conscription', *Cooperation and Conflict* 36(2): 153–76.

Kuus, M. (2007) '"Love, Peace and Nato": Imperial Subject-making in Central Europe', *Antipode* 39(2): 269–90.

Latour, B. (1987) *Science in Action: How to Follow Scientists and Engineers through Society*. Cambridge MA: Harvard University Press.

Latour, B. (2005) *Reassembling the Social: An Introduction to Actor-Network Theory*. Oxford: Oxford University Press.

Law, J. (1987) 'Technology, Closure and Heterogeneous Engineering: The Case of the Portuguese Expansion', in W.E. Bijker, T.P. Hughes and T.J. Pinch (eds), *The Social Construction of Technological Systems: New Directions in the Sociology and History of Technology*. Cambridge MA: MIT Press.

Law, J. (1992) 'Notes on the Theory of the Actor-Network: Ordering, Strategy and Heterogeneity', *Systems Practice* 5: 379–93.

Law, J., and Hassard, J. (eds) (1999) *Actor Network Theory and After*. Oxford: Blackwell.

Levitt, J. (2005) *The Evolution of Deadly Conflict in Liberia: From 'Paternaltarianism' to State Collapse*. Durham NC: University of North Carolina Press.

Lewis, S. (2005) *Challenges to Humanitarian Space*. Liberia: ECHO/Oxfam.

Lischer, S.K. (2007) 'Military Intervention and the Humanitarian "Force Multiplier"', *Global Governance: A Review of Multilateralism and International Organizations* 13(1): 99–118.

Loutis, W. (2006) 'Evaluation de la situation des femmes dans le cadre de la violence armée', UNDP and MINUSTAH Unit for Equality, Haiti.

McDowell, L., and Sharp, J. (1997) 'Gender, Nation and International Relations: Introduction', in L. McDowell and J. Sharp (eds), *Space, Gender, Knowledge: Feminist Readings*, 395–401. London: Arnold.

McGovern, M. (2005) 'Rebuilding a Failed State: Liberia' *Development in Practice* 15(6): 760–66.

Macgowan, K., and Melnitz, W. (1955) *The Living Stage*, 478–79. Englewood Cliffs NJ: Prentice Hall.

MacInnes, J. (1998) *The End of Masculinity*. Milton Keynes: Open University Press.

Mackay, A. (2001) 'Sex and the Peacekeeper Soldier: The New UN Resolution', *Peace News* 2443.

MacQueen, N. (2006) *Peacekeeping and the International System*. London: Routledge.

Mann, M. (1987) 'The Roots and Contradictions of Modern Militarism', *New Left Review* 165: 35–50.

Martin, S. (2005) *Must Boys be Boys? Ending Sexual Exploitation and Abuse in UN Peacekeeping Missions*. Washington DC: Refugees International.

Masquelier, A. (2002) 'Road Mythographies: Space, Mobility, and the Historical Imagination in Postcolonial Niger', *American Ethnologist* 29(4): 829–56.

Merleau-Ponty, M. (1962). *Phenomenology of Perception*. London: Routledge.

Mertus, J. (1999) *Kosovo: How Myths and Truths Started a War*. Berkeley: University of California Press.

Mertus, J. (2001) 'Gender in the Service of Nation: Female Citizenship in Kosovar Society', *Social Politics*, Summer/Fall: 261–77.

Middleton, P. (1992) *The Inward Gaze: Masculinity and Subjectivity in Modern Culture*. London: Routledge.

Mohanty, C.T. (1991) 'Under Western Eyes', in C.T. Mohanty, A. Russo and T. Torres (eds), *Third World Women and the Politics of Feminism*. Bloomington: University of Indiana Press.

Moran, M. (2006) *Liberia: The Violence of Democracy*. Philadelphia: University of Pennsylvania Press.

Morgan, D. (1987) '"It Will Make a Man of You": Notes on National Service, Masculinity and Autobiography', *Studies in Sexual Politics* 17, Department of Sociology, University of Manchester.

Morgan, D. (1992) *Discovering Men*. London: Routledge.

Morgan, D. (1994) 'Theater of War: Combat, the Military and Masculinities', in H. Brod and M. Kaufmann (eds), *Theorizing Masculinities*. London: Sage.

Muggah, R. (2005) *Securing Haiti's Transition: Reviewing Human Insecurity and the Prospects for Disarmament, Demobilization and Reintegration*. Geneva: Small Arms Survey, Graduate Institute of Social Studies.

Nash, C. (2000) 'Performativity in Practice: Some Recent Work in Cultural Geography', *Progress in Human Geography* 12(24): 653–64.

Nelles, W. (2005) 'Education, Underdevelopment, Unnecessary War and Human Security in Kosovo/Kosova', *International Journal of Educational Development* 25(1): 69–84.

Nettleton, S., and Watson, J. (1998) 'The Body in Everyday Life: An Introduction', in S. Nettleton and J. Watson (eds), *The Body in Everyday Life*. London: Routledge.

Nichols, R. (2005) 'Disarming Liberia: Progress and Pitfalls', in N. Florquin and E.G. Berman (eds), *Armed and Aimless: Armed Groups, Guns and Human Security in the ECOWAS Region*, 108–43. Geneva: Small Arms Survey.

Nyman, C. (1999) 'Gender Equality in "the Most Equal Country in the World?" Money and Marriage in Sweden', *Sociological Review* 47(4): 766–93.

Oas, I. (2005) 'Shifting the Iron Curtain of Kantian Peace: NATO Expansion and the Modern Magyars', in C. Flint (ed.), *The Geography of War and Peace: From Death Camps to Diplomats*, 395–414. Oxford: Oxford University Press.

O'Connell Davidson, J. (1998) *Prostitution, Power and Freedom*. Cambridge: Polity Press.

Olonisakin, F., and Levitt, J. (1999) 'Regional Security and the Challenges of Democratisation in Africa: The Case of ECOWAS and SADC', *Cambridge Review of International Affairs* 13(1): 66–78.

O'Tuathail, G. (1996) *Critical Geopolitics*. Minneapolis: University of Minnesota Press.

O'Tuathail, G. (2000) 'The Postmodern Geopolitical Condition: States, Statecraft and Security at the Millennium', *Annals of the Association of American Geographers* 90(1): 166–78.

O'Tuathail, G., and Dalby, S. (1998) *Rethinking Geopolitics*. London: Routledge.

Outram, Q. (1997) 'Cruel Wars and Safe Havens: Humanitarian Aid in Liberia 1989–1996', *Disasters* 21: 189–205.

Oxford Dictionary, Thesaurus and Wordpower Guide (2001) Oxford: Oxford University Press.

Paes, W.C. (2005) 'The Challenges of Disarmament, Demobilization and Reintegration in Liberia', *International Peacekeeping* 12(2): 253–61.

Pain, R. (1997) 'Social Geographies of Women's Fear of Crime', *Transactions of the Institute of British Geographers* 22: 231–44.

Palmer, A. (2002) 'Deceptive Transparency: Problems in the New Conceptual Framework of Global Communication', *Global Media* 3(4).

Paris, R. (1997) 'Peacebuilding and the Limits of Liberal Internationalism', *International Security* 22(2): 54–89.

Paris, R. (2001) 'Echoes of the Mission Civilisatrice: Peacekeeping in the Post-Cold War Era', in E. Newman and O. Richmond (eds), *The United Nations and Human Security*. London: Palgrave.

Paris, R. (2002) 'Peacebuilding in Central America: Reproducing the Sources of Conflict?', *International Peacekeeping* 9(4): 39–68.

Paris, R. (2003) 'Peacekeeping and the Constraints of Global Culture', *European Journal of International Relations* 9(3) 441–73.

Paris, R. (2004) "Still an Inscrutable Concept," *Security Dialogue* 35(3): 370–72.

Parker, A., and Sedgwick, E. Kosofsky (1995) 'Introduction: Performativity and Performance', in A. Parker and E. Kosofsky Sedgwick (eds), *Performativity and Performance*, 1–18. New York: Routledge.

Parpart, J., and Zalewski, M. (1998) *The 'Man' Question in International Relations*. Boulder CO: Westview Press.

Parpart, J., and Zalewski, M. (eds) (2008) *Rethinking the Man Question in International Relations*. London: Zed Books

Pease, B. (2002) *Men and Gender Relations*. Melbourne: Tertiary.

Peterson, A. (2003) 'Research on Men and Masculinities: Some Implications of Recent Theory for Future Work', *Men & Masculinities* 6(1): 54–69.

Pitts, M., (1999) 'Sub-regional Solutions for African Conflict: The ECOMOG Experiment', *Journal of Conflict Studies* 19(1): 49–68.

Polman, L. (1997) *We Did Nothing: Why the Truth Doesn't always Come Out When the UN Goes In*. Amsterdam: Rozenberg Publishers.

Pouligny, B. (2006) *Peace Operations Seen from Below: UN Missions and Local People*. Hurst: London.

Pugh, M. (2002) 'Postwar Political Economy in Bosnia and Herzegovina: The Spoils of Peace', *Global Governance* 8(4): 467–82.

Pugh, M. (2004) 'Peacekeeping and Critical Theory', *International Peacekeeping* 11(1): 39–58.

Pugh, M. (2005) 'Transformation in the Political Economy of Bosnia since Dayton', *International Peacekeeping* 12(3): 448–62.

Pula, B. (2004) 'The Emergence of the Kosovo "Parallel State," 1988–1992', *Nationalities Papers* 32(4): 797–826.

Razack, S. (2004) *Dark Threats and White Knights: The Somalia Peacekeeping Affair and the New Imperialism*. Toronto: University of Toronto Press.

Rehn, E., and Johnson-Sirleaf, E. (2002) *Women, War and Peace: The Independent Experts' Assessment on the Impact of Armed Conflict on Women and Women's Role in Peacebuilding*. New York: UNIFEM.

Reiter, D. (2001) 'Why NATO Enlargement Does Not Spread Democracy', *International Security* 25(4): 41–67.

Richmond, O., and Williams, P. (2004) 'Conclusion: What Future for Peace Operations?' *International Peacekeeping* 11(1): 183–212.

Robben, A., and Nordstrom, C. (eds) (1995) *Fieldwork Under Fire: Studies of Violence and Culture*. Berkley and Los Angeles: University of California Press.

Rubinstein, R.A. (1993) 'Cultural Aspects of Peacekeeping: Notes on the Substance of Symbols', *Millennium Journal of International Studies* 22(3): 547–62.

Rubinstein, R.A. (1998) 'Methodological Challenges in the Ethnographic Study of Multilateral Peacekeeping', *Political and Legal Anthropology* 21(1): 138–49.

Sangmpam, S.N. (1995) 'The Overpoliticised State and International Politics: Nicaragua, Haiti, Cambodia and Togo', *Third World Quarterly* 16(4): 619–42.

Schilling, C. (1993) *The Body and Social Theory*. London: Sage.

Schmidt, G. (ed.) (2001) *A History of NATO: The First 50 Years*. London: Palgrave.

Seidler, V. (1997) *Man Enough: Embodying Masculinities*. London: Sage.

Sesay, M. (1996) 'Civil War and Collective Intervention in Liberia', *Review of African Political Economy* 67: 35–52.

Shanks, L., and Schull, M.J. (2000) 'Rape in War: The Humanitarian Response', *Canadian Medical Association Journal* 163(9): 1152–6.

Sharp, J. (2000) 'Remasculinising Geopolitics? Comments on Gearoid O'Tuathail Critical Geopolitics', *Political Geography* 19: 361–64.

Sheller, M. (2000) *Democracy after Slavery.* Gainesville: University of Florida Press.

Shepherd, L. (2006) 'Veiled References: Constructions of Gender in the Bush Administration Discourse on the Attacks on Afghanistan post-9/11', *International Feminist Journal of Politics* 8(1): 19–41.

Shepherd, L. (2008) 'Power and Authority in the Production of United Nations Security Council Resolution 1325', *International Studies Quarterly* 52(2): 383–404.

Sida, L. (2005) *Challenges to Humanitarian Space: A Review of Humanitarian Issues Related to the UN Integrated Mission in Liberia and to the Relationship between Humanitarian and Military Actors in Liberia.* Monitoring and Steering Group, Liberia.

Sinha, M. (1995) *Colonial Masculinity: The 'Manly Englishman' and The 'Effeminate Bengali' in the Late Nineteenth Century.* Manchester: Manchester University Press.

Sion, L. (2008) 'Peacekeeping and the Gender Regime', *Journal of Contemporary Ethnography* 37(5): 561–85.

Smith, N. (2003) *American Empire: Roosevelt's Geographer and the Prelude to Globalization.* Berkeley: University of California Press.

Smith, S.J. (1989) 'Social Relations, Neighbourhood Structure and the Fear of Crime in Britain', in D. Evans and D. Herbert (eds), *The Geography of Crime*, 193–227. London: Routledge.

Soja, E. (1989) *Postmodern Geographies: The Reassertion of Space in Critical Social Theory.* London: Verso.

Sokolova, J., Richards, A., and Smith, H. (2006) *Small Arms and Light Weapons Survey of Kosovo.* Belgrade: South Eastern and Eastern Europe Clearinghouse.

Spencer, S.W. (2005) 'Making Peace: Preventing and Responding to Sexual Exploitation by United Nations Peacekeepers', *Journal of Public and International Affairs* 16, Spring: 167–81.

Sreenan, J. (2006) 'Doing "the World's Most Important Work" – from Cyprus to Liberia', *Irish Studies in International Affairs* 17: 15–22.

Stoddard, A., and Harmer, A. (2006) 'Little Room to Maneuver: The Challenges to Humanitarian Action in the New Global Security Environment', *Journal of Human Development* 7(1): 23–41.

Stuart, P. (2002) 'Camp Bondsteel and America's Plans to Control Caspian Oil', World Socialist Web Site, www.wsws.org/articles/2002/apr2002/oil-a29.shtml; accessed 15 January 2008.

Taw J.M., and Grant-Thomas, A. (1999) 'U.S. Support for Regional Complex Contingency Operations: Lessons from ECOMOG', *Studies in Conflict and Terrorism* 22(1): 53–77.

Teh, T. (2001) 'Dirtier Than a Lie', *The Perspective* (Liberia), www.theperspective.org/dirtier.html, accessed 4 March 2008.

Thrift, N. (1996) *Spatial Formations*. London: Sage.

Thrift, N. (1997) 'The Still Point: Resistance, Expressive Embodiment and Dance', in S. Pile and M. Keith (eds), *Geographies of Resistance*, 124–51. London: Routledge.

Tickner, A. (1997) 'You Just Don't Understand: Troubled Engagements between Feminists and IR Theorists', *International Studies Quarterly* 41(4): 611–32.

Tickner, A. (2001) *Gendering World Politics: Issues and Approaches in the Post-Cold War Era*. Columbia: Columbia University Press.

Tripoldi, P., and Patel, P. (2002) 'The Global Impact of HIV/AIDS on Peace Support Operations', *International Peacekeeping* 9(3): 51–66.

Tuck, C. (2000). '"Every Car or Moving Object Gone": The ECOMOG Intervention in Liberia'. *African Studies Quarterly* 4(1): 1.

Van Brabant, K. (1998) 'Cool Ground for Aid Providers: Towards Better Sercurity Management in Aid Agencies', *Disasters* 22(2): 109–25.

Valentine, G. (1989) *Women's Fear of Male Violence in Public Space: A Spatial Expression of Patriarchy*. Ph.D. thesis, Department of Geography, University of Reading.

Valentine, G. (1992) 'Images of Danger: Women's Sources of Information about the Spatial Distribution of Male Violence', *Area* 24(1): 22–9.

Van Mierop, E.S. (2004) *The Humanitarian Response in Liberia: Some Observations by the ICVA Coordinator*, Geneva: International Council of Voluntary Agencies.

Von Einsiedel, S., and Malone, D.M. (2006) 'Peace and Democracy for Haiti: A UN Mission Impossible?', *International Relations* 20(2): 153–74.

Weber, C. (1998) 'Performative States', *Millennium: Journal of International Studies* 27: 77–97.

Welch, A., Aliu, L., Cooper, I., Hasani, A., Jaka, B., Kamberi, A., Kastrati, B., Kondi, S., Stinson, D., Tolaj., V., and Page, M. (2006) *Kosovo Internal Security Sector Reform*. University of Kosovo and United Nations Development Programme.

Whitworth, S. (2004) *Men, Militarism and UN Peacekeeping: A Gendered Analysis*. Boulder CO: Lynne Rienner.

Woodhouse, T., and Ramsbotham, O. (2005) 'Cosmopolitan Peacekeeping and the Globalization of Security', *International Peacekeeping* 12(2): 139–56.

Woodward, R. (2004) *Military Geographies*. London: Blackwell.

Woodward, R., Winter, T., and Jenkings, N. (2008) '"I Used to Keep a Camera in my Top Left-hand Pocket". British Soldiers, Their Photographs and the Performances of Geopolitical Power', in K. Dodds, F. MacDonald and R. Hughes (eds), *The Observant State: Geopolitics and Visuality*. London: I.B. Tauris.

Yannis, A. (2004) 'The UN as Government in Kosovo: The Politics of International Administration', *Global Governance* 10(1): 67–91.

Zanotti, L. (2006) 'Taming Chaos: A Foucauldian View of UN Peacekeeping, Democracy and Normalization', *International Peacekeeping* 13(2): 150–67.

Zaremba, M. (2007) 'Complain in Azerbaijan', in *DN. Kultur*, www.dn.se/DNet/jsp/polopoly.jsp?d=2502&a=664659; accessed 15 January 2008.

Zarkov, D. (2001) 'The Body of the Other Man', in C. Moser and F. Clark (eds),

Victims, Perpetrators or Actors? Gender, Armed Conflict and Political Violence, 69–82. London: Zed Books.

Zarkov, D. (2002) '"Srebrenica Trauma": Masculinity, Military and National Self-image in Dutch Daily Newspapers', in C. Cockburn and D. Zarkov (eds), *The Postwar Moment: Militaries, Masculinities and International Peacekeeping*. London: Lawrence & Wishart.

Zeid, C. (2005) *Report to the U.N. General. Assembly: A Comprehensive Strategy to Eliminate Future Sexual Exploitation and Abuse in United Nations Peacekeeping Operations*, UN Document A/59/710.

Zisk-Marten, K. (2004) *Enforcing the Peace: Learning from the Imperial Past*. New York: Columbia University Press.

Index